FIGHT LIKE A GIRL

CLEMENTINE FORD

ONEWORLD

A Oneworld Book

First published in Great Britain and North America by
Oneworld Publications, 2018

This updated mass market paperback published 2019

ISBN 978-1-78607-603-8
eISBN 978-1-78607-364-8

Printed and bound in Great Britain by Clays Ltd, Elcograf S.p.A.

Oneworld Publications
10 Bloomsbury Street
London WC1B 3 SR
United Kingdom

For the girls

CONTENTS

INTRODUCTION

In 2016, I published this book, *Fight Like A Girl*. Part memoir, part manifesto, it took aim at the violence patriarchy inflicts on girls and the various ways in which we're conditioned to see ourselves as powerless against it. I've since been enormously privileged to have women from all over the country share with me deeply private stories and responses to this book. Thank you all for trusting me with your lives. Thank you for joining me in this fight, and thank you for letting me join you in yours.

I was motivated to write *Fight Like A Girl* because I was sick of the more heightened levels of misogyny I could see rising up around me, particularly as online discourse became more markedly toxic. As a feminist writer, I'd spent much of the previous decade dealing with online trolls: men of all ages whose fury (or fear) over what they saw as a misandrist agenda hell-bent on matriarchal world domination and the subsequent banning of all men led them to send me a slew of death threats, rape threats, treatises on how unfuckable I was, how mentally deranged, how I needed to be beaten, sodomised, murdered and in what manner. Whenever I complained about or even mentioned these threats, I was an overly sensitive baby who was scared of words and reacted by 'playing the victim'.

I'm a woman who lives in the world, which means it's been impossible for me to escape the impact of patriarchy. In *Fight*

Like A Girl, I wrote about the ways in which women are taught (and encouraged) to hate ourselves, starting from well before the time we enter adolescence. I explored how this self-hatred can cause fractures in our emotional selves, compounding our risk of mental illness and paving the way for the specific kind of torturously slow and violent self-harm that comes in the form of chronic eating disorders (which are really our attempts to wrest back some form of control over our physical and emotional selves, while literally attempting to make ourselves as small and unobtrusive as possible). I wrote about my difficult relationship with anxiety, a condition I was formally diagnosed with at twenty-one but that I've been living with for almost all my life. The intermittent disassociation I experience, which renders me emotionally incapacitated for weeks on end and feels like looking out at the world from the inside of a painting or a sealed glass bottle. My occasional suicidal ideation and obsessive-compulsive behaviours, both of which flared up in terrifying ways during my pregnancy. I advocated fiercely for abortion rights, detailing the two times in my life I've made that (easy) decision and how I refuse to allow anyone else to make me feel shame because of it. I wrote about the restorative value of female friendship, and the importance of finding yourself a good girl gang who can lift you up and provide a safe place to land. I discussed rape culture, men's violence against women, victim blaming and the fear of male disapproval, and how all these things are used to keep girls and women in line and obedient. 'It's okay for you to be angry,' I said, ending with a scorching takedown of everything we deserve to feel angry about; a celebration and acknowledgment of the blistering hot rage that runs through us but that we're made to deny and feel ashamed of and uneasy about.

I love women. I love our strength and our stamina in the face of structures and individuals who do us such significant harm and inflict such violence on us. I love how we survive, despite this. I wanted *Fight Like A Girl* to be both a call to arms and an embrace: the nurturing touch that says, 'I see you', while also saying, 'Go out and fuck some shit up.' I wanted it to be a kind of fire-breathing dragon of a book that women might read and find sustenance in.

Since its release, we've seen the global rise of the #MeToo movement and the downfall of some of its worst offenders. We have also lost more women than we can count. As I write this on 19 June 2018, Australia's annual death toll of women killed by men's violence has already reached thirty. Last night, I stood with over 10,000 people in Melbourne's Princes Park and held twenty minutes of silence for Eurydice Dixon, the twenty-two-year-old woman who was raped and murdered while walking home after work. In the past week, we have been advised (once again) to be more 'aware' of our surroundings. We have fielded endless complaints from men aggrieved by an outpouring of rage that has failed to acknowledge that *they* didn't do it, that *they* are good men. We have seen as well how much less attention has been paid to Qi Yu, the twenty-eight-year-old woman murdered only a few days before Eurydice, but whose alleged murderer was known to her and therefore considered less frightening to mainstream society than the thought of a *stranger* snatching a woman off the street.

It's easy to feel weary in the face of toxic masculinity, and what seems to be the unrelenting drive to silence women through the use of shame, fear and bristling hostility. People sometimes ask me how I cope with the onslaught of abuse and harassment that comes as part of doing this kind of work. The truth is, if you align yourself with an army of women who are prepared to fight for what they believe in, that stuff very quickly becomes meaningless background noise.

But I sail on a vessel made out of hope, too. Sometime after this book was first released, I received an email from a fifteen-year-old girl who, after reading it, felt buoyed by the realisation that she wasn't alone. She finished her email with the words, 'I am ready to create havoc and unapologetically disrupt the system.'

I do not care what opponents think about women's battle for liberation. I care that fifteen-year-old girls will grow up believing they can lead their own revolution.

We have much to be angry about. And so the fight goes on.

AUTHOR'S NOTE

The following book contains references to topics such as sexual violence, rape culture, eating disorders and mental health issues. Some readers may find certain descriptions or recollections triggering for them and are advised to take care while reading.

Fight Like A Girl is an exploration of my experience as a girl in this world. It is not intended to claim itself as a universal experience, even though many of the situations and feelings described herein are universal to girls the world over. Where I haven't directly cited my sources the information is widely disseminated online.

Some words or abbreviations you may not be familiar with are listed below, with explanations.

Patriarchy: A system in which masculinity is centered and structural power is held and inherited by men.

Cisgender: The description given to those people whose gender identity aligns with the sex they were assigned at birth.

MRAs: Men's Rights Activists. Typically refers to a specific kind of man who believes feminism is oppressing him with its mean words and women who won't stay in their place.

Thank you for reading *Fight Like A Girl*. I hope you enjoy it, and find it galvanising!

In solidarity,
Clementine Ford

—1—

BIRTH OF A FEMINIST

'Of course I believe in equality…but I'm certainly not a feminist.'

Such was the catch cry of my late adolescence, and it was just one of many sadly ignorant views on the world that I offered to anyone who would listen. As a teenager coming of age in the late 1990s, I had multiple explanations for my belief that I was Not A Feminist, and it will come as precisely zero surprise to you that none of them were particularly earth-shattering or well researched.

When I thought of feminism, I thought of a tired old movement filled with irrelevant ideas and even more irrelevant women. They didn't understand that the world had moved on. It wasn't the seventies anymore! Women were allowed to shave their legs and wear make-up and look like *women,* dammit! It didn't mean they were being subjugated by patriarchy, it just meant that they cared about looking nice. What could possibly be wrong with that?

Don't get me wrong. I didn't think we were living in some kind of utopia, a post-feminist paradise that sparkled with the reflective shards of a thoroughly shattered glass ceiling. I had been a loud and opinionated child and, with the exception of a stifling period of time between twelve and sixteen, I was a loud and opinionated teenager. Had I been a boy, this would have been considered acceptable. But I was a girl and, even worse than that, I was a bolshy one. I had already felt the sting of judgment and approbation that came from having opinions while female, and even if I didn't have the tools or skill to articulate what was wrong with that just yet, I could see that something definitely was.

Despite being a feminism-denying adolescent, I was still interested in the disparate treatment of men and women. I bristled each time domestic chores were handed down to my sister and I while our brother was given leave to play and explore, our femaleness apparently carrying with it a greater capacity for cleaning things. Why was there still this sticking point that assumed certain jobs were just the realm of girls? That we were 'just better at those kinds of things', as if we'd emerged from the womb only to look around at the mess, rip the obstetrician's rubber gloves off and get a start on scrubbing the blood off all the medical implements and washing out the sheets?

As the cracks of sexism started to appear at home, the outside world also began to change. An undercurrent of danger was slowly rearing its ugly head. I started to hear warnings about 'being safe' and to experience the unsettling feeling you get when you realise someone's looking at you. On the streets and at school, I became aware of the lingering threat that circled girls. The men who yelled crude sexual taunts and those who simply stared, both executions resulting in the slow and steady shrinking in on oneself that begins with the budding of breasts and never truly goes away.

Still, I did not call myself a feminist. Because even though I knew that women still suffered from inequality, I managed to convince myself that this inequality was a different kind of beast to the sexism and misogyny that had raged throughout the course of human history. It was sexism – but it wasn't *sexism*-sexism.

And so I continued, stockpiling examples and experiences of injustice that would later prove too heavy to bear anymore in silence. I was a camel crossing the desert, and I was starting to feel the rumbling strains of thirst.

■

There would be few people who haven't heard of Harvey Weinstein, the former industry heavyweight who used his power to make or break careers as a weapon against women and whose downfall marked the start of an international conversation about sexual harassment, abuse and the subjugation of women worldwide. In 2017, an article published in the *New York Times* brought long standing whispers and allegations of his abuse to the public's attention. By the end of that year, he had been accused of sexual assault or indecent behaviour by at least fifty-five women. The allegations ranged from appearing naked before them and requesting a massage to openly masturbating and, in some cases, rape. He was also accused of using his position of power to emotionally manipulate and abuse the women around him, particularly those who relied on his industry support. The testimony of Salma Hayek's experience with the mogul while making *Frida* left no doubt about the lengths Weinstein was prepared to go to bully the women he had power over, nor is it possible to ignore the impunity with which he felt entitled to act. Some people would call him a monster, but ascribing supernatural traits to him is too easy. The truth is that he is just a man, and that is far more frightening.

The exposure of Weinstein was followed quickly by that of Kevin Spacey, who was accused of decades' worth of abuse against male colleagues and industry crew members, including at least two rape attempts against teenage boys. Brett Ratner, James Toback, Louis C.K. and Danny Masterson were just some of the high profile names to follow. By January 2018, over one hundred men working across a range of powerful industries had been either accused of sexual harassment (or worse), or gone so far as to step down from their positions after admitting that allegations against them were true.

The floodgates had been opened. Women's testimonies of harassment and abuse began pouring out – first from the entertainment business and then far beyond that into the lives of average women all over the world – something began to shift. The #MeToo campaign (launched ten years ago by Tarana Burke, a woman of colour and an activist living in New York) resulted in a stunning outpouring of voices that echoed 2014's #yesallwomen phenomenon. It led to the formation of Time's Up, an activist organisation spearheaded by women (most of them women of colour) in the entertainment industry invested in bringing positive change for women everywhere who experience abuse and harassment in the workplace. According to statistics compiled by Time's Up, almost half of working women in the United States say they have experienced workplace harassment, with women who work in low-wage service jobs especially at risk. Most women never report it.

And really, who could blame them?

In 1991, Susan Faludi released *Backlash*, an eviscerating text outlining the persistent retaliation of patriarchy against the advances made by women's rights activists throughout history. *Backlash* may be close to three decades old, but the phenomenon it charted is as present today as it was back then. Even as the numbers of women empowered to break their silence with #MeToo increased, so too did the counterclaims against them. There were accusations that this was about attention-seeking and notoriety; that the silence breakers were 'in it for the money', as if the praise received for pointing fingers at men is only outstripped by the financial windfall a woman receives for doing so. Of course, neither is true. Exposing the sexual deviance of men – particularly white, straight, cis men with the kind of power that underpins their abuse in the first place – has always held far graver consequences for the victims speaking out. It took decades for Weinstein to be properly punished for his behaviour – but when he was still considered a kingmaker, it was women who either spoke out against him or rejected his advances who ended up having their careers destroyed.

Even those of us who weren't exposing men at all but simply talking about our multitude of experiences of being a woman in a male-dominated world were ridiculed for being 'too sensitive'. The distinction between sexual assault and 'clumsy sexual attention' was wilfully blurred, with all too many people (including a much publicised line-up of prominent French women, because never let it be said that the patriarchy hasn't done its job properly on us) willing to believe that this was about criminalising normal sexual interaction – as if millions of women around the world had declared war on flirting. Men wondered out loud in comment pieces if this meant they were no longer allowed to hug women in the workplace (as if the loss of this privilege presented a horrifying form of discrimination). The term 'witch hunt' began to be used more frequently, because of course people bending over backwards to defend men against charges of widespread abuse of power would have no problem co-opting a period in history where many thousands of women were murdered by their communities for stepping outside of the status quo and challenging male power. It felt like every time a brave woman spoke out, a thousand angry opponents would line up to malign her as an attention-seeker jumping on a bandwagon for money, fame and the opportunity to ruin men's lives.

Because *of course* that's how people responded.

Women learn early on about the backlash, and we adjust our behaviour accordingly. There have been long stretches of time where I've been silent about the pain I was in – the fear of not being good enough, not pretty enough, not small enough, not compliant enough, not *enough enough enough*. I have moved through the world desperately trying to figure out how this unwieldy body, with its unfeminine heft, loud voice and lack of physical fragility, could possibly fit into one of the tiny little boxes allocated to women. For all the progress we've made, we still live in a patriarchal system that ultimately values cis-heterosexuality, whiteness and masculinity. To be a white straight cis boy in this environment is to experience a degree of privilege beyond the rest. It seems to me that boys who conform to this are given the universe in which to carve out their identities, the promise of infinite space for them to expand into and contract upon. Girls are allowed only enough room to be stars, and we must twinkle, twinkle if they want anyone to pay attention to us.

Because as reaffirming as it is to see the rise up of women around the world finally banding together in a definitive 'mad-as-hell-and-not-gonna-take-it-anymore moment', the fact is we still have so far to go in actually getting people – men, mainly – to listen. The year might have ended with *TIME* Magazine awarding its Person of the Year award to the #silencebreakers who made 2017 an uncomfortable time for sexual predators and sexist assholes, but it began with the inauguration of a man who proudly boasted on tape about grabbing women 'by the pussy' because 'when you're a star, they'll let you do it.'

The election of Donald Trump in November 2016 speaks to the embrace of misogyny, racism and right-wing fuckery that still bubbles and rages throughout the world like a particularly toxic case of flatulence. At the same time as right-wing pundits, legislators and voters were gleefully indulging their mock outrage at the newly exposed (liberal) predatory men in the entertainment industry's traditionally left-wing enclaves, the number of women who had broken their silence on abuse allegedly suffered at the hands of President Trump had grown to at least sixteen. Trump enthusiastically endorsed Roy Moore as the Republican Senate candidate in Alabama, despite the fact at least one woman had alleged he tried to statutorily rape her when she was fourteen and he was in his early thirties. In response to that, Alabama State Auditor Jim Zeigler likened Moore and his alleged victim to Joseph and Mary – you know, Jesus Christ's mum and dad – telling reporters at *The Washington State Examiner,* 'There's nothing immoral or illegal here. Maybe just a little bit unusual.'

Actually Jim, the age of consent in Alabama is sixteen. Not only is it definitely illegal, it's also predatory and traumatising. But then, you do seem to put your stock in a story that sees an adolescent girl impregnated by God so I guess your ambiguities on this issue don't come as too much of a shock.

Moore lost that election, but that was only thanks to Alabama's black population (specifically its black women). The majority of white people wanted to elect Moore, with 57 percent of white college educated women and 73 percent of non-college educated women casting their votes for Trump's preferred candidate. These numbers are more or less in keeping with the ratio of white people who voted for Trump (a shit-tonne) compared with his black supporters (tumbleweeds rolling in the breeze).

Roy Moore's stance on abortion was no doubt considered favourable to the white voters of Alabama. In the age of #MeToo, Republican legislators (most of whom are white, cis-het men from privileged backgrounds) are increasing their assault on reproductive healthcare rights while continuing to remove access to welfare payments and social support systems that would actually help women raise the children they've been forced to have. We only have to look back as recently as 2012 to remember Republican Senate candidate Todd Akin sharing his extremely scientific views on pregnancy with a St. Louis television station, stating, 'If it's legitimate rape, the female body has ways to try to shut the whole thing down.'

But it didn't stop there (even though Akin's bid for the Senate did). Numerous states across the country have since tried to introduce heartbeat bills, which effectively outlaw abortion after around five weeks – at least a week or two before most women will even suspect they might be pregnant (and when, incidentally, the embryo is only the size of a sesame seed). In 2017, a minimum of forty-five bills aiming to roll back hard won abortion rights were introduced to state legislatures across the United States. In Idaho,

Senator Dan Foreman announced plans to sponsor a bill that would classify abortion as first-degree murder, making both the recipient of the procedure and the healthcare provider performing it both liable for prosecution. A similar bill was presented to the Iowa State Legislature. A blanket bill was introduced in Michigan to defund Planned Parenthood entirely (only around 3 percent of its services are the provision of terminations, meaning the success of this bill would, among numerous other things, remove access to the contraception that might prevent the pregnancies in the first place.) And numerous bills were sponsored that sought to outlaw Dilation and Evacuation Procedures (D&E), which would effectively outlaw abortion in the second trimester (gestational weeks fourteen to twenty-six), one of the implications being that women who've suffered late-term miscarriages would have to wait for nature to take its course and deliver a dead fetus, an inhumane assault that poses great risks not just for their mental well being but also their physical health.

And this is just in the legislature.

The impact of rape culture has also continued to be felt over the last few years, both in how the behaviour and presentation of girls and women is policed to evidently 'protect' them from the raging desires of boys and men and in the devastation caused by some of those 'raging desires' themselves. Schools across America have come under fire as girls have fought back against regressive dress codes that sexualise their bodies while providing little to no expectation for male self control. Judicial rulings around the world continue to draw from the victim blaming handbook, with altogether too much concern shown for the perpetrators of rape (most usually when they are white and considered pillars of their community.) In Utah, Judge Thomas Low described a Mormon bishop as 'extraordinarily good' after a jury found him guilty of ten counts of forcible sexual assault and one count of object rape. In California, Judge Aaron Persky sentenced Brock Turner to a paltry six-month sentence (he was out in three) after he was found guilty of sexually assaulting an unconscious woman besides a dumpster outside a fraternity party. In offering a character testimony, Turner's father said he shouldn't be punished for 'twenty minutes of action'.

■

The big business of sports continues to dismiss abuse meted out against women in favour of protecting its star players. In America, the public will rally around NFL players accused of beating and/or sexually assaulting women – men like Ben Roethlisberger, Jameis Winston, Mark Sanchez, Richie Incognito, Brandon Marshall and Phillip Merling, just a handful of the more than four dozen players accused of crimes against women in the last decade – but should they take a knee to protect racial inequality and police brutality, white audiences will bay for their blood.

In the UK, football players have been similarly protected when allegations against them have been put forward. The most famous recent example is that of Ched Evans, a striker for Sheffield United whose conviction for rape in 2012 was later overturned on appeal after a retrial that included a ruling that allowed the jury to hear testimony about his victim's entire sexual history. During the trial, the nineteen-year-old woman – who says Evans let himself into the hotel room while she was having sex with one of his teammates – was subjected to vicious abuse by members of the public, many of whom held strong opinions about life-ruining sluts but were strangely silent about how the degradation of women's bodies is viewed by some men as an effective bonding experience.

A year after his conviction was overturned, Evans returned to Sheffield United on a contract worth £1 million.

Online abuse and harassment has also increased exponentially the more technology becomes integrated with our lives. Image-based abuse and exploitation (more popularly referred to as 'revenge porn') continues to be downplayed by authorities, with women targeted by it blamed for having produced the content in the first place. When women working in the entertainment industry (such as Jennifer Lawrence, Scarlett Johansson and Vanessa Hudgens) have been targeted by hackers who've leaked their personal photographs online, they've been berated for 'not respecting themselves' and 'being so stupid' as to think their private property would remain private.

What's that old saying? Beware those who point the finger with one hand while jerking off with the other.

But then, victim blaming is a universal language.

■

In India in 2012, young student Jyoti Pandey Singh and a male friend both boarded a private bus together after seeing a movie. Jyoti's friend became suspicious when the men on board closed the door on the bus, but his objections were met with a savage beating in which he was knocked unconscious. Jyoti was dragged to the back of the bus and horrifically, brutally, gang-raped and sexually tortured with a rusty iron rod. When it was finished, the men threw both of the young students out on to the road where they were found by passersbys who rushed them to the hospital.

Jyoti had suffered monstrous injuries to her internal organs and genitals. She died two weeks later.

The attack spawned a wave of protests around India, with millions of women and some men taking to the streets to speak out against sexual violence. Yet some members of the establishment also condemned the twenty-three-year-old for being out after dark and in the company of a man who wasn't her husband. Manohar Lal Sharma, a lawyer for three of the male defendants, concluded it was Jyoti's fault because he had never seen a case in which a 'respected' woman in India has been raped. The spiritual leader Asaram Bapu said that 'guilt is not one-sided' and that Jyoti should have 'called the culprits' brothers and begged them to stop'.

If only it were that easy.

But we're so different, westerners proclaim, their racism settling over them like a warm and comforting blanket. We don't treat *our* women like that.

Oh no? You mean we don't demand to know what they were wearing, how much they'd been drinking, who they'd been talking to, how much sex they've had in their whole lives, where their boyfriends were, what who where why how whenever a woman becomes another rape and/or homicide statistic?

Men's Rights Activists (many of whom also express white nationalist fears that the 'white race' is somehow being bred out – if only!) love to behave as if western women's reports of gendered violence are self-indulgent whingefests that ignore the reality of the world's 'real' violence. Many of them took great pleasure in crafting numerous memes calling out those who participated in the global Women's March in 2017 (the world's largest protest to date) for being absent from feminist movements in the Middle East. I'm regularly targeted with Islamophobic hate speech by some of these men. In response to my comments about the rape and abuse of women in my own communities, they send me links to articles about forced marriages, female genital cutting, stonings and so on and so forth. It's like a perverted game to them. *If you really cared about women, you'd be fixing this instead of man hating all over my internet!*

Firstly, it's incorrect to assume that women need any help with coordinating their own liberation movements. There are vibrant feminist movements all over the world, run by women who have the knowledge and intelligence to lead their own movements. I know white people love to march in and take ownership over everything we see, but it's just more colonialism to assume we have the right to do that with liberation movements. But secondly, 'whataboutery' is rarely used as a genuine defense of human rights abuses and more often used to deflect attention away from the dismantling of privileges that people don't want to give up. These MRAs might well argue western women are ignoring the 'real' wrongs in the world in favour of their trivial complaints, but it's not as if they let the existence of, oh I don't know, *political activists being imprisoned in hard labour camps in North Korea* stop them from bitching about how the PC Brigade are trying to criminalise rape jokes.

■

Women are murdered in the service of patriarchy and male supremacy all over the world. On an average day in the United States, over 20,000 phone calls will be made to domestic violence hotlines nationwide according to the National Coalition Against Domestic Violence and roughly three women will be murdered. The presence of a gun inside a home where domestic violence is perpetrated increases the risk of homicide by 500 percent. Three quarters of murder-suicides involve an intimate partner, and *94 percent* of the victims of these crimes are women. Black women are the most likely to be murdered, followed by Native American women, Hispanics and finally whites and Asians. In the UK, where access to firearms is tightly controlled and largely prohibited, the murder of women remains surprisingly high – at around three a week, with more than half of them as a result of acts of domestic violence. The Crime Survey of England and Wales found that an estimated 1.3 million women experienced domestic violence in the year ending between March 2015 and March 2016. On average, UK police receive 100 phone calls every hour related to domestic violence complaints.

In fact, since the year 2001, while western political agendas have been fixated on hunting down would-be terrorists, more women have been killed by their partners than people have died as a result of politically or religiously motivated attacks. For that matter, while domestic terrorism in America is more likely to be perpetrated by white men with no connection to Islam than it is by men of Muslim faith, these men are treated as 'lone wolves' rather than representatives of an entire demographic of people or (to be more accurate) a symptom of social conditioning that breeds malcontented males. How interesting that so many of these lone wolves also have histories of perpetrating domestic violence against women? It's almost as if angry men gripped by a sense of rage and entitlement are dangerous in some way.

Still, you can't swing a cat in a western country these days without hitting a man eager to tell you all about how we women should be grateful for how good we've got it. ('We could treat you worse you know, so you better watch yourself!')

Anti-feminists hold onto the idea that misogyny was abandoned long ago in the way way back, and that it's paranoid fantasy to pretend it might still be a problem today. But the way way back isn't as far back as people like to think. In the US for example, it was still legal to rape your wife (it was called 'conjugal rights') in all fifty states up until the mid-1970s, when feminists began challenging legislative bodies and campaigning against sexual violence. It wasn't until 1993 that marital rape had been outlawed nationwide, and came only two years after England abolished marital immunity for the same crime.

Or, to put it another way, that legislation is younger than Taylor Swift.

Even then, does this mean men have stopped raping their wives? Of course not. Nor does criminalisation mean men have stopped raping women who *aren't* their wives. In 2017, the American Journal of Preventative Medicine published a paper that estimated the lifetime economic cost of rape at $122,461 per survivor. When you extrapolate this to cover the more than 25 million US adults who have survived rape, this delivers a lifetime population economic burden of $3.1 *trillion*. According to RAINN, one sixth of American women have been the victim of an attempted or completed rape. Women account for the vast majority of rape survivors and their highest risk period for being subjected to sexual violence is between the ages of sixteen and nineteen. Non-college educated women between eighteen and twenty-four are four times more likely than the general population to experience sexual violence. Native American women are significantly more likely than women of other races to be raped, but unlike other women they are almost as likely to be raped by a stranger as they are an acquaintance. Up to 13 percent of rape survivors will attempt suicide. Approximately 90 percent of women with intellectual disabilities will experience sexual violence; in Australia, one of the common judicial 'solutions' for this has been to allow families and carers to apply for medical dispensation to have women in this demographic be sterilised as they reach puberty – because why not throw some eugenics in with rape culture? In 2013, the Senate Inquiry into the Forced and Involuntary Sterilization of People with Disabilities ultimately decided against banning the practice in favour of 'regulating' it more closely – a fact that still does nothing to address the real problem, which is that nine out of ten women with intellectual disabilities are being subjected to horrific sexual violence.

Out of all those statistics, all those lives that have been forever changed and marked by violence, this is perhaps the most frightening one: only 2 percent of rapists will ever be convicted of their crime.

The reality is that patriarchy – the overriding system we all live under whereby men are privileged by structural and social power – is alive and well. For every step forward that women as a class of people take, the patriarchy and its enforcers use all of their might to try to push us back twice as far. Women suffer the world over, some more than others, and my heart throbs for us all.

■

Of course, I didn't know any of this back then. If I had, it would have saved an awful lot of trouble and angst. As it was, at seventeen I was Not A Feminist – but for all the intellectual justifications I could try to make now, the reason was pretty simple. I was overwhelmingly scared of how it would make other people think of me. And when I say 'other people', I mean 'boys'.

Securing the good opinion of boys had by this stage been a concern of mine for at least a third of my life. Since the onset of puberty, I had felt keenly awkward in my skin, undeserving of the label 'girl' and insurmountably far from the identity of 'woman'. I defined everything I was by everything I was not. I was tall, but I was not willowy. I was strong, but not thin.

I thought of myself as something separate to femininity, an unwieldy and unattractive blob whose very existence was an imposition on the boys who were used to being charmed by the small, slight and accommodating beauty of the delicate creatures around me. My sense of feminine disgrace was so profound that I quickly fell into the habit of apologising whenever I was introduced to a peer.

'This is Clementine,' a friend might say, and I'd cringe internally, bristling at the inconvenience of those three syllables, before rushing in with something reassuring like, 'It's okay, you can call me Clem.' I had unconsciously come to the conclusion that it was too big an ask to expect that a girl as galumphing and large as me could be called by her full name. 'Clem' seemed more suitable, an acceptance of the stocky androgyny I had not asked for but which I reasoned must be navigated without complaint.

If I were beautiful, I thought, I could call myself whatever I liked and people would be captivated by me. If I were slim hipped and slight, I could be a Clementine and my schoolmates would think me as graceful as a Shakespearean heroine, my features as delicate as fine bone china with a birdlike appetite to match.

I was not these things, and to pretend otherwise was to participate in a humiliating display of wishful thinking. Better to get on with it eagerly, as if being such a tragic outsider to the female condition had been my plan all along. No one would think that a 'Clem' was entertaining any fanciful notions of fielding evening phone calls from boys or joining other couples to kiss in quiet corners of dimly lit living rooms. A 'Clem' wouldn't mourn these truths or think about what it might be like to be suddenly lifted into the air, squealing with delight and demanding in mock indignation to be put down.

So I called myself 'Clem' and filled my wardrobe with men's trousers bought in charity shops, cargo shorts found in surf stores and sneakers which didn't pinch my toes. I did all this to let people know that I was in on the joke that was me. *It's okay*, I tried to translate to them. *I'm not even trying to be thought of as a girl, so it doesn't matter that you don't see me that way.*

I told myself that, and went to bed every night wishing to wake up different.

I wish I could sit here now, two decades later, and write brazenly and proudly about being the kind of girl who didn't give a shit, who told bully boys to go fuck themselves while subtly trying to recruit the girls who put so much stock in securing their good approval and the limited rewards that came with that. I would like my memories to be of a girl who didn't treat other girls with suspicion. A girl who didn't think that boasting about 'just getting along better with boys' was a way to circumvent the deep and devastating feeling of being irrelevant to their dicks and so instead became useful tools for their emotional egos. I wish I could say that I had integrity and strength, a girl with an unshakeable sense of self and a belief that I mattered as much as other girls, that they mattered as much as me.

But it's not the way things were. I was a nothing-girl, and adolescence was an obstacle course which needed to be both navigated and survived.

In her wildly popular book, *How To Be a Woman*, Caitlin Moran proposed this simple test for feminists:

Put your hand in your pants.

a) Do you have a vagina? and

b) Do you want to be in charge of it?

If you said 'yes' to both, then congratulations! You're a feminist.

How To Be a Woman was a game-changer in many ways. It was entertaining, funny and irreverent. It has been credited with being part of the groundswell to reinvigorate feminist activism, introducing ideas of gender equality to a mainstream audience who had fallen victim to the anti-feminist propaganda highlighted in Susan Faludi's *Backlash*. For those of us wandering in the desert wastelands of feminist activism and social awareness, it was like a sudden downpour that swept us back into the suddenly welcoming arms of the greater population.

But there are problems with Moran's limited scope here. Namely, that being a feminist isn't as simple as putting your hand in your pants and finding a vagina there. And it's not as simple as that because, as trans activists working against a tide of phobia and suspicion have brought into the mainstream, being a woman isn't as simple as what goes on in between your legs. To suggest otherwise is to dismiss fundamental aspects of womanhood and indeed personhood that go far beyond physicality, not to mention to ignore the multitude of ways we are oppressed by things like sexual violence, domestic homicide and discrimination.

Americans between the ages of fifteen to thirty-four face about a one in 12,000 chance of being murdered, according to the National Centre for Health Statistics. But for black transgender women in the same age bracket, that risk increases exponentially to a rate of one in 2,600 (and that's just based on the known numbers). The media organisation Mic found that between 2010 and 2016, 'at least 111 transgender and gender-nonconforming Americans were murdered because of their gender identity'. Of this number, 72 percent were black trans women and gender-nonconforming femmes. Consider the words of transgender activist and actress Laverne Cox, who appeared on Katie Couric's show alongside transgender model, Carmen Carrera only to be repeatedly asked about their genitalia. Having failed to get a response from Carrera on what the activist called a 'really personal' topic, Cox responded by criticising the focus on transition and surgery as an objectification of trans people that erases their lived experiences.

'The reality of trans people's lives is that so often we are targets of violence,' she said. 'We experience discrimination disproportionately to the rest of the community. Our unemployment rate is twice the national average; if you are a trans person of colour, that rate is four times the national average. The homicide rate is highest among trans women. If we focus on transition, we don't actually get to talk about those things.'

But also, it's just pretty fucking rude and creepy to ask people about their junk. If you wouldn't want someone doing it to you, don't do it to somebody else. That's basic human decency 101.

Later in *How to Be a Woman*, Moran offers what is perhaps a better – or at least broader – definition of what it can mean to be a woman: 'When a woman says, "I have nothing to wear!" what she really means is, "There's nothing here for who I'm supposed to be today."'

As individuals, we have a vast and magnificent range of identity expressions, desires, hopes, passions, beliefs and fears. The terrain of possibilities that exists inside our hearts is immense – and yet, so often the experience of *being* a woman in this world is one that is suffocating and heartbreaking.

■

Part of being a woman, regardless of what you look like under your clothes, is the knowledge that other people will assume the right to decide who you are allowed to be on any given day. There is a little flexibility (particularly if you have privileges that other women don't, like being white or having money), but there are also rules so strictly enforced that you must suffer the consequences for disobeying them. Be whatever you like, but do not be this. Do not be loud. Do not be sexual. Do not be prudish. Do not be disagreeable. Do not challenge. Do not be too fat. Do not be too skinny. Do not be too dark skinned. Do not be too masculine. Do not take up too much space. Do not say the things we don't like. Laugh when we tell you to. Smile when we tell you to. Fuck when we tell you to. And you will be free.

In *Princesses and Pornstars,* Emily Maguire writes that her own hesitation to label herself a feminist came from one very basic place. She was afraid that if she called herself a feminist, boys wouldn't want to have sex with her. When I first read this, I nodded in wry recognition. Because isn't this what it fundamentally comes down to, when you strip away the quasi-dense language and the analysis of social codes? That women alike (particularly those in their adolescence) have been trained to desire the approval of men? And that the way a sexist society teaches its men to show approval for women is by deciding they want to fuck them?

I feared all the irrelevant things that women are even now still taught to fear, and I worked my hardest to avoid being associated with them. I didn't explicitly know any feminists (in the same way that some people think they don't know any gay folks), but everything I heard said about them made it seem they weren't very well liked. Feminists were loud and shouty. They overreacted to everything. They didn't know how to relax and have a laugh. They had to turn everything into a goddamn *issue* and spoil everyone's fun. Worst of all, they were *ugly*. Everyone said so. Girls are raised to believe that the most important thing we can be is pretty. We learn early on that this won't just garner us attention and rewards, but is in fact the rent we must pay in order to negotiate even the most illusory of powers. If we aren't offering something pleasant for men to look at while they're forced to listen to us, what's the point of us at all?

The message isn't so much banged into us as it is kneaded into the fabric of our identities. To be granted an audience with the Gods, we must bring the appropriate tributes of beauty, complicity and deferential admiration. Those who turn up empty-handed will be punished severely.

How many times have you heard or seen someone dismiss a woman's opinion by calling her ugly? By calling her a slut? Maybe even a dumb cunt?

When there are so many people willing to degrade women so horrifically just for having the nerve to express an opinion it doesn't take long for us to regress into silence. Think of how Donald No-One-Respects-Women-More-Than-Me Trump characterised the journalist Megyn Kelly as having 'blood coming out of her wherever' just because she had the audacity to do her job during the Presidential debates, or the time he suggested Senator Kirsten Gilibrand was willing to do *anything* in exchange for campaign contributions. Think of how his supporters whooped and brayed over the outrageous fun of it all, his actions empowering them to be more brazen and open about their own hatred for women who challenged their sense of authority. For that matter, think of the times you might have personally been labelled a 'bitch' or a 'slut' or a 'cunt' because you've said something a man doesn't like or disagreed with him in something as meaningless as an online comment thread. In the face of such overwhelming hostility and virulent payback, it's nothing short of remarkable that any of us have the courage to claim space at all in the verbal marketplace.

As a young girl and then a young woman, I felt all of these things keenly. At its heart, this is why I was so frightened to call myself a feminist. Everything I observed about the world screamed for women to take up arms against gender inequality once more, but I was afraid that this was a move I couldn't come back from. I already suffered from the overwhelming sense that I wasn't good enough to be judged positively by society's standards of womanhood – but I wanted to believe that I might one day be. That if I played the game hard enough, smiled at all the right moments and giggled in collusion whenever men put my gender (or even just me) down, that I might one day be deemed worthy of their attention and respect.

Realising that the likelihood of this happening was slim to none was one of my first steps towards embracing feminism not just as a theoretical concept but as a label and identity. I enrolled in a gender studies course at university and, almost immediately, everything I thought I knew about the world was completely deconstructed and then rebuilt again. I learned about concepts like 'symbolic annihilation', the idea that women have been ritually erased from history, storytelling and pop culture to make it seem like we have only ever been bit players.

I learned phrases like 'hegemonic power'* (which I have admittedly used rarely) and 'structural violence'† (which I have used much more). Both were useful tools in recognising how women have been oppressed by the enforcement of gender inequality and invisible discrimination. I started dropping 'patriarchy' into my conversations. Referencing patriarchy fell out of favour for a few years, because it seemed cheesy and retro – a throwback to the humourless feminists of old, saddled as they were with their earnest and daggy descriptions of *shit that had evolved, man.* Thankfully, it's back, along with words like 'sexist', 'misogynist' and 'dickhead', all beautiful words which can be used separately or strung together, your choice.

I didn't understand everything I was learning in my gender studies classes, and I don't agree now with some of the ideas I formerly embraced. My feminism has changed dramatically over the years, tempering in some areas and becoming more radical in others. I have become much more aware of my own privilege since my days spent ranting about inequality on the university lawns. My father is Australian and my mother was from Guyana, but I have white skin and have lived with its benefits my entire life. I'm cisgender, middle class, university educated and I have a platform that isn't afforded to the majority of people. I'm queer, but I am partnered with a cis man so I currently experience straight passing privilege too. Reckoning with the privileges I have will be a lifelong task, because the assumption that we can somehow

---

* Predominance by one group within a society, typically a group that exerts undue influence. e.g. White people have hegemonic power over people of colour
† Violence inflicted by social structures or institutions e.g. the structural violence inflicted by a lack of access to universal healthcare

transcend the need to have those conversations with ourselves just by reading a few of the right books is where a lot of damage is caused. I have caused damage before and I will probably do so again, because the privileges that I do have are representative of structural oppressions that I cannot possibly hope to understand. What I can and must do is be open to acknowledging my fuck-ups. To offer not just apology, but an ongoing commitment to being better.

This process isn't easy, but it's necessary. And again, this is one of the great joys that feminism and the activists engage with it have given me. I am prompted continuously to think in ways I never have before, and I'm challenged continuously to defend my viewpoints but also be okay with letting go of the ones that no longer make sense to me or that can't be defended by any metric of intersectionality.

Above all, there are two fundamentally important gifts feminism has given me, and I received them the moment I opened myself up to it. The first was a sense of community among like-minded individuals. Women whose bodies had been violated in various ways, whose integrity had been called into question when they spoke out about it and who had learned, as a result, to expect such treatment and just get on with things.

I was welcomed into this community alongside other newbies. The more our minds expanded to accommodate this startling, secret history of the world, the more strength we gleaned. We sat together in huddled circles on the university lawns, around pub tables, on the floor of the student newspaper office, and we talked excitedly about things that had, throughout all of our adolescent upbringings, seemed verboten. It felt powerful and liberating. It felt like we had spent our whole lives stumbling blindly through the dark. But at last, someone had turned on the light and we gazed around the room in awe, blinking, realising suddenly that we were not alone.

Those women remain my friends today. They were my first comrades and my lasting saviours. Without them, I don't know what I would have done.

And this is the second thing feminism gave me, and it is more valuable than words can possibly say. It taught me that *my thoughts and feelings were real*. It took the edges of myself that I had rubbed out, tried to soften, tried to erase, and it made them sharp once more. It's always been convenient to use the tropes of stereotypes to scare women away from embracing feminism, because it has the double whammy effect of diminishing the movement's reach while reinforcing women's subjugation. But the only people who care whether or not a woman is hairy, ugly, fat, lesbian, butch, 'man-hating' or aggressively opinionated are the people who are so terrified of the idea that women might be real humans in their own right that they can literally find no other way to attack them other than relating it back to whether or not a man wants to fuck them.

I have, thankfully, long been at the point where I don't give a shit whether or not someone wants to fuck me. The threat of some dude's disapproval or disappointed flaccid cock doesn't tie me up in knots anymore. There are only so many times you can be called an ugly-fat-hairy-bitch-slut-cunt-with-daddy-issues before the words become utterly meaningless. Once upon a time, the threat of those words would have been enough to stitch me into silence. Now, they just sound like the pathetic last wheezes of a dwindling breed in its death throes.

The dull throb of learning what it means to be a girl in the world had the result of making me cower inwards. I tried to shrink myself and my opinions so as to make myself more palatable to the people around me, taking the whirligig of sadness, frustration and anger that stirred so violently in my chest and hiding it behind acquiescent giggles and Cool Girl behaviour. I didn't know that what I felt was blessedly normal; that there were legions of girls out there just like me who wandered through this emotional wilderness with the same crushing weight of loneliness and uncertainty, fearing that there was something wrong with them, unable to see the extent of their perfect clarity or the solidarity that awaited them once they found their people.

Nothing hurts more than realising you've been complicit in your own silence. Nothing feels better than unleashing your voice. A friend of mine once said to me that feminism helped her to figure out a way of being a girl that doesn't hurt. I was floored. She'd captured everything about this movement and ideology that I had always known, but never thought to articulate. A lot of the time, being a girl in this world *hurts*. Before you are aware of it, it just presents as a persistent throb. A slow and steady sense that something isn't quite right. You wonder if the world you're experiencing is the same one that everyone else is living in. Do they see colours the same way you do? Do their senses work differently? Is there something wrong with you? This feeling builds and builds and – if you're lucky – it suddenly hits you, out of nowhere. *This* is what it's like to be a girl. To feel subjugated and alone, to know that the words you say, the ideas you have and the gifts you can contribute are all considered null and void unless you offer them in a way that maintains the status quo.

In the end, this is the simplest answer that I can provide for why I'm a feminist and how I came to be that way.

Feminism helped me figure out a way of being a girl that doesn't hurt. It is my constant companion, my life saver, my oxygen tank. Without the collective of ideas, women and strength that feminism has given me, I wouldn't know how to breathe. I wouldn't know how to laugh. And most importantly, I wouldn't know how to fight.

I am a girl, and this is my manifesto. Welcome to the war room.

–2–

READY FOR MY CLOSE-UP

Before the advent of digital technology and mobile phones smaller than a chequebook (a form of monetary exchange popular among our ancestors), families used to record their precious moments on gigantic whirring bricks. These things were called 'video cameras', and they were able to harness the magic of space and time to record anywhere up to fifteen minutes' worth of moving pictures, which could then be transferred to a machine called a 'video player'. The whole process took about four hundred years from start to finish. It was truly like living in the future.

My family got our first video camera when I was roughly seven years old. I remember being completely blown away by how cool it was. We had a video camera! We could make videos! We could actually record ourselves living our own lives and then watch it back!

Now, unless you're a parent, this is the kind of thought that only a seven-year-old could have about the life of a seven-year-old. I was a goober, not a Goonie. The various excitements of my day were limited to eating margarine on a spoon while standing in front of the fridge, and using my mother's double-handed exercise tyre to pretend to be one of the Wheelers from Return to Oz. No one would have been interested in watching a montage of moments from my day with the possible exception of my parents – and I'm pretty sure even they would have taken a raincheck.

But still, I thought this video camera was sensational. Whenever my parents pulled it out of its gigantic box and hoisted it onto their shoulders, I started prepping myself to 'perform'. I was always ready for my close-up, preparing for the time when I'd become a famous actress, live in a mansion and suddenly look exactly like Goldie Hawn.

Those video tapes are lost now, but some of the scenes are etched so deeply in my memory that I can replay them at will. There I am at nine, singing 'Under the Sea' from The Little Mermaid while prancing up and down the staircase. I am chubby and freckled, my fluorescent bike shorts stretched across my thick thighs and with a visible gap between my front teeth. I am also joyful. Clearly, this is before I started to learn that chubbiness and joy were supposed to be mutually exclusive.

Another tape, and there I am shovelling birthday cake into my mouth. It's a glorious pink sponge smothered in even more glorious pink frosting, and half of it is smeared around my mouth and in my hair. Save it for later, I'm probably thinking to myself, already imagining the unbridled comfort that would come from sucking dried cream and sugar off a ponytail lollipop.

I have always loved to eat. As a child, I could consume entire packets of chocolate-covered Hobnobs in one sitting. I knew where my mother hid the sour cream and chive Pringles (top level of the pantry, behind the flour), and I'd sneak up there after school to snatch fistfuls. Terrified of getting caught, I'd quickly lick the radioactive dust off of each crisp and then mash the entire handful into my mouth. I'd hoover them down before anyone could discover me, my heart beating fast against my chest from the adrenaline (or possibly even the vast quantities of MSG). My idea of an after-school snack was mayonnaise and ham slathered on half a loaf of white bread and washed down with a litre of chocolate milk.

I indulged in these things freely, partly because my parents' frequent absence gave me unregulated access to the fridge, but also because I had no idea that my femaleness meant I shouldn't. I didn't know that girls weren't supposed to be loud and rambunctious. That we weren't supposed to be obnoxious or bossy, or horde our possessions and power. That girls were only allowed to love food – to take pleasure in consuming it, yearning for it and daydreaming about it – if our bodies were small enough to be granted permission.

At seven, eight and nine, I barrelled through the world with a loud voice, in loud clothes and with a loud, large appetite. I didn't understand yet that this way of living wasn't considered a birthright but a crime, and that punishments awaited the loud girls like me who ate too much and took up too much space and behaved as if our place in the world was a given and not a negotiation.

■

I spent most of my childhood living in the Middle East. My dad's job had taken him all over the world (at least, to the parts of the world where gas and mining were kind of a big deal), and when I was three that meant moving to Oman, a large sultanate on the eastern border of the United Arab Emirates. It's a beautiful country, with stunning desert landscapes and spectacular ocean coves. Our house was washed in white paint to reflect the sun and tiled with marble to radiate the cool. When I was little, my house and the haven it offered felt like the safest place in the world.

On weekends, my family and I would drive to the beach with our fins and snorkels piled into the boot. It's been more than two decades, but I'm pretty sure I could still find my way from our old house, across the sprawling Arab city and over the mountain that separated it from the ocean. Those last five minutes were the best part of it. As we circled down the cliff towards the sea, us kids would start to bounce in our seats a little, anticipating what was coming next. And then, just when we thought we couldn't stand it any longer, there she'd appear, glittering in the sunlight – a marine playground. We'd pull into a park, drag the esky to one of the permanent umbrella stands, wrestle our fins on and then waddle out into the drink.

About fifty metres out from the shoreline, a sturdy wooden raft was anchored to the ocean floor. I liked to swim out there and float on my back, spreading my arms and legs like a starfish and closing my eyes against the sun. Lying in this position, all the sounds from the outside world disappeared and were replaced by the muffled pressure of moving currents. I listened to the chk chk chk of the ocean, the magnified sound of fish talking to each other as they nibbled at the coral.

In the water, you're weightless. And even though you're alone with your thoughts, you're also wrapped in a cocoon of something much bigger than them. It's hard to feel too anxious when the sheer magnitude of your environment is reminding you how irrelevant you are to the bigger picture. As an adult, this recognition instils a very particular kind of relief. As a child, it simply feels like the long summer days will never end and there will always be more time.

On land, it's a different story. One afternoon, I was sitting under our beach umbrella when three kids approached me. Let's call them Tom, Dick and Sally. I knew them from 'around the traps' which, at nine years old, meant I'd been forced by necessity to play with them at various grown-up parties and occasionally at the pool. I didn't like them, but kids are curious creatures; we'll play with pretty much anyone the same height as us, even the people we hate.

Tom and Dick were boys a little bit younger than me, and Sally was a girl of my age. They asked me if I wanted to go rock-pooling with them. I couldn't imagine anything less fun, but I said yes anyway because as boisterous and confident as I was within the safety of my family's home, I was also insecure about making friends and I wanted people to like me. I traipsed behind them along the beach, already regretting my decision. Tom and Dick were whispering to each other and giggling, and Sally was marching imperiously to their right. My skin was tight from the salt water, and the sand was rubbing uncomfortably on my feet. Why was I here? Why wasn't I swimming around the raft pretending I was a mermaid?

I trudged on.

We reached the rock pools at the far side of the cove and started to poke about in the shallows. Just as I was bending down to reach one of the pools, I heard the three of them giggling behind me. I turned my head, my bottom still stuck in the air. They were pointing at me and making a grand show of whispering behind their hands. I stood up, feeling ambushed.

'What's so funny?' I asked.

It was Dick who spoke up. 'You're fat,' he said.

Sally sneered at me from next to him while Tom guffawed.

It wasn't the first time I'd been called fat. I'd even used the word myself. My brother and sister I hurled it at each other like a weapon when we were mad, and it always stung. It was different to the torture we usually inflicted on each other, which mostly involved using one sibling to sit on the other so they couldn't move while the third one tickled their feet or farted on their head. Although neither of these things was all that fun to be on the receiving end of, there was something vaguely jovial in their application. Fat was different. Even as kids, we knew it was a word designed to humiliate and silence.

My cheeks burned. But worse was my feeling of furious injustice. I wasn't the only fat girl in attendance.

'Sally's fatter than me!' I protested. I know it's not admirable to throw someone else under the bus, particularly when it's another girl, but it does go to show just how deeply entrenched those feelings of patriarchal capitulation are. It didn't occur to me to tell them there was nothing wrong with being fat, or to defend myself or even to call them a mean name in return. On some level, I must have agreed with the assessment. I was fat. My only defence was to prove that I wasn't as fat as one of their allies, and therefore render their arguments null and void.

'She is so not as fat as you,' piped up Dick. 'She is this big' – he pulled his hands apart to mime the measurement of someone's waist – 'and you are this big.' His hands widened considerably. Standing beside him, Sally beamed.

I must have protested further, because the next thing I remember is being told to stand back to back with her while the boys judged which of us was the most disgusting. Definitely me, according to Tom and Dick. The matter of my repulsive girth settled, the boys rapidly became bored and wandered back along the beach while Sally chatted animatedly next to them, her laughter carried back to me on the breeze.

I was quiet on the drive home that night. Underneath my damp t-shirt, my tummy loomed up at me.

Fat, it whispered.

■

I started to notice all the ways in which my body was different to my friends'. I was larger, wobblier and thicker. My legs were covered in a rugged coat of hair. I wasn't yet wearing a bra, although it's unclear whether or not the things protruding from my chest were actually breasts or just two lumps of fat that had sought refuge there after turning up at my middle and finding there was no room at the inn. There's a school photograph of me from around this time, self-hatred and depression already starting to write themselves across my face. I recall this picture for two reasons. The first is that I've taken furiously to one of the other girl's faces with a pen and scratched deep marks into it. Beside her head, I've written: Bitch! The second is because it was the first time I seemed properly able to articulate the sharp stab of disgust and self-loathing that I would feel looking at any photograph of myself from that point on.

When I was eight, I spent a couple of years at boarding school. To say this was an unhappy time for me would be an understatement. Although I would never trade the experience now (strength through adversity etc.), it was my first glimpse into how horrible children can be and the particular weapons made available to girls just trying to survive. The fact that there was only a handful of girl boarders in my year level was both an upside and a downside. We were forced to be friends through sheer proximity, but this also meant we couldn't escape each other.

One Saturday afternoon, we were sprawled on the wooden deck outside one of the classrooms. I remember it as being like a wooden hut, which I suspect is the universal attempt by school architects to create the illusion of healthy outdoorsiness to parents considering banishing their children to a prison of morning wake-up bells, prescribed dinner times and detentions for having wet hair at breakfast. As we sat there in our mandatory civvies uniforms of blue jeans and maroon jumpers, the circle tried to find a girlfriend for the unpartnered Josh.

Of course, nine-year-olds partnering up sounds absurd to an adult, but it was very serious to us. Couples who 'went together' had a particular kind of gravitas. They didn't actually do anything, but that wasn't the point. The point was to be chosen. I guess that makes a lot of sense when you consider these were all kids whose parents, for various reasons, had sent them away.

This charge to find a match for Josh was being led by Sarah, who was the most popular girl in our year but coincidentally also the nicest. Sarah threw my name into the ring, deciding that Josh and I should 'go together'. He grudgingly accepted. I was elated, not because I secretly fancied Josh but because it was a big deal to be singled out by Sarah. We all chatted happily for the next minute or so, until Josh suddenly piped up with, 'What about Cheryl? Can't I go with her?'

The group exclaimed their approval, each high-pitched shriek puncturing my ego further. I joined in, acknowledging that yes, that pairing made much more sense. Why hadn't we thought of it before? But inside, I wailed. Cheryl was a two-faced moll.

These people were the closest things I had to any kind of friends or normality, and even they thought I was nothing. Realising this, the tiniest part of my heart broke away. When it found its way back to me, it came with the belief that, given the option, there would always be someone better, prettier and more preferable than me – someone who just made more sense. Irrational though it may be, I've never been able to shake it. Relationships have been sabotaged before they've even begun, the thought of someone liking me filling me with a deep and abiding disgust. Why would you like me? I mentally sneer at potential partners. What's wrong with you?

For a lot of us, self-love is a hard mountain to climb. And it's not made remotely easier by the messages we receive about which of us deserves love and which of us doesn't. I started to feel some sense of this on the wooden deck that day. I was already tall, loud and lumpy. Realising I was 'fat' and 'undesirable' just added to the trauma. As the girls around me blossomed, my resentment for them increased. Why did they have it so easy? Why could they eat what they like and still stay so thin? Why were all the labels that made a girl too much of one thing the same traits that made her not enough of another?

■

A few months after I turned twelve, my parents announced that we were moving to England. I dreaded the prospect, and exercised my disgust by stomping up and down staircases and dramatically telling my parents they were 'ruining my life!' When the time came to leave, I exchanged tearful goodbyes with my friends – girls I had secretly cursed for being considered more popular and attractive than myself, and boys whose admiration I desperately yearned for and hence didn't punish to anywhere near the same kind of level – and began a new life in a picturesque seaside town on the Norfolk coast.

Sheringham was a world apart from Muscat. For a start, the kids there were wild. They drank alcohol and smoked cigarettes, both things I swore I would never do but enthusiastically took up within a year. Sartorially, it was unlike anything I'd experienced growing up in a modest Muslim country. Girls with tiny waists and thigh gaps draped themselves in short tops and shorter skirts, while boys who put in no effort at all looked on half approvingly and half bored. Once again, I found myself simultaneously hating and envying my female peers.

That tremulous period between turning double digits and becoming a teenager can be difficult enough, but it didn't help that I was settling into a new school with what I felt was a weird name, a weird accent and an entirely undesirable body. I longed to return home to the life and people I understood, but relief never came. With no means to control my environment, I did what so many girls and women have done and tried to control the one thing I felt sure I could conquer – my rebellious, unwieldy body.

■

I had tried to diet before, copying my mother when she ate nothing but cabbage soup for days on end or grimaced her way through sour grapefruit halves. Nothing had worked, because those diets are both medically irresponsible and completely disgusting. And so I began to cut back on meal sizes instead and started walking the thirty-minute distance to school. Portion control and daily exercise are widely praised as the kind of 'sensible' methods people should use to lose weight, with little regard for how easily they can escalate into obsessive behaviours. Soon, my new eating plan had turned into a punishing diet; everything became about the limited calories I allowed myself to consume, and the rigorous order in which I could have them. Anything above my self-imposed daily calorie allowance sent me into a hysterical, obsessive cycle of measuring my body with a tape measure over and over to check that I hadn't suddenly become 'fat' again.

At night, I would lay in bed with my hand on my stomach, enjoying the feeling of the protruding hip bones that were growing more prominent every day. I am in control, I'd think to myself.

The weight loss was rapid. My clothes became baggy and shapeless almost overnight. My parents congratulated me on a job well done, telling me how good I looked and how proud they were of me. (Side note: Don't do this to your kids.) I began to wear shorter, tighter skirts to school, feeling suddenly inducted into a secret world of girlhood that I'd never been privy to before – the one where you're allowed to feel good when people look at you instead of feeling exposed. As I continued to shrink, I thought of my body as a monster eating itself. I starved it, because in starving it I thought I could defeat it. I closed my mouth to stop it from making a sound, from telling me how hungry it was. Instead, I looked for nourishment from other things. Appreciative glances from boys at the park, smiles that had never been turned my way before with lips that moved to offer me cigarettes and alcohol. The spiteful glances of other girls, whose envy I took as a compliment. Acknowledgment from my parents that I was succeeding. Even the prick of smug self-satisfaction that came from thinking my ability to control my body might turn me into the favoured daughter.

'It's so easy,' I would say when my sister was in earshot. 'Really, anyone can do it if they just try hard enough.'

I lost a lot of weight in a really short amount of time. The loss was so unhealthy that my period stopped. I'd been so desperate to get it and so excited when it finally arrived, but I wasn't sorry about its departure. Being undernourished enough to stop menstruation mightn't have been ideal, but to my anorexic mind it felt a little like having a secret savings account in the bank. My budding breasts withered up and never really followed in the footsteps of my more buxom mother and sister. My shadowed ribs enveloped me like a suit of armour.

But it still wasn't enough. The slender body I'd been so thrilled to carve out from a mountain of flesh was no less terrifying to me than the gruesome mass I'd left behind. I knew I was thin, but I could never take pleasure in this newfound thinness for fear it would abandon me. I was obsessed. When I wasn't counting calories, I was thinking about calories. I stood in front of the mirror, poking and prodding at the skin stretched over my bones, pinching all that I could between my fingers and recoiling in disgust. I looked at myself from every angle, pulling my clothes flat against me so I could check that I was as thin now as I had been three hours ago. I began to deprive myself even further, instituting a series of bizarre rules. If the morning's measurement had shown I'd gained half an inch overnight (please note, it is totally normally for your weight to fluctuate throughout the day), I would gasp in horror and swear off breakfast. If I'd stayed the same or even lost a millimetre or two, I'd shiver with excitement – but I'd still skip food just to be on the safe side.

Becoming thin was easy. Staying thin defeated my mind, my body and my spirit. Escaping the hatred I felt for myself was like trying to run away from a tidal wave. I wrote endless pages of self-hating poison in my diary, paragraphs and paragraphs dissecting my ugliness and physical grotesqueness. In these disturbed ramblings, I drew picture after picture depicting what I thought I looked like, the scribbles illustrating delusions of a misshapen duck's body: no tits, massive arse, enormous saggy stomach, ham legs.

My fixation with controlling my body crossed over into an anxiety disorder, and I started throwing up after meals. Bent over the bowl, I rid myself of the food I did not deserve and fed myself instead on self-loathing.

The boisterousness I had exhibited as a child had given way to shame and self-doubt, the way it does for most girls who spend their childhoods exploring imaginary castles in the garden, singing loudly without fear, and proudly telling anyone who'll listen about all the things they're good at and all the adventures still to come. As our bodies expand and the volume of our voices decreases, we enter the territory that lies beyond the familiarity of our garden boundaries. Here, we learn about what happens to the girls who break the rules. The ones who have too many opinions, who eat too much, talk too much, fuck too much and act too much like we might have the right to decide what happens to us and why.

We learn what happens to those girls, and it teaches us what not to do. Don't grow, but shrink. Use your inside voice at all times. Pick at your food, and pretend you're full before you actually are. Dress for your shape. If your shape isn't willowy and thin, drape yourself in layers of fabric and silent apology. Don't offer opinions before confirming that other people, especially boys, share them. Don't say no to things when people want them from you. If people take things that you didn't want to give them, be prepared to explain why you didn't say no. Keep your legs closed – on public transport, in the living room, while watching TV, while lying in bed, while lying with someone else. Be the gatekeeper. Know that boys can't help themselves, that it's your job to help them learn self-control, but you must never, ever, ever tell them that, because it's not fair to treat boys like they're dangerous. Sacrifice yourself so that they might become better people. Be the scaffold they need to climb to heights greater than you'll ever be supported to reach.

Be aware that the space you take up is borrowed and your right to occupy it is dictated by your willingness to offer something in return – prettiness, acquiescence, unquestioning agreement, a fuckable rig, the right balance of morality and sexuality (which – surprise! – turns out to be impossible to achieve because the goalposts change whenever you move towards them), and an unassuming smile that says, 'Frankly, it's just an honour to be included.'

Absorb the message that other girls – the girls you tumbled with and played fairies and space heroes and mermaids with, the girls you curled up with to whisper secrets in the dark, the ones you choreographed dances with, painted with, climbed trees with, ate ice-creams with, learned to swim with, fought with, made up with, fell in love with, wore flower crowns with and developed secret languages with – are not your friends. That women can't be friends because women are each other's own worst enemies. That it is women – not men, not society and certainly not patriarchy – who are responsible for the trauma, self-doubt and hurt that is part and parcel of being a woman.

Above all, understand that whatever happens to you is always your own fault.

Yes, #metoo.

At thirteen, it seemed clear to me suddenly that this world, the one which had previously brought so much unbridled delight and laughter, that had made me feel ten feet tall, was no longer interested in having me play in it. I had danced up and down staircases, roly-poly and resplendent in lycra shorts stretched tight over a round tummy, and I had never been made to feel like this was wrong. When I dressed myself in the morning, it wasn't in a state of panic or worry, my brow furrowed as I pondered which outfit would make me feel like fewer people were pointing at me. I didn't catch glimpses of myself in the mirror and feel a sudden burst of shame at having seen the contortion of a double chin or a flabby arm that seemed able to announce my presence in a way my mind and heart could not.

I was yet to experience that sudden and uncomfortable shift in perception that would become so familiar later: that feeling you get when your awareness wrenches itself from your body to float above you and calculate all the ways you and your inherent womanhood don't belong.

When you're a child, you consider yourself as a whole being. Heads, shoulders, knees and toes. If you're happy and you know it, clap your hands. But the process of becoming a woman involves the stripping away of key parts of yourself by outside forces as you look on a bewilderment that quickly turns to shame. Eventually, it doesn't matter how you try to do the sums. All that's left is an assortment of pieces, and none of them seem to add up.

I am thirteen, and I think I'm worthless. I am thirteen, and I hate myself. I am thirteen, and all I want to do is disappear.

■

For girls, the pursuit of thinness is so often tied up with the desire to take up less space. The adults who monitor our childhood watch as we grow up and out, and then suddenly absent themselves when adolescence creeps in and marks the start of what can be the lifelong attempt to fold ourselves neatly away. We are like little Alices, searching for perfect potions to help us shrink and dreading the bite that will send us shooting up through our house and into a state of monstrosity. Eat me. Drink me. Up. Down. In. Out.

What kind of world do women occupy when we experience an average of 4745 negative thoughts about our bodies every year? When 97 percent of women admit to thinking 'I hate my body' at least once a day?

According to a study conducted by the University of Central Florida, nearly 50 percent of American girls aged three to six are already concerned about their weight. Could it be because diet and diet-related industries bring in an annual revenue of $33 billion? Or could it just be that misogyny has always been the happy bedfellow of capitalism, and distracting women from realising our true potential by encouraging us to find self-worth through invisibility is sweeter when you can make a profit from it?

Why is the measure of a man's worth the size of his power while the measure of a woman's is the size of her waist? Why do we sit by and participate in this spectacle of judgment, picking over photographs of women taken at beaches and noting not their grins but their fat rolls or rib cages or cigarettes or stretch marks or wrinkles or whatever else we want to pluck out of a modern-day still life to use as ammunition against her right to just exist in peace?

How can we move through the world each day, all seven billion of us, and not hear that piercing shriek that emanates from the souls and hearts of girls and women the world over?

It's the shriek that screams notice me even as it also yells don't look.

■

When I think back on those days now, on the self-hating, the purging, the heartbreaking self-analysis that took place in my journals, I'm astonished that nobody seemed to notice. I lost over a third of my body weight in the space of a single school term, and the only person (outside of a brief interaction with my mother) who thought to check if everything was okay was a kindly teacher whose enquiry I summarily discarded as jealousy. Beyond that, I was adrift in the same ocean of poisonous messages as all girls seem to be. Being thin is good. Being thin is healthy. Being thin is pretty. Being thin will make boys like you. Being thin will solve all your problems. Being thin brings you worth. Being thin means you are in control. And never underestimate how fiercely girls will grab onto the opportunity to feel in control of *something* in their lives.

The flip side of these messages is almost too terrible to contemplate if you're an average girl raised in an average world where the average person averagely hates you, based on the law of averages. Being fat is bad. Being fat is unhealthy. Being fat will make boys loathe you. Being fat will cause you problems. Being fat makes you worthless. Being fat means you have no control.

Poor body image – the pain girls are conditioned to think is normal – is hereditary. As my weight loss hit its most extreme level, my mother fretted one night that it had gone too far. I had gone downstairs wearing nothing but a bra and my brand-new school trousers to show her what they looked like, but instead of admiring them, she recoiled at the sight of my sunken breasts and prominent bones. 'You need to stop,' she pleaded with me. Her concern seemed jarring, because it came after weeks of hearing nothing but praise for my efforts. She had even happily agreed when I made her promise to pull out the tough love card if I started to 'get fat' again. Jealous! I screamed later to my diary.

Some years later, when we'd left England for Australia and I'd regained most if not all of the weight I'd lost at thirteen, my mother admonished me one night as I reached for a second helping of whatever we were eating for dinner.

'Clementine,' she chided, 'do you really think you need that?'

I stared at her, my hand in mid-air, a mixture of humiliation and indignation beginning to swirl inside. 'Why?' I asked.

'Because I think you could do without eating it,' she replied. My face must have signalled something like fury, because the next thing she said was, 'Don't give me that look. You once made me promise to tell you if you started to get fat again, and I'm just keeping my promise.'

I was astounded, not only by the fact she'd remembered a silly thing said years ago by a child who was clearly in the grips of an eating disorder, but because the existence of that eating disorder seemed to have been completely erased from her memory.

Don't be tempted to rest all the blame squarely on my mother's shoulders, though. For all his excellent qualities, my father was also squeamish about the idea of having fat daughters. I think he believed, as so many do, that fatness offered the world a negative impression. Fatness, particularly in women, was a sign of weakness or failure. It was more important for a woman to be pretty than it was for a man, because women had a responsibility to make the best of themselves. I remember my father getting very agitated one day because my stomach was peeking out between my shorts and my t-shirt (this was the summer of 1999, when it was basically impossible to find a t-shirt that wasn't designed to be three inches shorter than was comfortable). I was just schlepping about at home, but he suddenly pointed at the exposed flesh and yelled something about how my stomach was 'hanging all over the place'. Another time, he observed how unfortunate it was that a woman he knew was fat because 'she would be so pretty if she lost some weight'.

Again, before you condemn my parents, take a breath. Yes, parents or guardians can play a significant role in perpetuating the patterns of self-hatred that are inflicted by an obsessively poor body image. But having a child doesn't make you a suddenly perfect person, nor does it instantly allow you to release the baggage that was built by others for you to carry when you were a child yourself.

My mother often talked of being chubby when she was little, teased for being bigger than her younger sister. Her own mother, renowned as a Great Beauty, had sustained permanent emotional damage from being interned and sexually abused in a Russian concentration camp during World War II. She spent the rest of her life simultaneously hating men for the violence they'd inflicted on her while believing she had no other options but for them to take care of her. Feminine beauty was highly valued in my mother's home – for many years, my mother felt inadequate in comparison to her sister and mother, the latter viewing her daughters as competition for the affections of the many men who came in and out of her life. To understand how I learned to hate myself by watching my mother, you have to understand how she was taught to hate herself too. Never satisfied with her efforts to achieve the impossible task of becoming less than what she was, she tried every fad diet going except the one which gave her permission to love herself exactly as she was.

It's a bitter tragedy that she spent her life trying to be thin only to have her ability to eat taken from her by stomach cancer when she was fifty-seven. For weeks, she lay in bed wasting away as we waited for death to come and relieve her of her suffering. At her funeral she lay there in the open casket wearing a formal suit she hadn't been able to fit into for many years. Her cheekbones were majestic, and sharp enough to cut my heart in two.

Shit happens to everyone, not just ourselves. I didn't grow up hearing that it didn't matter what my body looked like, only how it felt, because my parents didn't grow up hearing those things either. My mother didn't have the benefit of internet op-eds and women's websites dismantling all this stuff for her. All she had were the lessons she'd learned in childhood, delivered by a mother who wasn't capable of loving her to even a tenth of the degree that my mother loved me and my siblings. I've learned many things about love from her and my father. I've learned that it's important to talk to each other, which we always did. I've learned the benefit of laughter and play, which we always had. I've learned, based on the reports from some of my friends, how lucky I am to have family who aren't afraid to kiss and hug and say 'I love you' every time we say goodbye or goodnight. But I've also learned not to teach children that their body is an enemy. I've learned how important it is to model self-love as a rule, to demonstrate to impressionable young minds that they are so much more than the sum of their parts.

As a girl, all I ever wanted was to have some control over my life and the space I was told I was entitled to occupy. Being big and loud and awkward did not earn you a place at the table. This acceptance was only granted to women whose bodies indicated an awareness of How Things Worked. I resented the girls for whom this privilege seemed to come naturally, and I hated myself for having to work so hard to achieve it. From that first moment in the car when I looked at my belly and heard it whisper fat to me to the moment this morning when I stood in front of the mirror and tried to see if my exercise plan was working, I have spent more than two decades worrying about whether or not my body is small enough to excuse my womanhood. More than two decades feeling emotionally convinced of the intrinsic connection between my worth and my size, even when every rational part of my brain tells me that's ridiculous. I know it's ridiculous. I believe it's ridiculous. I tell other women it's ridiculous.

But it doesn't seem ridiculous when you're walking down the street and you're struck by the self-loathing belief that the whole world is pointing at you and thinking to themselves, 'That fat cow really shouldn't be wearing those shorts.'

Imagine how much precious time and energy we would save if we could just figure out a way to let all of this shit go. If girls and women could wake up in the morning and smile at themselves in the mirror instead of turning from side to side, measuring all the ways in which our bodies have let us down again today. And imagine how much easier it would be for us to believe this if everyone else would stop measuring women's value by whether or not our thighs touch in the middle, offering their unwanted commentary about what women should and shouldn't wear or sneering at us for having the audacity to act as if we deserve respect rather than derision.

■

I learned to like myself more when I began playing roller derby. Being in a community of women athletes was fun, but it was also empowering. I began to look at my body as something with a use and a purpose, something that could do things, rather than something that existed just to be looked at and critiqued. On the track, using my body for sport and play, I feel like a child again in a good way. I am powerful. I am good. I am worth something. Other people see it and, more importantly, I see it.

This is one of the secrets. It's finding the things that your body likes to do and then doing them. It might be swimming. It might be running. It might be lying on the grass and feeling a hundred different green blades tickle your skin. It might be standing in front of your bedroom mirror and dancing just for yourself. I do that a lot.

Find something that your body likes to do and let your body do it. Let your body do it because it deserves as much as any other body in the world to shake itself to the rhythm of the beat, to plunge into the roiling waves and surf itself in to shore, to drape itself in beautiful colours, to stride through a crowded room and announce itself with confidence rather than apology, to be kissed, to be touched, to fuck and be fucked, to run, to be nourished and fed, to roller skate in teeny-tiny shorts, to recline, to sleep, to be at peace. All bodies are good bodies, and that includes yours.

This is part of the self-love that we so often deny ourselves.

Write down a list of all the things that you're good at and all the things you enjoy doing. When you're feeling down or insecure about yourself, take that list out and remember that your body is a good body.

Thank your body every day for the way it cares for you. Care for it in return. Do nice things for it. Have a bath. Get a massage. Go for long walks in the countryside and feel the unique pleasure of going to bed with tired legs that have taken you to see the world in all its glory. Masturbate – frequently! Your body and you deserve to feel good in every way. Don't be ashamed about touching yourself. It's your reward for being so awesome. I reward myself for being awesome two, sometimes three, times a day. Because I'm worth it.

Try to banish negative thoughts by replacing them with something positive. Or, as comedian Luisa Omielan says, grabbing her tummy, 'Do you know what this means? This means I go out for dinner with friends. This is my present to myself.'

Help your friends to love themselves too. If someone you know says something negative about themselves, say, 'Hey! That's my friend you're talking about! Don't be mean to my friend!' Think about the way you talk to yourself as well, and ask if it's something you'd be comfortable saying to someone else. Chances are it's not. So don't say it to yourself.

A lot of guff is spoken about 'health' and fatness, as if the real reason people feel entitled to shame other people's bodies is out of concern for their welfare. Do you know what's not healthy? Being at war with yourself. Hating yourself is not healthy. Fixating on the bodies of other people and how they compare to yours is not healthy. Starving yourself to fit in with the arbitrary ideals created and policed by other people is not healthy.

Fatness is not a disease, and it's not contagious. The only thing that's contagious is the temptation to pile hatred into a completely random and often genetically determined physical self and turn it into a symbol of disgust and worthlessness. We need to stop passing on the toxic messages that have travelled down from generation to generation and start creating a new paradigm of what it means to be good. Of what it means to be different. To be diverse. To be valuable. We need to tell our children that they are everything they need to be. We need to tell our girls that their bodies exist for them to use, not for others to look at.

Remember this, above all else: there is no wrong way to have a body. You are perfect just as you are. You are exactly the way you are meant to be. Love yourself. Because you are worth loving.

Get ready for your close-up, baby. You're gonna be a star.

—3—

REAL GIRLS

Learning to love your body is one thing, but convincing manufacturers to make clothes that will fit it is another thing altogether. Incredibly, women didn't all fall out of the Woman Factory in five different perfectly ascending sizes of the exact same shape. So instead of using standard numerical sizing on clothes, why not divide items according to what women's bodies actually look like and the different tastes we have? We're all genetically coded to store fat and muscle differently. For example, my sister was blessed with a magnificent cleavage. Her breasts form the kind of narrow chasm that looks like it might be hiding diamonds or maybe even the crushed bones of those men who, mesmerised by the glittering jewels, slipped into its crevice one day never to be seen again.

I, on the other hand, ended up with a set of misshapen poached eggs that were obviously plopped out from tiny, angry chickens. Their position makes it clear to me that they disagreed with each another once upon a time and now languish miserably on my chest refusing to look at each other. If I push them hard enough, I can make them touch at the tips but not quite in the middle. The end result is a little bit like watching two frenemies hug by moving their hips in the inverse direction from where their shoulders are heading. Don't misunderstand me. It's not that I don't have any cleavage at all. I do. It's just that it all happens to be on my butt. Whoever drew up the blueprints for my body obviously got distracted when it got to my bottom and trailed the pencil up about four inches too high. And you know what, I'm okay with that. Because my arse is majestical.

The point is, women's bodies are all different. Even women who ostensibly wear the same size clothing are predisposed to wear it in different ways. That's how human biology works – and given that women *almost* qualify as human beings, it stands to reason that the same logic would apply to us. We're not matryoshka dolls who reproduce by cracking open our midsections and pulling another one of us out, only smaller. (It would be easier and more convenient if it were the case, because then I could summon a mini-me every so often to handle Twitter for a bit so I could take a break from the man-babies whining about how feminists make their down-theres have a little cry.)

Throughout my adult life, I've swung wildly between sizes. I've been much thinner than I am now and I've been a little fatter too. At the moment, I'm stuck in that frustrating stage where the clothes on high street fashion racks lie about being XL or a size 16 and refuse to shimmy up over my calves, but the smallest sizes in 'plus size' stores are all too big in the bazoongas and might as well be sold in a shop called Fatties Must Be Punished By Wearing Ugly Shit And Everything Fringed With Lilac, Also We Hate You.

Look, it may come as a shock to retailers, but not every woman larger than a traditional size 16 wants to cloak her body in frills and drapes and the seemingly mandatory decoration of giant purple flowers. Nor do we all respond enthusiastically to the palate of 'alternative' vintage designs, with their nipped-in waists, various animal prints and general va-va-voomery. I'll be the first to put up my hand and admit I like the sultry silhouette of a Betty with Rubble in all the right places, but it's not one I necessarily want to emulate myself. Aside from the expense, it's always seemed to me as if committing to the vintage aesthetic would take a lot of time. Most mornings, I can't even be bothered brushing my hair let alone wrestling with a set of hot rollers. High heels are the devil's way of torturing people with wide feet. And pencil skirts are not especially practical for gals with a long stride. Also, while the 1950s may have looked quite pretty, it was not an especially excellent time for women – with the exception of readily obtained Valium prescriptions and it being okay to drink before noon.

That's before we even address the uniformity of these 'curves' that vintage styles are meant to enhance. Not everyone has the naturally cinched-in waist and generous bosom that seems to be favoured by pin-up clothing. This idea that 'real women' are bouncy in all the right places is just as offensive and limiting as the one that asserts women have to be waifs. Because to be honest, I have more chance of whittling my body down to look like Keira Knightley's than I do waking up one morning with the measurements of Christina Hendricks. In fact, in most cases, what is celebrated and held up as 'real' is just another unrealistic and limited aspiration of beauty that excludes the majority while pretending to create space for them.

I am a unique individual, and my body is uniquely mine. I do not have perky breasts, a narrow waist and curvy bedroom thighs. Until I discovered the heavenly comfort of Kmart's multipack of high-waisted knickers, most of the underwear I could afford to buy was too low in the back, too narrow in the torso, too close together in the cup and too uncomfortable overall. My feet are wide, which makes buying shoes a nightmare. My shoulders are broad, which makes tidy blazers impossible. And I've yet to find a pair of pants whose gusset doesn't seem to want to take up permanent residency in the cupboard under the stairs.

Like I said, women are different. And if fashion retailers weren't so invested in trying to make women spend money by making us feel utterly shit about ourselves, they would realise that there's probably a better chance of us spending even more of it by making us feel good.

So here, in no particular order, is a list of suggestions for how outlets can not only make clothes that fit a diverse range of women, but also label them appropriately:

- Big arse, small titties: dresses are for everyone
- Hockey player calves: looks great in skinny jeans
- Thick waist with legs to die for: rocks a miniskirt
- Flabby arms decorated with awesome tattoos that should be required by law to be always on display: get into these singlets stat
- Giant shoulder sockets, broad back: wants to cross her arms comfortably in a jacket
- Bodacious bosom, tiny waist: prefers the androgynous look
- XXL booty, chubby thighs, sway back: here are some trousers that get the job done

- Narrow hips, enormous cans: rocks a shirt and tie
- Legs like a gazelle, arms that deadlift the weight of a Prius: likes things in lace

You get the idea.

Look, bodily perfection should not be measured based on the size of our waistbands, the length of our legs, the colour of our skin or the mapping of our genetics. All bodies are good bodies, no matter what shape they come in. All bodies help us in varying ways to travel through the great adventure that is life. And all bodies are entitled to be treated with kindness and respect, regardless of whether or not they fit into rigid and arbitrarily determined ideals about what those bodies are supposed to look like. Fat, thin, tall, short, round, oblong, large-calved, giant shoulders, tiny waist, stubby neck, long neck, small breasts, massive breasts, perky breasts, saggy breasts, augmented breasts, one breast, no breasts, wide-set vaginas, small penises, short vaginas, long penises, genitals that are both a vagina and a penis, bodies that were assigned one gender at birth and turned out to be the opposite, bodies that express no gender, bodies that express both genders, bodies that use wheelchairs to move around in, bodies that use speech-generation devices to talk, bodies that use sign language to talk, bodies that have fewer limbs than other bodies, bodies that have tattoos and/or piercings decorating them, bodies that have birthmarks and/or scars decorating them, dark skin, light skin, blemished skin, sensitive skin, skin grafts, loose skin, thick hair, sparse hair, hairy armpits, hairy bush, hairy toes, hairy belly, hairy face, no hair, thigh gap, thighs that rub in the middle, knees that rub in the middle, calves that rub in the middle, butt cleavage, bodies that look like nobody else's bodies at all – the list goes on and on ad infinitum because of the beautiful, diverse complexity of the human race.

None of these wildly different attributes should be seen as anything other than a descriptor. By themselves, they carry no moral judgments, no ranking of good, better, best and precisely zero ability to speak on behalf of the bearer. In fact, the only thing responsible for assigning meaning to the appearance of totally random body parts is the unwanted and unnecessary input of other people. Bodies that don't conform to generalised standards of beauty aren't *bad*. But they're transformed into something bad by the critical, abusive policing of a society that is both subject and master to the whims of capitalism and power.

Conversely, there is nothing inherently better or superior about fitting into the 'right' category of body. Bodies that conform to generalised standards of beauty aren't *good* – they just happen to be prioritised as such by a society subjected to the same whims of capitalism and power.

What's 'good' and 'bad' anyway? To herald something as 'good' implies a moral superiority, and there's no such thing as moral superiority as far as bodies are concerned. Bodies come in such vastly different shapes, sizes, expressions and identities that it's not only impossible to declare any kind of moral superiority as far as they're concerned, it's also a ridiculous exercise in vanity. Diversity is what makes the world and all its inhabitants interesting, not homogeneity. And who gets to decide what qualifies as better? We might think as individuals we're capable of determining our own tastes, but newsflash – we're not. Pretty much everything we value is decided for us by an external source that wants either to control us or make money from us, and very often wants both of these things together.

And here's another revelation – no matter what we do, we'll never succeed in attaining the 'perfect' body or the 'perfect' face. This isn't just because perfection is an unattainable goal; it's because capitalism relies on people being constantly unhappy so it can keep selling us the promise that consumerism will make our lives better. As human beings, it's amazing how we allow corporations to tell us how rubbish we are while we gratefully lap up their bullshit with a spoon. I once stood in the supermarket and marvelled at how Schwarzkopf had managed to make every single one of their bottles of shampoo and conditioner sound like a necessary remedy for something more akin to snakes growing out of a woman's head than actual hair. Buy this one for 'rebellious, frizzy hair'. Slather this one on for 'dead, brittle ends'. Soak your noggin in this potion to cure your 'lank, lifeless strands'. Not a single bottle there for gals with an average barnet that just wants washing every so often.

And it's not just hair, oh no. Yesterday, I absent-mindedly moved to close a pop-up ad on a beauty website (don't judge me, I ain't done baking yet) so I could get back to reading about this season's hottest trends in socks or eyebrows or something equally pointless. The ad was for some kind of fancy moisturiser that probably costs $900 for a fingernail's worth because a clever marketing executive discovered that writing something about Amazonian tree juice makes people think magic is real. There were only two options in response to the question of whether or not I wanted to learn more about Miracle Face Crap. They were 'Yes please!' and 'No, I don't care about my skin'. I mean, they might as well have followed it up with a picture of that guy who chooses the wrong cup at the end of *Indiana Jones and the Last Crusade*. Look at what happens when you don't spend $900 on a fingernail's worth of Miracle Face Crap, you repulsive piles of stinky cow dung who think you're too good for our product! Your entire head will *literally* have all its moisture sucked out until it blows away in the breeze and you die a sad, forgotten old hag! Because you thought you were *too good* to care about your own *skin*.

Capitalism will always come after us. Once upon a time, it was nothing for a woman to have a bountiful bush marking the entrance to her lady cave. Hair wasn't considered to be abnormal, a nosegay of stench so foul it needed to be expunged from the earth. Look at any nudie magazines or vintage porn up until the 1970s and it's a beacon of bush.

Now, hair is out, smooth is in and vitamin E cream is a bathroom cabinet must-have.

Of course, it's not just hair on your down-there that causes such offence. I mean, isn't it funny that we've made it all the way past the events of *Back to the Future II*, when humanity was supposed to have developed flying cars and self-drying clothes (excellent for all those Busy Mums out there), through worldwide war and famine, past the development of smartphone technology and over the rainbow of how the internet even works, and the thing that still manages to both terrify and astonish us in equal measure is the sight of underarm hair on a woman. We'll raise approximately zero eyebrows at Japanese sex robots or the thought of sending a bunch of humans to Mars in a box, but NO UNDERARM HAIR PLEASE, IT'S UNNATURAL.

Yes, you're perfectly entitled as a feminist and indeed as an autonomous human-being woman person to grow or remove as much or as little hair as you like. But grooming is a personal choice only in so much as everything is a personal choice – which is to say that 'choices' as we generally understand them aren't made in a vacuum. Imagine you woke up in an actual vacuum one day, with no memories or concept of life outside the vacuum. On a table in front of you is a packet of wax strips. Aside from sheer boredom, do you think it would even occur to you to spend the next few hours painfully and painstakingly removing all the body hair below your neck? I put it to you, madam, that it would not.

So the thing is, 'fashion' and the whims of beauty are so transient and ever-changing that it's an almost wholly useless exercise to try to morph ourselves into something dictated by an external force. There are so many different variables and influences, and almost none of them are designed to make anyone feel good about themselves. Deeply entrenched racism, for example, has always instructed preferential treatment be given to white or light-coloured skin (check out Lupita Nyong'o's must-hear/read speech on black beauty from the 2014 Black Women in Hollywood luncheon). Angular, skinny bodies might be considered an aspirational benchmark today, but fifty years ago those same bodies were derided as unfeminine. Instead, advertisers encouraged women to purchase products with names like Wate-On and 7-Power in order to make their undesirable skinny rigs more voluptuous. Corsetry and girdles sucked women's waists in while pushing their T&A out, because having an hourglass figure was meant to make you a more worthwhile human-being woman person.

The 1990s spawned both the supermodel and heroin chic, Amazonian women as tall as trees acclaimed alongside the long-limbed, slight-framed girls who began modelling almost as soon as they began puberty. If anyone questioned how using fourteen-year-old girls to sell expensive clothes to adult women was sensible or fair, it was an argument that didn't gain much traction. In response, Riot Grrrls printed postcards and stickers calling for women to 'riot, don't diet', asking, 'Can you pinch an inch? Do you care?'

But the problem was, women *did* care. Because it doesn't matter how much you want to riot against a system that's inherently predisposed to hate you, actually resisting its influence is a different matter entirely. Even while women were being told to 'embrace your curves!' by the same women's magazines whose business models relied on them being shills for Miracle Face Crap and advising readers on How to Get a Better Beach Body, the allure of the so-called perfect chassis remained. What this actually is has never been settled on because, as I've said, the success of selling it and all the products required to get it secretly relies on it never actually existing. The perfect body is like the mirage of an oasis in the desert. It shimmers on the horizon as we tell ourselves that if we can just make it over the next dune, it's *bound* to appear. So we trudge towards it, sweating and thirsty, wondering when this fresh hell will end and we can splash in the cool, refreshing pool that awaits us. But we will never reach it.

In the 2000s, we were told that 'real women have curves'. Women weren't fat, they were 'curvy' because the prospect of assigning any kind of value to the word 'fat' was (and still is) so terrifying to people. 'Real women' were hailed as superior, sexier, better in bed, more attractive, more interesting, smarter (which is simply illogical as an argument), funnier, fitter etc. Real women had personalities. Real women were fun to be around. Real women ate real food like burgers, steaks and fries. They drank beer and laughed heartily. Real women were just like men, but with Sexy Curves. Men preferred women with curves because they looked like 'real women' and were hotter than a 'bag of bones' (which only dogs liked to pick at). This frequently offered explanation and seal of approval was supposed to make all of us feel better and more superior to the gazelle-like figures of the Skinny Bitches, because as everyone knows the presence of male desire always solves the problem of women's low self-esteem. I mean, there couldn't possibly be any other reason for self-hatred in a woman's life than the fear that men don't want to fuck her, amirite, ladies? Without a man to qualify our existence with an appreciative erection, what's the point of even being alive?

Excuse my ignorance, but isn't the idea that we need that validation part of the problem in the first place? Apart from the grossly heteronormative ideas behind it – i.e. that all women are interested in the sexual approval of men as if all women are exclusively sexually interested in men, and not, possibly, the mythical unicorn creature known as A Lesbian – it also assumes that the only thing standing between women and some sense of self-worth is a man's dick. And I'm sorry, but I couldn't give a flying fudge what a man or a penis thinks about the way I look.

Because let's not discount the contributions of men here. While it's true that men can also be affected by poor body image and the number of men admitting to having eating disorders is rising, the goalposts for male beauty are still miles further apart than the ones for women. Men are given the liberty to exist in a way denied to women, and a lot of them have the cheek to turn around and act as if women are just being overly dramatic about the whole thing. They'll very freely offer their opinions in this regard, despite the fact most women never ask them and will rarely be swayed by what they think. 'Relax, girls!' they instruct us casually. 'We think you're all beautiful! We don't care what you look like!'

The problem with this kind of boring, arrogant attempt at reassurance is twofold. First, the poor self-esteem and terrible body image shared by most women has nothing to do with the fear of being loathed by individual men (but what a fucking surprise that they would immediately make it about themselves). Fear of being loathed is part of it, but only because part of patriarchy's great power is in tethering women's identities to how men construct them. If a woman stands up and a man isn't around to see it or comment on it or admire it or acknowledge it or criticise it or offer any kind of unasked for and unwanted observation on it at all, does anyone care if the woman actually even exists? No. Because what we're conditioned to be afraid of is the omnipresent male gaze, and that tends to be far more brutal than jocular blokes using the internet or dinner parties or vox pops to once again position themselves at the centre of something that has nothing to do with their dicks. Now that I'm old enough and smart enough to realise how and why I've been taught to hate my body, I realise that my compulsion to do so is completely unrelated to whether or not Joe Average down the street wants to bone me. Perhaps I'm unusual in this regard, but I grow more and more immune to the 'fat-and-ugly' insults that men frequently send my way. I give zero fucks whether or not an identifiable man expresses disgust for me or my body. In fact, it would be hard for me to care less than I already do about men's critical thoughts on women, especially what we look like.

Caring about the omnipresent male gaze though, the one that dictates which people in society get to be seen and heard and made real, living flesh, and which have to contend with being dehumanised on a daily basis? Yeah, I care about that a lot.

And this is something the calm-your-farmers-we-love-you-just-the-way-you-are gang of dudebros will never understand, because while patriarchy subjects them to a lot of toxic bullshit, it will never teach them *as a rule* from an early age that having a modicum of fat on their bellies means they are less than a piece of shit on the bottom of some guy's shoe.

Think about Margaret Cho, who recounted the following in the must-watch documentary *Miss Representation*. In the 1990s she created a ground-breaking show called *All American Girl* featuring an Asian American family with a Valley Girl daughter. It was cancelled by the network after just one season because they said she got too fat. They then replaced it with *The Drew Carey Show*, a sitcom about a fat man who dates skinny women and whose nemesis at work is a fat woman who wears actual clown makeup. Even the sets were imported from Cho's show.

But relax, ladies, it's all good! Don't stress, yo. You girls are the ones creating this problem! Girls are their own worst enemies! Chill! We love you just the way you are.

Fuck off. Because this leads to the second part of the problem, which is that most men who claim to have a broad diversity policy when it comes to dating are gigantic liars. The men who'll skulk around the comments section of the *Daily Mail* claiming to love 'real women' with 'meat on their bones' are the same men who get out their red markers and draw figurative crosses over all the things wrong with Lily Allen's body as she tries to do a Saturday shop at the supermarket. They're the same blokes who bleat about how fat women shouldn't be allowed to wear nice clothes because it 'promotes obesity', as if the prospect of a fat woman existing for one minute without thoroughly despising herself isn't just intolerable, but also dangerous.

To me, it seems perfectly obvious that the real enemy is the benign permission we give to society to own women's bodies. We have been allowing culture to tell us for so long what our worth is that we barely even blink anymore. Instead, we apply all these bandaids to the problem and hope that it will go away of its own accord. We tell women that it's brave to go make-up free, and that to document this Important Act of Bravery they should take a selfie and show the world how brave they are. Look at me, world! See how brave I am? I'm not wearing make-up! LOVE ME! #brave

Awareness of these different beauty ideals (if not actual understanding) leads a lot of well-meaning people to mourn for a time in which women were supposedly praised for their plumpness rather than vilified for it. *Marilyn was a size 16!* they remind us, posting twee memes (or twemes, as I call them) of the decidedly not-size-16 Monroe alongside messages like: *Before anorexia and implants, there was something called SEXY.*

But as Mel Campbell, author of the must-read *Out of Shape: Debunking Myths about Fashion and Fit*, once told me, 'Breast implant surgery has been practised since the late nineteenth century and clinical anorexia nervosa, which has been described since medieval times, got its name in 1873. "Sexy" has always existed but has been expressed in different ways in different eras and societies.' As Campbell says, we shouldn't need to retreat into an 'illusory, imagined past' in order to express the frustrations we feel with objectification in the present.

It's frustrating that women are forced to waste precious time and resources staging rebellions over how much space (both physical and visual) our bodies are entitled to take up. Even though we weren't party to the negotiations of that social contract, we're still expected to adhere to them. Because of this, it's a defiantly political act any time women brazenly flout these unwritten rules.

Obviously, the day will come when we'll be able to select an outfit on a screen and then stand inside a 3D imaging/printer capsule and have it directly crafted onto our bodies. Having a high crack won't matter as much then, because technology will allow for waistbands to mould perfectly against a sway back. This may occur at the same time or slightly before robots rise up to take over the planet and enslave humanity – but at least we'll *feel* good as we're burned to a crisp by shape-shifting humanoids and their perfectly formed laser beam eyes.

LIKE A VIRGIN

I must admit, when I climbed aboard my bathtub that afternoon I had no idea of the magical mystery tour it was about to take me on.

Although I had casually rubbed up against it before, it was in more of an accidentally-on-purpose kind of way. You know. Like, 'Whoops! It seems I have carefully slipped over while stepping out of the shower and my legs have found their way on either side of the rim of this tub and it's obviously a bit of a shock so I'd better just hover here for a moment and use my thigh muscles to closely grip onto the ceramic so that my core can have a moment to stabilise while I very gently bob up and down!'

I was a roly-poly child not given to regular exercise, but I suppose this was at least a kind of yoga.

My affected clumsiness in the bathroom was the natural evolution of a childhood spent fascinated by sex and the feelings it was supposed to provoke. My mother was the kind of person who insisted on referring to genitals by their medical names instead of in euphemisms like hoo-hoo or winkle or the God-awful wee-wee. (Unfortunately, I was also certain that everyone saying the word 'vagina' had a speech impediment, and that it was actually pronounced 'pagina'. I still think this is a very lovely name for it, calling to mind a kind of warm, snuggly pair of thermals made available to a willing and consensual suitor to wrap themselves up in.) Pagina or not, I knew that there were certain things that created funny, good kind of feelings somewhere in the region of my lower tummy. Exactly why and how it felt good was a little hard to describe, but it reminded me of things I liked – ice-cream, for example, or swimming on a hot summer's day.

But my knowledge was patchy, limited only to knowing how babies were made. When I was five, my mother dragged out a ream of butcher paper after dinner one night and drew in minute detail the journey of the sperm from penis to egg. (It was one of many strange and serious lessons she would impart about life, including the forced annual screenings of a a doe-eyed Nicole Kidman in *Bangkok Hilton* so we could understand the consequences of accepting gifts from handsome strangers met in Asia. Spoiler: You always end up in jail.)

I remember my mother nudging the point of a pen just slightly onto the paper so that it made the tiniest mark. 'There!' she declared triumphantly. 'The egg is even tinier than that!' My brother and sister and I gazed at the mark, sheer wonder at life's design momentarily wrestling our attention away from wondering whether or not there would be a post-dinner pudding option.

The microscopic size of a human egg was easily the most accurate fact I had to hand, despite my efforts to secure more information. When I went off to boarding school at eight, my attempts were further confused by other children. One day,

I heard a grade five boy talking about condoms with one of the junior housemasters.

'What's a condom?' I asked.

The boy flicked a knowing glance at the housemaster. It was a look that said, 'Ugh . . . children.'

'It's a rubber ring that you you put around your dick to stop girls getting pregnant,' he explained confidently.

Of course I had no idea that my schoolmate was as ignorant as I was, and had somehow mistaken a prophylactic for a cock ring. Indeed, I would think of it as such for years to come – which probably explains the two abortions. (It's okay, you're allowed to laugh at that.)

I recall another time, when I was around nine, suddenly blurting out at the dinner table, 'What's oral sex?'

My parents exchanged an uncomfortable look.

'Er . . .' my father hedged. 'It's when you talk about it.'

'Oh!' I replied again, once more illuminated by the wrong information but feeling older and wiser anyway. Years later, I would reflect on how lucky it was for my parents that I hadn't gone to school the next day and answered any questions about what I'd done the night before with an enthusiastic, 'My family and I ate spaghetti Bolognese and then we had oral sex around the table!' This may have been the eighties, when you could eat vegetables that had been chopped on the same board as raw chicken, but there was still some semblance of child protection.

Despite my questions, I still knew nothing about what sex really entailed. But the romantic movies and badly lit thrillers that my family regularly brought home from the video store and to which I had unfettered access due to a lack of any real parental supervision taught me that it was either called 'fucking' or 'making love'.

The former was done in a frenzy of breathless passion, mostly up against a wall and either between enemies or co-workers. It typically lasted around thirty seconds and, if the mutual squeals and carefully choreographed moans were anything to go by, everyone always had a very good time.

The latter was a more sedate affair. The women wore satin nightgowns (or 'teddies', as I'd heard them called) and lots of rouge, while the men moved slowly above them. There were always lots of long, lingering looks and closed-mouth kissing.

Making love didn't seem as appealing to me as fucking, but it was still better than nothing. I eagerly recreated everything I'd learned upstairs with my Barbies, my door firmly shut against what I was sure would be disgust and disappointment if anyone was to happen upon the seedy evidence of my childhood sexual desire. In secrecy, I dressed Ken and Barbie up for their date, made them flirt awkwardly for a few minutes and then stripped their clothes off and frantically humped Ken against Barbie's crotch with wild abandon. It wasn't that different from Tinder, when you think about it.

When I needed something a bit more risqué than my adventures with Barbie and Ken, I'd pull down the typewriter in the study and write notes to myself.

Dear Ms Smith, they would say. *I'm coming over to your house tonight to fuck you. Love from your boss.*

In these fantasies of illegal workplace sexual harassment, I played both boss and secretary. Just typing the word 'fuck' made my belly flip-flop. When I put the final full stop on the page, pulsing from the erotic dirtiness of the whole thing, I'd rip the paper from the typewriter, gaze at it for a few seconds and then tear it up into tiny pieces, making sure to carefully slice through any incriminating words.

The excitement this activity aroused in me was mingled with guilt and shame. As much as it turned me on to play sex games with myself, I was terrified that people (read: my parents) would find out. I was sure that my perversions were written all over me, and that one would only need to look close enough to see it. I began to turn my head away during innocent kissing scenes in movies, feigning disgust so that my family wouldn't know that I was a closet sex fiend. When a boy at school asked me a few years later if I masturbated, I replied pompously, '*Well*, I have *heard* that masturbating is when women put their fingers inside themselves and I most certainly DO NOT do that!' He nodded approvingly. Women weren't supposed to touch themselves. It was disgusting and embarrassing.

And then . . . the bathtub.

My yoga sessions had been growing more frequent. I had taken to acting out girl-on-top, bobbing up and down on the ceramic rim and leaning forward to kiss the wall in front of me. I assumed this was what sex was like. Something warm and relaxing, the way a cat must feel to get its tummy stroked. On this particular day though, the pussy rub was fated to turn out *quite* differently. As my rhythm grew more furious, a hot feeling began to spread throughout my . . . area . . . My heartbeat began to quicken until it was racing. My cheeks grew flushed. My thighs started to shake, the pressure of holding a squat both adding to my excitement while making me weaker. So taken was I by the sensations that I even had to stop kissing the wall.

Suddenly, an explosion! My stomach dropped out from beneath me, and what felt like an electric shock ran up between my legs and back down again. I felt like the deepest, most secret part of me had erupted in a dazzling fireworks display.

What I haven't told you yet is that as a child I was a hypochondriac. Every twinge of pain heralded cancer. Blurry vision was the onset of blindness. Terminal illness lurked around every corner. So my enjoyment of my very first orgasm was hampered somewhat by the fact that I was convinced I was having a stroke. My thighs suddenly re-energised from the adrenaline, I leaped from the bathtub and whipped around to stare at it accusingly. WHAT HAVE YOU DONE TO ME? I screamed silently.

This was what happened to dirty girls.

If only I had kept my perversions in check! If I survived, I promised myself and God and whoever else might be listening that I would never touch myself again.

As you've probably gathered, I did survive. My stroke symptoms disappeared as the after-effects of my climax subsided, and I soon realised what it was that had actually happened. Still, I kept my promise to keep my hands firmly where the good Lord could see them . . . for about two days. Now that I'd discovered this marvellous secret, I couldn't stay away. This was better than ice-cream and swimming.

Rhonda, it was better than 'Dancing Queen'.

Now, I do it everywhere – in the shower, in aeroplane toilets when I'm bored, sometimes in the car for a real thrill ride. I do it on the couch when I'm procrastinating with work. My friend Ben calls this 'procasturbation'. I have honed it to a fine art – I've got so good at it that I can rub one out in fifty-nine seconds or less. I am so passionate about the importance of self-love that some friends call me a masturbation evangelist. I'm so good at it that sometimes I orgasm accidentally without even touching myself. Reading porny stories or watching pornier videos can be enough to get me off. Once, I came in a gym class while doing push-ups on an exercise ball. The instructor had us rolling in and out and engaging our cores, and what can I say? I just have a really good core, I guess. I realised I was about ten seconds away from 'arriving' when she told us to take our balls and use them to squat against a wall. Well, you're not going to throw something like that away, so I had to feign great interest in checking that my alignment was okay and that I was 'doing the exercise properly'.

Trust me, that is definitely the proper way to exercise.

Look, masturbating is awesome. And it makes sex awesome! I truly believe that discovering the abilities of my body at such a young age has led to an easier experience with sex in general. Pleasure has always been within easy reach, and I've been able to communicate to partners exactly what floats my boat. I've always been bothered by the narrative that holds it's the responsibility of someone else to 'give' a woman an orgasm. No! How can you expect someone else to invest that kind of time in you when you don't even want to do it yourself?

I'm speculating here, and I don't think I need to point out that I'm not an expert in anything other than my own clitoris and *Buffy the Vampire Slayer* – two concepts that are brought together far more often than you'd think – but it's always seemed to me that the reason some women find it difficult to come is precisely *because* they didn't accidentally stumble onto their own pleasure at a young age. If you don't know how to jerk off, it can take a long time to 'get there'. The bonus of starting young is that usually you aren't sure of what to expect. You can take your time and go the long way round, and when you finally reach your destination it comes as a nice surprise – one you're eager to keep revisiting and figuring out shorter and shorter paths to.

I'm alarmed at the number of women I've met over the years who've told me they don't mazz because they get bored or because it doesn't work. They give up after twenty minutes and decide that it's not for them. Trust me – masturbating is for everybody. But you wouldn't think that given how uncomfortable many folks still seem to be with the thought of women venturing into the basement and having a good rummage around. Obnoxious magazine articles berate women's partners (who are always assumed to be men) for not being able to get them off, while jokes still persist about how rubbish men are at figuring out how to find a clitoris.

If you know how to get yourself off, you don't need anyone else to do it for you. Any expertise they bring to the table is just a nice bonus.

It's concerning that pleasure, and the pursuit of it, remains so absent from youth education programs. To the uninitiated, orgasms can be a perplexing and unpleasantly overwhelming experience. I've met women who, even as adults, have talked themselves out of climaxing because they find the feeling too intense and anxiety-inducing. When pleasure isn't taught as a key component of sexual engagement and intercourse (particularly for girls and particularly in hetero contexts), female participation is reinforced as something passive and secondary to the male role.

What is it that society finds so troubling about the idea of young girls learning about sex and pleasure? Perhaps it's the puritanical fear that it will encourage them to rush off and 'sleep around', as if their bodies belong to them and not to the society intent on controlling them. Absurd, I know.

I want to tell you about someone I went to school with.

Alisha Brown was the youngest girl I ever knew to be having sex. I met her when we moved to England. We were twelve years old, but she was years ahead of me in terms of experience. She seemed wild and free, and I thought that made her dangerous. She did things with her body that both terrified me and made me feel childish. There were some moments when she seemed to have a secret knowledge about the world, a knowledge that I would never be able to acquire no matter how hard I tried. At other times, she just seemed like a bit of a cliché. She enjoyed the kind of popularity that seems motivated more by the fear of other people rather than any genuine admiration – she was bitchy and mean, and totally unapologetic in her cruelty towards other girls. I didn't like her very much, and used the fact of my dislike to justify the way I judged her sexual behaviour.

'Twelve is just SO YOUNG,' I would say to my friends. 'She's obviously just using sex to get love. I almost feel sorry for her.'

I criticised Alisha because a part of me felt that her sexual confidence made her a better, worthier girl than me. I was jealous of her because she knew things that I didn't and because I was too scared to find those things out for myself. It was easy for me to deride her, because I was reading from a script that had been passed down from generation to generation. Alisha was a 'slut', I thought, and I had no problem calling her that. She gave things away that she should have held on to, and behaved in a way that she should have known was strictly forbidden. Verbalising this didn't just give me an opportunity to put her down – it also allowed me to reframe my own sexual insecurity as a moral superiority. Boys might want to fuck Alisha, I thought to myself, but they would *respect* me.

Internalised misogyny is a powerful thing, and it starts from the moment girls learn that they're considered inferior. Policing women's sexuality is perhaps forgivable in a twelve-year-old girl trying to navigate her way through a world that has taught her to fear and mistrust other women, but not everyone lets go of those childish and petty cruelties. There are grown-up Alishas all over the place who are still subjected to judgmental bullshit from people whose only actual responsibility towards them is to mind their own fucking business.

The thing is, maybe Alisha was just having sex to get love. Maybe she was too young. Maybe she grew up regretting her experiences and wishing that someone had intervened. Maybe she wishes she had waited, maybe she wishes she had loved herself more, maybe she wishes she had done it first with someone she loved, maybe she hopes her daughters will be different.

But maybe she doesn't.

Maybe she grew up to be a completely fine, normal, adult woman with memories of regret and triumph in equal measure across a broad range of formative experiences, the least of which might be the ways she chose to have sex and with whom. Maybe she grew up to be just like me, a girl who either by design or lack of opportunity waited until she was almost nineteen to fuck someone else for the first time, and feels neither pride nor remorse about that. Maybe it just is what it is, and maybe we're both okay.

Sex education is about so much more than biology. It's bigger than the conservative ideals we continue to force on young people, which includes the furphies that women use sex to get love and men use love to get sex. Pleasure isn't a peripheral by-product of sexuality but an inseparable part of it. And there's something desperately wrong with a world that is okay with making the control of female sexuality the domain of everyone other than the woman who owns it. It's important that women be aware of this, but also that men are too.

Patriarchal society might be afraid of women's bodies, but that doesn't mean women should be taught to fear them too. We should be teaching girls to feel pleasure instead of shame, and giving them a framework to express sexual autonomy and confidence. Remember: if you build it, they will come.

I have come many, many, many times in my life – in different ways, with different people (or just by myself) and with different implements. I haven't *always* orgasmed during sex, but I find it a pretty easy thing to do.

The first time I had sex with someone else, I was eighteen. I was in my second year of university and had moved out of home at the start of the year. I had done so with a very clear picture of what awaited me in my new grown-up life. Simply put, I expected to have sex. Lots and lots of sex. Lots and lots of sex with lots and lots of different, interesting people. It was just what happened: you turned eighteen, moved away from your parents and – ta da! – instant bonage. After all, I was in a share house now.

Would it hurt? I wondered. The instructional guides I'd consumed voraciously (see: Judy Blume's *Forever* and the 1980 movie classic *Little Darlings*) indicated that it probably would. But this was okay, I decided, because it was like a rite of passage. It was a mark of the journey you'd take from being a girl to becoming a woman.

I pictured myself in cosy bars, wearing glamorous outfits while drinking sophisticated wine. Carnal knowledge would make me glow, transform me from the awkward child still wrapped in puppy fat into the kind of woman I was desperate to become.

Men would flock to me to exchange witty banter and I, knowing already that their answer would be yes, would casually invite them to come back to mine. We'd laugh as we stumbled up the garden path and then kiss at the front door. We'd tiptoe across the hall to my bedroom, me being ever so slightly theatrical in my whispers so that my flatmates were made aware there was a gentleman caller in the house, and then undress each other in the soft glow of the lamplight. He wouldn't feel repulsed by my body. I would feel light and delicate beneath him. We would always come.

I'm sure it will come as no great shock to you to discover that reality turned out to be quite different.

I had moved in with a new friend who was the epitome of sophistication. What this means is that she wore silk dressing-gowns and Samsara perfume and had done it loads of times. I figured I could learn a lot from her.

Amazingly, I found a fellow I liked who also liked me back. After a short courtship involving copious amounts of alcohol and the Travis song 'Driftwood' played on repeat, he became my boyfriend. I prepared myself for what was to come – specifically, me. It only took a few short weeks into us being 'official' for me to inform him one day that I was 'ready'. We'd gone to all the bases already. I'd seen a penis close up and I thought I had it pretty well figured out. The next step would be Full Penetration. I was excited and nervous and scared, but mainly hopeful that everyone around me would be able to tell that I'd finally Gone All The Way and was now one of the initiated. I looked forward to being able to reminisce about my first time, staring off wistfully into the distance and offering the occasional knowing chuckle. I anticipated instructing younger, more naive ladies in the ways of the world. They would hang on my every word and marvel at how I managed to stay so grounded despite all my experience. 'She's so cool,' they'd say, 'but also just *so nice*.'

It happened on a Saturday morning, the day of the Adelaide University Law Ball. Beth Orton's 'Central Reservation' (carefully selected for the occasion) played in the background. Did it hurt? Yes. But not exactly in the way I thought it would. It wasn't so much like a constant dull ache as it was like a thousand needles stabbing you all at once and then screaming at you. And then, suddenly, it didn't hurt that much at all.

Afterwards, I wrapped myself in a blanket and went into my housemate's room under the guise of borrowing something. It was very important to me that she see I had become A Woman. She spotted it immediately (which was probably more to do with my nakedness and massive clown grin) and we giggled like teenagers, which of course we were. So this was sex, I thought – fun, silly and adventurous.

Which is a pretty good way to be initiated into it, don't you think?

And yet, this is not how many women experience it and nor is it encouraged. The sexuality of boys is considered sacrosanct. Not only are they thought of as entitled to pursue sex, but many boys aren't provided with the option of *not* wanting to have sex or wanting only to have sex with people they feel intimacy with. For girls, the opposite is true. We're told to get our hands out of our pants, not to pleasure ourselves, not to seek pleasure from other people and to guard our bodies with our lives. Sex for girls is still too often treated like something we have to police – an activity we can only enjoy and benefit from when done with a committed partner, and something we definitely shouldn't do with too many people because it makes us dirty and sluttish and a gross bag of garbage that men don't want to touch.

But we deserve more than this. We deserve not only to have our choices and autonomy respected, but to be given the information from the outset that lets us know it's okay to be connected with our bodies in that way. Frigging myself stupid on a bathtub changed my life. And you know what? Even if it had been a stroke, I think it would have been worth it. Because to this day, I don't think I've ever re-created the intensity of that moment.

Oh, I've had more intense interactions, for sure. I've fucked people, made love to them and done a whole lot of other stuff in between.

On a night bus from Sydney and surrounded by dozing passengers, a boy I was secretly in love with gently rubbed the crotch of my jeans until I came, shuddering, in his hand. Like all of our sexual interactions, we never spoke about it again.

A humid evening in Adelaide, stoned with a girl I'd just met but who felt as familiar to me as my own skin, stroking each other beneath the sheets of a friend's bed. Once invited, I hesitated for less than a second before lowering my mouth to her and crossing yet another frontier.

A park late at night, fucking my boyfriend on a park bench and giggling as another couple softly padded over the grass on their way home. It was more an exercise in adventure than anything driven by sexual need, because sometimes that's exactly what makes sex good and interesting and fun.

Email confessions, exchanged between me and men I've never met, talking about what we like and what we would do to each other if given the opportunity. Photographs sent, sexual hints and desires discussed, secrets shared that we either felt too nervous to tell to our partners or that happily existed only in the safety of this private, safe and totally raw space.

If virginity is the maintenance of certain boundaries and codes, then I have lost my virginity countless times. I have lost it to men, I have lost it to women and I have lost it to myself. Some of these incidents have proven more profound and life-changing to me than the generic understanding of 'virginity loss' that's inflicted on all of us, particularly women with vaginas. In the current cis-heteronormative discourse, women become inducted into the act of sexuality only when we open our legs for the first time and let a man fuck us. But the simple act of being penetrated isn't enough to define the course of a life. Why should the moment I first experienced a dick inside me be any more important than any other transformative moment that opened my eyes to the possibilities my body held for me?

Something's being fucked here, and it's not the pussy.

—5—

A LEAGUE OF THEIR OWN

Before I became radicalised as a man-hating, separatist feminazi hell-bent on installing a matriarchy and imprisoning men as its slaves,* I possessed a nominal amount of internalised misogyny about the value of women. Women were bitchy and mean. They cared about irrelevant rubbish and talked in loud, shrill voices. Their laughter was annoying and tinny, and they did it too often and performatively. Women were boring to talk to, and they were especially boring if they were pretty and nice and well liked – coincidentally, all the things that I felt I wasn't and that thus excluded me from the club of womanhood.

---

* I am required by law to state that this is a joke. There will be no male slaves in the matriarchy because there will be no men. This is also a joke, and must be outlined as such otherwise the internet's resident man-babies will take this line and use it as incontrovertible proof that I am indeed conspiring to kill all men and establish matriarchal order. But such a mammoth task would be impossible in my lifetime, so all I can do is hide instructions in the hivemind so the next generation can fulfil my destiny. That was a joke too.

There were even a few years in my late teens when I congratulated myself on eschewing the company of women. I was full of praise for men, and prided myself on 'just getting on better with boys'. I flattered myself that, even though they didn't want to date me like they did my female peers, they wanted to confide in me. I thought this was better. I thought it meant I was more important, that they saw something in me that was more valuable than physical desire.

To me, other girls were the enemy and they had an arsenal of complicated mind games and underhanded tricks they'd use to make you feel like shit. Boys were easier, smarter and less complicated in their bullying. If a boy was going to be mean to you, he'd call you a nasty name or laugh at you. But girls, on the other hand . . . well, girls froze you out. Girls did peculiar things like pretend to be your friend and then have everyone at a party ignore you. Like boys, they made up stories about you but it hurt more coming from them than because somewhere, deep down, you thought they were supposed to be on your side.

Were I born a few years later, I've no doubt I could have easily fallen into the horrifying hole that is the Women Against Feminism movement. Being down on other girls wasn't just about a general antipathy towards the way they behaved; it was a gesture to reassure all the boys around me that while I may have looked vaguely like a girl on the outside, I wasn't really like a *girl*-girl.

But I'm getting ahead of myself. The point is that at the age of sixteen and seventeen, I was what you would call a 'gender traitor'. Girls were dumb. Their empty heads could think of nothing more interesting or important than how they looked (the great irony being that about 90 percent of my time was spent obsessing about how ugly I thought I was) and their ignorance about 'important issues' was embarrassing. That I had a pretty flimsy grasp on what these 'important issues' were supposed to be was irrelevant, because factual accuracy is never the issue when pointing the finger at an entire group's supposed failings. It was easy to pretend that ignorance was a particularly female trait, because it tied neatly into the other idea I was helping to prop up, which was that boys' heads aren't filled with the petty concerns of women. It took a special person to be able to distinguish herself from those stereotypes, but I was determined to have boys see that I was different. *Look at me*, I could say to them. *I'm not like all the other girls.*

Like so many girls caught in this trap, it wasn't enough for me to want to be considered an intellectual and social equal by men (because, really, that's what a lot of this scrabbling for their approval comes back to – the misplaced desire to achieve equality for ourselves by being welcomed into the inner sanctum rather than to destroy the sanctum altogether and redefine the dynamic entirely); I also had to climb a tower made out of the discarded, disdained bodies of other women in order to prove myself worthy to enter. Clearly, I had absorbed the patterns of thinking bell hooks outlines in *Feminist Theory: From Margin to Centre*, when she writes:

> It is sexism that leads women to feel threatened by one another without cause. While sexism teaches women to be sex objects for men, it is also manifest when women who have repudiated this role feel contemptuous and superior to those who have not . . . Sexism teaches women woman-hating, and both consciously and unconsciously we act out this hatred in our daily contact with one another.

Because I was born a girl, I was taught to fundamentally distrust other women. So in saying that, I have to also accept and forgive the ways many of them were taught to mistrust me. The first twenty years of my life are filled with uncomfortable experiences of girl-on-girl crime. Whether it arises as bullying, cruelty or viciously applied sexism, girls are separated from each other (and from organising into a bloc of power) by being encouraged to view other girls as competition. And if I'm being truly honest, I'd say for me this began with my sister.

Despite being almost five years older than me, Charlotte has always been a much gentler soul. She seems to care for people in ways that I don't, sacrificing her own comfort at times to make sure everyone around her is properly looked after. Her patience is in inverse proportion to mine, to the point where I sometimes wonder how we came from the same parents. Growing up, I took advantage of this kind nature and was often vicious to her. As siblings, we all called each other the nastiest of names at times (isn't this normal?), but the ones reserved for me and Charlotte (either levelled at each other or spat at us by our brother) often related to the way we looked. The go-to barbs were 'fat' or 'ugly', but we weren't shy in spitting 'bitch' at each other either. I had the advantage of being more outspoken and willing to really go to the edge with my cruelty than Charlotte, and I'm ashamed to say I often pushed her long after she'd conceded defeat. We're extremely close now, but it took us a long time to get there.

I might have begun that fractured relationship with women at home, but it absolutely followed me out into the world. There are many times when I have not been a good support to other women and times when they've let me down too. I think of these moments now with a prickly sense of shame and an everlasting regret at all the opportunities lost.

Because the fact is, if we don't stand by and for each other, then no one else will.

■

Pop culture has a pretty patchy record when it comes to representing women, but it occasionally gets it right where our friendships are concerned. In fact, when I'm feeling down or pissed off about something, it soothes me to think about all the great female pairings that exist across screen or page. Like the devotion Anne Shirley has for her 'bosom friend', Diana Barry, in the *Anne of Green Gables* series. Or how much Leslie Knope loves Ann Perkins in *Parks and Recreation*, frequently raving about how wonderful and beautiful and smart she is. The best thing about it is that Leslie, an eternal optimist, truly believes that everyone sees this greatness in Ann, even though she's deliberately written as a character a lot of other people find weird and annoying. Then there's *Broad City*'s Ilana and Abbi. Their relationship is particularly excellent because their creators (Ilana Glazer and Abbi Jacobson) have subverted all the major tropes about friendships, where one girl is supposedly cool and the other is her sidekick. In any other depiction, Ilana would be the duo's leader. She's more adventurous, more sexual and just a lot more out there than the conservative Abbi (who's so neurotic that she schedules masturbation time into her calendar). Typically, Abbi would be depicted as Ilana's dogsbody, because cautious, sexually inhibited girls are always dismissed as boring and shit. But in *Broad City*, the opposite is true – cool, vivacious, sexy Ilana completely ADORES Abbi, and is always raving about how beautiful she is, how she's so smart and funny and how she has 'the ass of an angel'. And much like *Parks and Rec*'s Leslie, Ilana is so sold on Abbi's essential brilliance that she treats it as self-evident. It's a perfect disruption of the pervasive idea of girl-on-girl competition – because if a goddess like Ilana sees herself as lucky beyond all belief to hang out with a dorkier, more anxiety-ridden friend, then maybe there's hope for all of us.

Then there's the recent outing on Netflix of *Jessica Jones*. Much has been written already about the brilliant construction of patriarchy as the Big Bad in season one, but I'm drawn as well to the central love story. Not the romance between Jessica and fellow superhero Luke, but between Jessica and her adoptive sister Trish. Trish is the only person Jessica truly loves, and certainly the only one she can count on. In fact, the whole first season basically builds up to (spoiler alert) Jessica telling Trish she loves her before breaking the villainous Kilgrave's neck. Awesome.

There are so many more examples. I still bawl every time I watch *Beaches*. The general vibe on that movie is that I'm supposed to be embarrassed about liking it, but fuck that noise. Why does every single man breathing in the world today get to list *The Shawshank Redemption* as one of his favourite movies and not be shamed for it, but women are supposed to roll their eyes at *Beaches*? *Shawshank* is basically a celebration of the same thing (thirty years of platonic friendship and its various trials and tribulations), it just had to be set in a prison so men could give themselves permission to cry over it. Yet we're supposed to turn our noses up at tearjerkers like *Beaches* because women and their relationships with each other are pathetic and the theme song was (apparently) annoying. Get over it, haters! *Beaches* was an epic story of two women who really ended up being the loves of each other's lives. It covered everything in the handbook of female friendships – adolescence, adventures, petty jealousies, love, loss, what happens when you hate your friend's kid. It's really more of a documentary, when you think about it.

And what about Muriel and Rhonda in *Muriel's Wedding*? I think I could watch that movie once a week for the rest of my life and still find new things in it. Muriel has to go on a bit of an emotional journey to figure out what it means to be a good friend and a woman's woman, but Rhonda is right there from the start. Who doesn't fist pump during the island scene when Tania 'You Can't Talk To Me Like That, I'm Beautiful, I'm A Bride' Degano and her gang of bitches invites Rhonda to sit with them because 'it's not like in high school where you should feel like you're not good enough to talk to us'? And after a bit of back and forth, Rhonda replies, 'Shove your drink up your arse, Tania. I would rather swallow razorblades than drink with you. Oh, and by the way, I'm not alone. I'm with Muriel.'

Right on.

There are so many more women whose friendships I've fallen in love with in books, movies or TV. Benny and Eve in Maeve Binchy's novel *Circle of Friends*; the southern belles of *Steel Magnolias*; Daria and Jane in *Daria*; the complex women on *The 100*; Ruth and Idgie in *Fried Green Tomatoes* (although in Fannie Flagg's original novel, *Fried Green Tomatoes at the Whistlestop Café*, Ruth and Idgie weren't 'just good friends' but actual lovers, and the movie is irreparably harmed by choosing not to portray that). The list goes on.

Unfortunately, there's also a truckload of terrible representations of female interaction on screen. In numerous cases, it either doesn't exist at all (because too many writers still think it's okay to only have a woman present if she can double as the prize for the hero at the end) or women's relationships are defined by bitchiness and competition. This accounts for some of the many complicated feelings I have about the 1980s girl-made-good story *Working Girl*. As much as I love watching Tess McGill rise like a phoenix into the power zone of shoulder pads and the corner office, I also hate that her major nemesis is her female boss, Katharine. I mean, we're meant to be on Tess's side and for the most part that's easy. But then you remember that Katharine's boyfriend Jack not only begins an affair with Tess (without disclosing his relationship), but gets to stay with her at the end because we just accept that his moral compass had been devoured somewhere along the way by Katharine's ambitious, brunette vagina. Tess does have other friendships with women, but they're minor. Her major interactions throughout are with businessmen (all of whom she's able to charm with her raspy voice, sexy hair and a business acumen that manages to be both sweetly naive and disarmingly cunning) and Katharine, who ends up trying to steal her ideas and denigrate her ability. I mean, I guess you could take that as a lesson on how not to support your fellow women in the workplace, but it's a long bow.

Then there are the examples where multiple women exist but fail to talk to each other about anything other than a man. Cartoonist Alison Bechdel made light of this phenomenon in one of the early strips for her cult series, *Dykes to Watch Out For.* One of her characters invites another friend to see a movie, but the friend declines, saying she only watches films these days if they meet three specific criteria:

1. There has to be at least two women in it . . .
2. . . . who talk to each other . . .
3. . . . about something other than a man.

The Bechdel Test, as it's become known, might be imperfect (namely because there are examples of films that don't pass but still contain feminist messages, and films that do pass but feel still like they've been crapped out of a Men's Rights Activist's butthole, and none of its parameters account for the overwhelming lack of racial diversity in cinema) but as a rough guide it's helpful to see just how often movies fail, particularly when they're the kinds of blockbusters millions of people end up watching. When you don't see women talking to each other about anything other than the men who dominate their stories, it reinforces the pernicious view that women exist only to be supporting players in men's lives. Worse, it further convinces women of what patriarchy has tried to tell us all along: that we are not allies but enemies, and that our only hope of succeeding in life is to win some weird, unspoken competition against every woman we ever meet so that we can win the ultimate prize of men's admiration and love. Taylor Swift's early work was basically all about this.

These messages are filtered to us right from childhood. Think about the role of women in fairy tales and (if you're an eighties kid like me) how these relationships were depicted in colourful, intoxicating Disney animations. With the exception of the occasional kindly fairy godmother (whose existence I can actually only recall in two stories, *Sleeping Beauty* and *Cinderella*) women are depicted either as innocent young princess-types or jealous old crones trying to steal their beauty. Snow White, Cinderella, Aurora and Ariel are all victimised by other women, who are in turn all vanquished by story's end, leaving the heroines to enjoy the great thrill of becoming child brides to handsome older princes. If that weren't bad enough, these 'witches' aren't even taken out by the heroines. The spells cast on Aurora and Snow White are both broken by men they don't know but who can conveniently bestow 'True Love's Kiss' on them (while they're sleeping, because that's not creepy and gross). Cinderella's Prince Charming rescues her from a life of indentured servitude because her feet are the only ones in the kingdom tiny enough to fit into the glass slipper, and apparently that provides better proof of her secret identity than looking at her face or, you know, having a conversation. And after spending the majority of the movie being unable even to speak (still not enough of a deficit to stop Prince Eric from falling for her), Ariel isn't even given the kudos of being able to kill Ursula in the final battle. No, Eric runs a boat through her abdomen.

And they all lived happily ever after.

But at least those movies had other women in them. The only other woman of significance in *Beauty and the Beast* is Mrs Potts, and she's a fucking kitchen appliance. Let's not even get into the fact that the story is about a young girl falling in love with the abusive man who imprisons her in his mansion, because we already know that's fifty shades of fucked up. The less said about *Pocahontas* the better, aside from the fact it's a disgustingly racist rewrite of the life of an actual Native American woman who was kidnapped by the British and then later paraded throughout Europe as an example of the 'civilised savage'. Not exactly a love story. *Aladdin* and *The Lion King* may not have evil witches as their antagonists, but they also only have one significant woman character apiece.

It is changing, and not just with Disney (2013's *Frozen* was the kind of capitalist success a company like Disney dreams of, so we can only hope to see more. And Disney Pixar's *Inside Out* featured a pretty even split not only between women and men but in the amount of time each group spoke for – in fact, it's one of the very few films made in which women have slightly more than 50 percent of the lines). 'Girl power' is back in vogue, but this isn't the primary reason we're seeing better and more prominent relationships between women on screen. It's because more women are being funded to produce content that portrays what it's really like to be a woman, not merely what a man thinks it might be like.

That's the major difference I see when I think of how women and our relationships with each other are reflected in pop culture. When women have been given creative control, either as writers, producers, directors or performers, I am more likely to see the kinds of rich, positive and complex interactions between women that have been my life experience (well, at least since I wised up and started to work with women rather than against them). That's why shows like *Broad City* are so fantastic while being irreverent and silly – because the relationship between Abbi and Ilana, the things they do together and the things they talk about, seems like it's actually informed by female life as something that exists on its own and not as a depiction of how that life sits in relation to men.

It is also why every single available copy of the movie *Bride Wars* needs to be taken to a field, arranged in a gigantic pattern that spells What Were You Thinking, Anne Hathaway?, doused in petrol and set so thoroughly ablaze that the magnitude of that monstrosity can be seen from space.

Lest we forget.

■

In 'Ready for my close-up', I talk about the anorexia I developed at thirteen. I went from being round-faced and pudgy to having sharp angles and a sunken chest. This weight loss wasn't achieved by healthy means, and I can't say it had too much of a positive effect on my mental state either. Still, there were flashes of satisfaction at being able to wear clothes that had previously been off-limits to me. Our school dress code was more of a suggestive colour scheme than a uniform policy, and one of my proudest achievements as a closet anorexic was the day I found I could fit into the kind of short, tight black skirt worn by the worldlier girls in my year level.

I wasn't used to wearing the costume worn by other girls. I'd spent the majority of my life not only chubbier than them but also living in a country where wearing a tiny black skirt would have been considered culturally inappropriate; thus I hadn't seen much of them until I'd moved to Norfolk. Now that I could finally wear one myself, I felt like I'd ascended into the official state of womanhood – or at the very least, was doing a good job of faking it. My school skirt was more than just an item of clothing. It was a sign that I'd achieved something. (Calcium deficiency? Interrupted menstruation? An obsessive eating disorder? All of the above?) I liked to double roll it at the waistband so that it sat just a couple of inches below my butt, my suddenly lithe legs stretching out beneath it in opaque tights.

I always believed this kind of physical ideal was what girls were meant to aspire to – and that once we arrived, the cruel taunts of being 'tubby' or 'gross' would stop and we could enjoy the satisfying privilege that involves being both respected and left alone. But having never spent any time on this side of the girl fence, I didn't realise that there's never a moment in which any of us are considered to have 'earned' the right to have scrutiny withheld. I didn't expect to suddenly find myself dealing with sly whispers and giggles.

She thinks she's so good.

She just wants boys to like her.

Look at that skirt.

Slut.

The funny thing is that I had said these things about other girls myself, racked as I was with envy over the privileges I thought their beauty gave them. I had projected my own insecurities on them by calling them names, calling their moral worth into question and bitching about them with other girls. It gave me little stabs of pleasure to denigrate them, to punish them for their good fortune. I told myself this was fair and justified, because why should being beautiful mean they were automatically loved by everyone?

Perhaps the thing that really allowed me to forgive my behaviour, though, was my belief that they wouldn't care. Why would they? I didn't know that beautiful, popular girls were just as likely to be hurt by other women calling them sluts and bitches as the plain wallflowers. That they would find the experience just as confusing and isolating, and it would make them feel just as likely as anyone else to turn away from the possibilities that friendship with other women offers.

Women are supposed to be beautiful, accessible and gaze-worthy, and we know this on a very deep level. But we're also keenly aware of how unfair this measure of value is, and how arbitrary the judgment that ascribes it to us. Unfortunately, instead of tearing the whole facade down and taking control of the rules ourselves, we turn to the patterns of behaviour that teach us to work against other women instead of with them. Rather than banding together to reject the system entirely, the ones who feel let down by it make it the fault of the women it supposedly rewards. We tell ourselves that they might be pretty, but they're empty-headed. They might be sexy, but they're a slut. They might be desirable, but they can't offer anything more than physical pleasure. We are so used to feeling the gaze on ourselves that we learn to look at each other with men's eyes.

How powerful would it be if we used our own eyes instead? If we could look at other women and say, 'She's beautiful and she makes me laugh.' Or, 'She's really intelligent and I can tell why so many people enjoy her company.' Or even, 'She has sex on her own terms and I really admire her confidence.'

We don't have to like every woman we meet. That would be impossible. But we have to stop disliking them because we're afraid they might be a rival for the male attention we've been taught to want or because we think that destroying them for being too slutty/too pretty/too arrogant/too bitchy/too unpredictable will earn us patriarchy points.

When I was sixteen, someone wrote the words *Clementine is a slut!* on the fence of my family's home. My uncle found it early one morning and fetched my father to help him scrub it off. I didn't find out about any of this when it happened, because neither of them wanted to bring it up. When my father finally told me years later, I treated the news with a curiosity that can only be made easier by the passage of time. I knew that it wouldn't have been any of the boys I went to school with, because they were far more likely to call me fat or ugly. I have a fairly good idea that it might have been the girls who once invited me to spend the evening with them at the town's annual show, and then spent the whole night pointedly ignoring me and acting as if I was a bad smell that had latched on to them and which they couldn't shake. They reminded me of a group of girls I'd been friends with briefly in England; the ones who'd invited me to meet them in a meadow one afternoon and then never shown up. I waited for half an hour before deciding I'd got the message wrong and leaving. I found out later they'd been hiding on a ridge the whole time, watching me and laughing.

Does the fact that a bunch of girls were bitches to me in high school mean that no girls are to be trusted? Of course not. I don't buy into the bullshit argument that tells us women are each other's worst enemies. The idea that women's greatest oppression comes from the lateral violence inflicted by other women is simply another tool developed by thousands of years of patriarchy to deflect our attention away from trying to destroy it. If women can be convinced to mistrust one another instead of working together, patriarchal order is secured for another day.

Men are often oblivious to the fact these power dynamics exist, which is why it can be so frustrating to try to explain it. How do you tell someone what air looks like? Just because you aren't aware of something doesn't mean you don't benefit from it. If women and teen girls are taught to vie for the attention of men, those men have to do very little to feel themselves admired. And so it becomes unconsciously assumed that women will embody the practice of flattering men, be that through their conversations with them, their attempts to aesthetically please them or their willingness to tear down the other women who present as rivals for the crumbs thrown out as reward.

Lateral violence isn't a by-product of women's nature but is designed to protect the stability of a structure that relies on women's subordination. Patriarchy acts to alienate women from one another and teach them instead to seek value and approval in the good opinion of men. It encourages us to work at being the Official Woman, the only one in the clubhouse, the woman above all other women, the woman good enough to hang with the boys – in short, the woman who excels so much at proving her allegiance to men above women that she earns the right to eat their leftovers.

But striving to be the Official Woman is a learned practice. This means we can unlearn it.

■

I began the process of unlearning this sexism when I went to university. It wasn't just that I took up gender studies, although that certainly helped in providing me with a framework to talk about issues that had always bothered me but for which I lacked the language. It wasn't that I discovered my male friends from that time were terrible human beings. They weren't, and I still value their impact on my life today. What helped me was discovering the transformative power of female friendship, and the importance of having a good girl gang in your life. The girlfriends I made in those early days of tertiary education remain my friends today. We've grown up together, stayed out late together, got drunk and silly together, fought and made up with each other and shared almost two decades worth of emotions.

It wasn't until after I rejected that ideology that I realised just how suffocating it was to perform the role of Official Woman. When you measure your value based on how proficiently you validate men's behaviour and flatter their intellects, you cannot help but live in a mild state of fear that you might make a mistake one day. This stereotype of hierarchical power in friendships is often ascribed to women, but I've found that the true model of the girl gang is as far removed from this pattern of jealousy and recrimination as you can possibly get.

As I write this, I've just completed a two-week residency at Varuna, a writers' retreat in the Blue Mountains west of Sydney. While not specifically for lady writers, I was fortunate to spend my time there in what turned out to be a female-only space. I lived with six other extraordinary women, all of them writing vastly different things but with whom an intimacy was quickly and organically established. Our paths sometimes crossed during the day, a warm word shared here and there while making tea in the kitchen, but we mostly worked in comfortable solitude. At night, we'd gather in the dining room for hearty meals prepared by Sheila, a glamorous octogenarian who's been providing evening sustenance to writers there for the past twenty years. Unlike our brief daytime interactions, these dinnertime conversations were rich and expansive. Each day, we'd enter that space with new stories, writing triumphs or frustrations we were eager to discuss or seek advice on and questions about each other's progress. It didn't take long before we were sharing our own secret histories with one another. In the final week, we began practising what Mag called 'the five joys'. Over dessert, we'd share five of the moments or thoughts that had brought us joy that day. Without fail, each of us would mention something to do with the others – either the support we felt we were receiving, the happiness that came from having participated in a particular conversation or simply the privilege we all felt at being there in each other's company. These were intimacies that could only have been shared in this particular dynamic, with women left free to be themselves in supportive company. And while there are one or two men I can think of who would have done a fine job of slotting in, the particular intimacies shared between women still remain distinct. That is a rarity that's not only valuable but worth fighting for.

On my final evening at Varuna, when almost everyone else had left, I walked with Mag and Anna to watch the sun set at the nearby Three Sisters lookout. Although I had known them for only a fortnight, I felt strongly connected to them both. As the waning sun turned the mountains a burnt orange, we hiked down to one of the Sisters and took in the awe-inspiring view of the land beyond. The vastness of it seemed a good metaphor for how much space and intensity we had covered with each other in such a short time. When we arrived home later, we decided it was a 'dinner in the kitchen' kind of night, and this too seemed to signify something special. Kitchen tables are where friends and family say farewell to formalities and congregate comfortably and without artifice, and that's exactly what we had come to feel like – family. When the morning came, I was sad to say goodbye. But as with any family member, I knew it wouldn't be forever.

I love the company of women. Given a choice, I probably value it more than the company of men. But where once no one batted an eyelid when I said the same thing of male friendship, now I'm made to feel strange or hostile when the situation is reversed. Being effusive about my fondness for women turns me into a man-hater or a shrew. Some people treat me with suspicion, or feel the need to urge me to reconsider. I'm entreated to admit that men are wonderful, even when the only thing I've said is that I think women are great. Even the act of asking a man not to just assume he can join a group of women is seen as subversive, as if we only come to life when a man is there to talk to us. In fact, it's my experience that women are more likely to shrink than we are to expand when men are present. This doesn't necessarily mean that men are wilfully oppressing us. In all honesty, they're probably not even aware it happens. But as with so many things, what is once seen cannot be unseen – and I have watched as even I, *le boner killer extraordinaire*, subconsciously adapt and modify my behaviour or conversation when confronted with the possibility that a man might find it inaccessible or dull. Spending time with women is therefore not only necessary to give one pleasure, it becomes a vital salve against the invasive restriction of constantly existing as the Other. I think of these moments of resistance as akin to Roald Dahl's gathering of witches. In the safety of our own covens, here we can all stand and whip off the bindings that hide our various layers from the world, scratch the itch of suffocated scalps and look at each other with honest eyes.

Listen to me when I tell you this, because it might be the most important thing in this whole book: the best thing you can do for your self-esteem, your sanity, your sense of accomplishment, your happiness and your inner strength is to find yourself a solid girl gang.

Instead of feeling judged by my girlfriends, I find relief in their company. They make me feel safe and supported, because they don't respond to my shared experiences of being a woman with the suggestion that I might be exaggerating or imagining things. Their reciprocal stories make me feel validated amid a narrative which still wants women to believe we are overly sensitive and humourless. When we are together, we have each other's backs against whatever obstacle or Neanderthal might be blocking our paths. With the support of my different girl gangs, I feel stronger and more equipped to live freely and confidently in the world as I choose to rather than according to the outdated, gendered ideas of womanhood which reinforce the comfort of men.

I promise you that if you give yourself over to relationships with good women and allow them into your heart, your feelings of value and positivity will skyrocket. I don't mean women who treat you like shit or bully you or make you feel like every moment with them is a competition you didn't sign up to participate in. I mean the kinds of women who'll listen to you without judgment when you're baring your soul, who'll hold your hair back when you vomit after too much booze, who'll have your back when you tell a guy to leave you alone at the pub, who'll sing loud songs with you while stumbling down the streets at night, who'll drop everything to take off on a girls' weekend to get high and watch *Magic Mike*, who'll always tell you you're a hot babe, who'll listen to you when you speak and really hear what you're saying, and who will, above all, let you know through their love and kindness that you matter and that you mean something.

If you have a girl gang, you'll never be alone. The world can be hard and unforgiving for us women, but with a girl gang by your side you will build with them a barricade. It will act as your protection, your fortress and your castle, and your enemies will never be able to tear it down, no matter how hard they try. Find your Steel Magnolias, the Thelma to your Louise, your own Broad City and a League of Your Own. Find it and never let it go.

To the members of my girl gangs, I love you all. Thank you for saving my life by loving me back.

—6—

ARE YOU MY MOTHER?

When I was twenty-five, I got knocked up.

Twice.

Both of these pregnancies were unexpected and both were decidedly unwanted. My reasons for this were pretty standard, but they all basically boiled down to the fact that it seemed unwise to bring a small infant into the world when I still had little to no idea how to navigate it myself. What if I forgot to feed it? I barely knew how to feed myself, evidenced by the fact dinner for me regularly consisted of a bag of fancy potato chips, a bottle of wine and an episode of *Survivor*.

It wasn't just the inability to navigate nutrition that concerned me. There was also the fact of my dearth of prospects. At the time of Pregnancy No. 1, I was only barely out of university and still not entirely sure as to the status of my graduation, i.e. had I actually qualified for one. (Note: this is still uncertain. Adelaide University, please advise.) I was living on a combination of Newstart payments and pocket money gleaned from the three hours a day I worked making lunches in a rickety old vegetarian cafe in Adelaide. While my then-boyfriend and I were in love, it's fair to say that the riches of this alone wouldn't put food on the table or shoes on the feet of our progeny.

Instead of feeling a connection to the cells dividing inside me, I felt nothing but anxiety and fear at the thought of what might happen if this biological process went unchecked. I knew that being pregnant was different to being a mother. I also knew that while I didn't want to be in the first situation, I wanted even less to be in the second. A thing was growing inside me, and I wanted it out as soon as possible.

So contemplating abortion wasn't especially difficult. I had been raised knowing that abortion was a woman's right. This word 'knowing' is important. It wasn't an opinion, as if there was room for debate around the topic. In my family, it's always been an acceptance of fact that matters of reproduction and birth are the business of nobody but the woman involved. No one could tell her what she should and shouldn't do with her uterus, especially not someone who would never be in the position of finding that happily vacant lot suddenly and unexpectedly slapped with a planning permit for a house that would take eighteen years to build and require a lifetime of sacrifice.

'Girls,' my parents reassured us, 'if one of you ever comes home pregnant, you don't have to be afraid to tell us. We'll support you no matter what you decide to do – but you should probably get an abortion because you're only sixteen and you have your whole life ahead of you.' (The latter half of this message was usually reiterated by my dad, whose biggest nightmare seemed to be having his daughters 'throw their lives away' on a two-minute roll in the hay.)

Being suddenly thrust into the reality of an unwanted pregnancy only strengthened my belief in the freedom of reproductive choices. Even in the early days of my first pregnancy, before I'd seen a doctor and when suspicion and intuition were all I had to go on, I knew exactly what I was going to do. I was going to 'get rid of it'. It was a choice that never caused any particular kind of distress or conflict within me. At twenty-five, all I had were my dreams and aspirations. I knew what I wanted my life to look like (sort of), but I was still trying to figure out how I could get there. I wanted to be independent. I wanted to achieve a measure of success that satisfied me. I wanted to be happy. I wanted to be a mother one day, but I wanted it to be when I had something of substance to offer a child. I wanted to be supported by a partner, and not necessarily financially (although there's no denying that if we want new mothers to be primary caretakers in at least the first few months of a child's life, we also have to accept that those mothers need financial assistance). And more than anything, I wanted to know that parenting had been a choice made on my terms. I believe that all people with the biological capacity to bear children have the right to make that choice, primarily because pregnancy is such an invasive and overwhelming experience. We require consent for all other medical procedures, particularly if it involves the use of our bodies by another person. Why is pregnancy treated differently, just because fundamentalists have created an easy moral narrative around the supposed innocence of life in the womb?

The decision was made. I consulted with my parents and booked myself in for a termination. When it was over, I felt nothing but relief – psychological relief over the fact I had been saved and instant physical relief from the horrendous cocktail of pregnancy hormones that had been wreaking havoc on my body and mind. I was free.

I was *free*.

■

This would normally be the point where I'd feel obliged to offer an explanation. You know the kind. *I was too young. We were in love, but it wasn't enough. I wish things could have been different. I think about it every day.* I'm not going to do this though because: a) none of that is true, and b) it's nobody's business. Too many women feel like we owe explanations to strangers for the whys and wherefores of our reproductive medical choices, but we don't. In fact, I think the only explanation anyone else is entitled to is: 'This is my choice and I don't care what you think about it.'

Refusing to justify your reproductive choices to anyone is a brazenly political act. The attacks on women's bodies extend far beyond just the matter of abortion, and it's well past time we stopped lending our support to this intrusion. With regard to abortion in particular, the tactics used by extremists range from spreading false propaganda to demonisation and even criminal attacks on individuals and organisations. As far as I'm concerned, these people are terrorists waging a war against women and our fundamental right to be in charge of our own bodies and destinies, and I will not negotiate with terrorists by operating within their own arbitrary, misogynist set of rules.

But it isn't just extremists who force women to justify their behaviour. There are people who consider themselves pro-choice who do this too; people who may not even realise that they've created a checklist of requirements that women must fulfil if we want to claim the right to control our own bodies. You've probably heard some of these before. Hell, you might have even said some of them.

'I'm pro-choice, but women shouldn't be allowed to have more than one abortion. Haven't they heard of contraception?'

'I'm pro-choice, but I think there are too many women who consider it the easy way out.'

'I'm pro-choice, but only in circumstances where the woman has been raped or there's something wrong with the baby.'

'I'm pro-choice, but I think too many women have too many abortions.'

'I'm pro-choice, but married women have no reason to have an abortion.'

'I'm pro-choice, but I think abortion is too readily available.'

'I'm pro-choice, but not when women use it as a form of contraception.'

What all of these really translate to is: 'I'm pro-choice, but only in situations where I am allowed to dictate the moral terms of reference.'

To my mind, a truly pro-choice position is one that's pro-choice regardless of the reasons. If I don't want to carry a pregnancy to term and become a mother, it shouldn't matter if that pregnancy was the result of the worst kind of thing a man can do (i.e. violently assault and rape a woman) or the result of the worst kind of thing a woman can do (have consensual sex with a man to whom she isn't married). As far as I'm concerned, there's no scale of morality when it comes to terminating a pregnancy (which is why I refuse to talk about the specifics of how I got pregnant). Abortion is a matter of healthcare, and the reasons behind choosing abortion are the business only of the person choosing it, their healthcare practitioner and their partner. Even then, all other input is properly overridden by the person whose body is at stake.

I understand why women offer their abortion stories as context for the overarching topic of abortion rights, but it's not something I personally have much interest in doing. I find it much more interesting to observe how opponents of abortion – particularly those invested in maintaining the enforcement of reproductive labour in cisgender women – characterise women who *own* their abortion experiences (which is very different to 'confessing to' or 'admitting to' abortion experiences, because never forget that asserting autonomy and choice over our own bodies is still a shameful matter that we must beg forgiveness for). If I discuss abortion as a practical option rather than one for which I must apologise, I am automatically cast by anti-choice zealots as a 'whore', a 'slut', a 'selfish bitch' and a 'loose woman' who needs to 'learn how to keep her legs shut'.

Don't be fooled into thinking we've moved on from the old-timey mindset that saw women institutionalised for having sex. The old trope of the harlot is very much alive today. The speed with which certain people race to brand women as immoral is phenomenal, and it pales only in comparison to the satisfaction they take from spitting the accusation at us. If they could get away with it, these people would be pinning scarlet letters to our chests and making us crawl on our bellies in the streets while the righteous gather around to pelt us with rotten tomatoes. Or, to refer to a more recent entry into pop culture canon, they would march us through the village, naked and shorn, as onlookers gathered to spit at us, curse us, throw things at us, gawp at the bodies they despise and yet simultaneously want to fuck into submission – all while a buttoned-up nun strode behind us, pushing us through the rabble and intoning, 'Shame!' with every third step. *Game of Thrones*' Cersei might have been duplicitous and conniving, but even she didn't deserve that treatment.

Eternal apology is not the toll women are duty bound to pay in exchange for making a basic healthcare decision. We certainly don't owe it to the world's misogynists to self-flagellate over our choices – choices that, when discussed free from the bogus rhetoric of regret and enforced grief, most of us are happy to reveal we made with unqualified relief. It's no secret that women's bodies and choices are considered to be held under the jurisdiction of everyone who isn't them, but that doesn't mean we actually have to tolerate that. Fuck those guys who try to make us feel guilty about putting ourselves first. Fuck those religious zealots who gather outside clinics waving photoshopped propaganda in our faces and telling us we're going to hell. Fuck all those people who think that the body of a living, breathing, actual human is of less value and importance than something smaller than a thumb.

■

There is an important point to be made here about the dialogue around abortion. You may have noticed that I swing between referring to 'people' and 'women' when I discuss pregnancy. This is in recognition of the complexities around bodies, trans inclusivity and biological make-up. Not all cisgender women can become pregnant. Not all women have vaginas. Some people who seek abortions are trans men with uteruses. Some identify as gender non-conforming. The body and identity is a wonderfully diverse thing. So when I say 'biological make-up', it is absolutely not my intention to create a barrier between cis and trans women. It is merely to acknowledge that the definition of womanhood and biology is far more nuanced and complex than mainstream society considers it to be.

However, in discussing the specific attacks levelled on abortion clinics and the rights to access termination of pregnancy, I think it's unwise to move completely away from a narrative which centralises the word 'women' and into a broader 'people' based one. While it is absolutely true that not every person who chooses abortion identifies as a woman, the vast majority of people accessing these services are cis women. More to the point, the reason abortion is so heavily policed is precisely because of archaic, binary notions of gender and reproductive labour. The anti-choice conservative is unlikely to even believe in basic gender diversity let alone acknowledge how broadly it can be defined. Their motivation to protest abortion isn't *just* to save 'innocent little babies'. I'd go so far as to say that it's actually not really about babies at all. Their motivation is to reinforce their personal idea of what women are and should be – to wit, cis women with the capacity to bear children and who thus need to be indentured into the kind of gendered domestic servitude that supports male power in a patriarchy by feeding it, clothing it and cleaning up after it. Capitalism plays a helping hand here by positioning the domestic sphere as something women are uniquely capable of controlling – think of all the hapless husbands and dopey dad advertisements you've seen over the years. These are not, as Men's Rights Activists frothingly argue, evidence of a society that is anti-man. Rather, they are tiny tools employed in the fight to maintain the status quo. Such an idea is issued in a double whammy:

1. Men are hopeless around the home, and that is why they need to dominate in the less difficult task of being Masters of the Universe.
2. Women can't compete in the workplace or in leadership, but that doesn't matter because they are Boss of the Home.

A significant driver of opposition to abortion is the social construction of the Ideal Woman. In a culture that rarely, if ever, allows women simply to be people, value is ascribed based on a woman's relation to something other than herself. A woman on her own is like a bit of driftwood floating in the ocean. She is a broken object with no purpose, waiting either to wash up on the shore and be put to use as part of something else, or to sink and be forgotten forever.

A woman's life only finds meaning when it becomes defined by another person's. Her value increases once she becomes a wife, because finding a man to love her *publicly* forever is the goal that society, pop culture and history have conditioned most little girls to aspire to. For what are we without a man to not only love us but transform us from invisible peasant girls into princesses adored by all the kingdom? (This is also why one of the go-to, bet-a-million-dollars-on-it-happening, I-hear-it-at-least-once-a-day insults used against women from anti-feminists and angry men especially is the time-honoured 'You'll never find a husband with that mouth' or the more aggressive 'No wonder no man wants to fuck you, good luck being single and alone forever'. They always seem so confused when I tell them that being single forever sounds amazing and certainly a lot more financially rewarding.)

After being validated by a man's love, the next step for a woman towards nominally recognised personhood is to bear his children. Note that they have to come in this order – a woman who has a child before finding a husband isn't a beatific vision of feminine power in the eyes of society. No, she's an irresponsible wench who 'got herself pregnant' and is now probably sucking on the teat of the welfare system and cheating everyone out of their hard-earned tax dollars. There's no shortage of irony in the fact that the same people who argue that abortion is the act of selfish sluts who can't keep their legs shut will often express opposition to supporting single mothers (especially those further disadvantaged by youth, race or class status) because 'if you can't afford children, you shouldn't have a baby'. Pregnant women who don't want to have children shouldn't be allowed to have an abortion because it's selfish murder, but if you get pregnant and have a child don't go sticking your hand out for benefits because you should have thought of that before you gave birth. (Look, logical thinking has never been the strong suit of people who think terminating pregnancies in the uterus is the evil murder of God's children, but bombing the shit out of brown babies in the Middle East is necessary to preserve our way of life.)

Anyway, after marriage comes a baby and the women who follow this prescribed step are allowed to become their authentic selves. These two things are assumed without question to be the pinnacle of female desire – for what could we possibly want other than to become somebody's wife and somebody's mother? This is evident in the way unmarried women over a certain age become the objects of ridicule. Sad, desperate, shrivelled-up old things who've missed the boat on love and are therefore destined to roam the earth in a perpetual state of misery. Think about the money tabloid magazines have made from writing about Jennifer Aniston over the years. Poor,

FIGHT LIKE A GIRL

lonely, barren old Jennifer Aniston – a woman who actually had managed to 'land' a husband, only to have him leave her, childless, to run off and start breeding prolifically with someone else. He also managed to avoid public criticism of his actions because stories of the catfight between Aniston and Angelina Jolie – pathetic women fighting over a man – were way more saleable than that of a cad husband.

Think about the derision and suspicion levelled at women who are open about their lack of maternal aspirations. 'I'm not interested in having kids' is rarely met with enthusiasm or even grudging acceptance. Instead, the women who say this (and who are never respected enough to know their own minds or breadth of emotional history) are told that they'll change their minds one day or end up regretting it. 'But who'll take care of you when you're older?' people ask. 'You'll end up lonely and alone!'

Haha! As if anyone cares about old women.

If women in general are already considered to be a social afterthought, old women especially are framed as irrelevant nobodies. Once a woman has passed marriageable and reproductive age, what's the point of her? Who'd want to spend time with an old woman when they didn't have to – apart from the children who are obliged to? It says a lot about how these people see women that they can't conceive of a rich life for them, one that's full of friends, intellectual stimulation and no children, beyond the age of fifty.

All of these expectations can be traced right back through the purpose of women in history. While men are busy exercising their right to run the world, women are expected to stay busy providing them with comfortable homes, a sense of respectability and a male heir to keep the family name alive. The thrill of supporting a man with our bodies, our children and our unpaid labour is not only supposed to make us happy but is offered as some kind of vital ingredient in the world's evolution. It's why absurd, insulting platitudes are thrown around to appease us, platitudes like 'behind every great man there is a woman'. I prefer to think of it like this: 'behind every well-respected man, there's a woman who probably does his washing.'

Of course, the reality is that women are human beings with just as many aspirations as men. For every woman who might regret not having a child, there is a mother who, in her heart of hearts, wishes she had chosen to remain childfree and single. Why is it that men who prioritise adventure and independence over family are called 'committed bachelors' and 'wanderers' who just can't be tied down, but women who similarly pursue a life free from burdens are called 'spinsters' and 'cat ladies' and are viewed as pitiful cautionary tales? It's because men are given the complexity to be fully rounded individuals while women are still treated like plants in need of a man's attention to fully bloom.

But the possibility that women might exist in their own right didn't really become a problem for patriarchal order until the advent of the contraceptive pill. As pregnancy became more preventable in the upswing of the sexual and feminist revolutions (and as abortion became safer and more accessible), women's options rapidly expanded. They no longer needed to rely on men to provide for them financially and they certainly didn't need to bear their children if they didn't want to. The Independent Woman was born – and to some people, she was terrifying.

Rebecca Traister references this fear in a 2014 article published in *New Republic*. In 'Let's Just Say It: Women Matter More than Fetuses Do', Traister addresses the insidious tactics of the anti-choice movement and how, seemingly with the permission or at least acquiescence of pro-choice lobbies, it has managed not only to centralise developing fetuses over the fully formed humans who carry them, but also establish them as more valuable and important. She writes:

> After [US Supreme Court decision on abortion] Roe was decided in 1973, the varied experiences of mothers, grandmothers, aunts, sisters, friends and selves suddenly seemed drained of their value. It was as if in gaining rights, not just to abortion, but also to greater professional and economic and sexual opportunity, women lost any claim to morality – a morality that had, perhaps, been imaginatively tied to their exclusively reproductive identities.
>
> What rose up instead was a new character, less threatening than the empowered woman: the baby, who, by virtue of not actually existing as a formed human being, could be invested with all the qualities – purity, defencelessness, dependence – that women used to embody, before they became free and disruptive.

The idea of a baby as the symbol of perfect innocence has resonance with many people. Most of us are at least somewhat invested in the idea of protecting the children who can't protect themselves, even people who aren't particularly sold on having children themselves. Where things become dangerous is when the word 'baby' becomes automatically synonymous with everything that happens throughout the process of gestation. While characterising what happens from conception as a 'baby' might satisfy those invested in maintaining the false narrative of abortion as murder, it's not scientifically true. If life begins at conception, it's only in the sense that cells which divide and grow are alive, and it takes a few more steps than doing the boudoir hokey-pokey to create what we could reasonably identify as a baby. Of course, none of that matters to the mostly male legislators who persist in trying to equate the 'life' of a blastocyst with that of an actual fully formed human-being woman person. Science? Psshhht.

■

Here's where I tell you a different story.

One morning late in 2015, I stood in a hotel room on the Balinese island of Nusa Lembongan and stared at a pregnancy stick. There was one solid line on it, the same single, solid line I'd seen in the three tests I'd done the day before, the day before that and the day before that. But there was something else as well, something new. A faint second line.

Did a whisper of a second line mean you were pregnant, or did it just mean the test wasn't entirely sure so had decided to take an each-way bet?

I turned to Google, the omnipotent oracle from which I'd previously sought advice on everything from whether or not a sore leg meant I had bone cancer or if taking half a Valium with three glasses of wine would definitely cause your heart to stop.

Pregnancy test faint second line pregnant? I typed in. The search results told me all I needed to know: a second line, however faint, was almost certainly a sign of pregnancy.

I looked at the stick again, just to be sure. Two lines, one faint. Pregnant.

My grin was silly and large, spreading across my face with seemingly no input from my conscious thought. I was going to have a baby.

I spent the rest of the day sitting at a restaurant on the shore-front, chatting excitedly with some of my girlfriends on Facebook. Common theory holds that women should wait until the first trimester is over before announcing their pregnancy because the risk of miscarriage is so much higher in the early stages. It makes sense to a certain extent, but I've also wondered why women are expected to keep that secret to themselves. Perhaps I just lack the self-control and patience that we're told is a virtue in motherhood, but I told five women within two hours of peeing on that stick and I hadn't even confirmed it to my boyfriend yet. The feeling, though – the feeling was overwhelming. I was excited and terrified and thrilled and terrified and grateful and also terrified. Most of all, I was happy. This was a good result. This was a desired result. This was something I'd spent the last year dreaming of and looking forward to, floating baby names with JB and joking with him about how he'd finally be able to talk about his records with someone whose limited mobility meant they'd have no choice but to listen.

The jubilation I felt that day on the island couldn't have been further from the distress I'd felt almost a decade earlier, the first time a home pregnancy kit told me there was something taking up residence in my uterus. Back then, all I saw in those two lines was loss and suffocation. I saw myself being landed with a responsibility I didn't want and certainly wasn't equipped to handle. I felt trapped and sick and scared. I also felt nothing for the thing inside me – no love, no connection and certainly no hope.

At thirty-four, seeing two lines on a stick still terrified me, but it was a different kind of terror. It was the terror that comes from wanting to do something well. It was the terror of knowing that this choice, the choice to go ahead and have a child, would divert the carriage I'd been riding in and take all three of us – me, JB and the baby – into completely uncharted territory. It was the terror of knowing that I'd spend every day for the rest of my life always being terrified – terrified that my child was safe, that they were happy, that they were making choices that were right for them, that they didn't feel overwhelmed by the life I had brought them into just to satisfy my own craving for something different.

As fierce and deep as this terror ran, I also knew I could do it. I knew I was ready. At twenty-five, I had so many reasons for not wanting a baby, but most of them boiled down to the fact that I barely knew who I was. If I'd had a child, I would have become completely defined by them. Everything about me would be about them. Having a child before I was ready would have sent me hurtling along a path that took me far away from the life I lead now. Would it have derailed my life completely? No. I'd have managed. But it would have been hard. I would have been mostly alone and definitely unqualified. Every day would have been a struggle to earn money, to pay bills, to live and breathe and carry on and just keep going.

Crucially, I wouldn't have been able to pursue a career as a writer. That might not mean much to others, but it means a lot to me. With a baby and then a toddler and then a child in what would likely be a single parent household, I wouldn't have been able to focus on the topics that have consumed my life for the last few years: things like rape culture, men's violence against women,

women's poor representation in governance and leadership, the ways we are taught to hate ourselves, the intense hatred some men seem to have for us that partly manifests in online abuse and harassment – in short, the things that I discuss in this book, which is the culmination of all those years of work.

I don't think it's arrogant to believe that one can make a difference in the world. And I believe that the work I've been able to do because I have been able to throw myself into it wholeheartedly has made and is making a difference. My life has mattered. The choices I've made, including the choice to end two separate pregnancies that came at the wrong time, have been worth it. But because I'm a woman, I'm expected to not only defend but also apologise for those choices in ways that men just aren't.

Life, if we can help it, should be about more than simply carrying on and keeping on going. If we are lucky enough to have the opportunity to shape our lives, we should grab it with both hands. For some women, that involves embracing an unexpected pregnancy at twenty-five and funnelling all their love into that child. That's wonderful. Good for them. I am truly happy to know that there are women who can make it work. But there are a shitload more women who can't, and who do it either because they believe they have no other options or because legislated misogyny means they *literally have no other options*. These women carry on and keep on going. They love their children – of course they do. If you ask them, they'll say they can't imagine their life without them. Because this *is* their life now, and we make the best of what we've got. We have to find joy in our lives, otherwise what's the point?

But in their heart of hearts, in the deep well that traps our secrets in whispers and keeps them safe from ears that would not understand, they may sometimes wish they'd been supported to make a different choice. To put their own lives first, and move on without regret. If I hadn't been raised to believe so fiercely in my right to choose, if I hadn't had parents who would drive me to the clinic and wait to wrap me in a blanket of love afterwards, if I hadn't lived in a place where these choices were accessible and straightforward, I would be that woman. I would love my child, but I would regret them too.

That isn't the life I wanted, for me or the person I would have otherwise brought into the world. No one should be resented while their mother wonders what else might have been. With the best of intentions, pro-choice advocates come up with all manner of reasons besides self-interest to justify the act of abortion. We hear lines like 'It's the hardest decision a woman will ever make' and 'Nobody makes the choice to have an abortion lightly'.

But these things aren't always true either. They're said as a way of sanitising women's realities and offering apology for our actions. Worse, they play right into the myth of the nurturer, a woman whose greatest primal instinct is to create a life that she can then protect. We need to be more honest about the fact that, while having an abortion is certainly not something anyone looks forward to or enjoys, for many women the choice to have one is actually very easy. More importantly, let's stop using the word 'selfish' like it's always a bad thing (particularly in women), as if considering yourself worthy of prioritising automatically strips you of emotional complexity and feeling.

I *was* too selfish to have a child before I was ready for one, and there's no shame in admitting that. Women should be selfish about our choices, for as long as we have the privilege of being selfish. Selfishness in women isn't the great crime that people like to pretend it is. We are as entitled as men to prioritise ourselves and our desires, and we are as capable as men of knowing what's best for us. Why is everyone so pathologically terrified of selfish women? The word is thrown around like an insult, as if the worst thing a woman could possibly do (aside from being fat, having sex with whomever she pleases and whenever, swearing, having an abortion, drinking alcohol, standing up for herself and being a working mother) is to decide that her life matters.

But women are allowed to be selfish. It shouldn't be considered a 'privilege' to be able to control our own bodies nor should it be treated like a favour done to us by the state. It's a right that, by and large, has been stolen from us and used to keep us in thrall to a paternalistic body that pretends to know what's best for us but is really only interested in maintaining the order that has proved best for them.

I use words like 'lucky' and 'fortunate' to describe the ease with which the state legislature of South Australia enabled me to seek out an abortion. I use these words even though they imply that what should be enshrined in law is something we should feel grateful to be granted. But when women are being imprisoned all over the world for reproductive-related 'crimes' such as having a miscarriage (like Purvi Patel of Indiana, sentenced to twenty years in prison for 'foeticide' after her pregnancy ended in utero, or rape survivor Guadalupe Vasquez, sentenced to thirty years in El Salvador for a miscarriage resulting in stillbirth), and when women are being left to die instead of being given life-saving abortions (like Savita Halappanavar, who died of septicaemia at Ireland's Galway University Hospital after doctors refused to abort the seventeen-week-old foetus that had begun miscarrying, triggering the infection in the first place), it is still prudent to refer to myself as lucky.

But this doesn't mean there aren't things about the situation that have made me sad. When I told my boyfriend I was pregnant the first time, his response was to pat me on the shoulder and say, 'I'm sorry.' I don't really have any way to tell you what it feels like to have the man you've let inside you explain that he won't be accompanying you to your abortion because Holly Throsby's playing a gig that night and he missed her the last time she was in town. It feels utterly shithouse, that's how it feels. Or how months later, after you've made your peace with him and you find yourself unexpectedly pregnant again (because it appears all you need to do is sit next to each other to have fertilisation occur), he'll disappoint you again when he tells you over the phone from the conservation site he's working on 3000 kilometres away that the reason he didn't call after your abortion appointment to see if you were okay is because he forgot it was happening. This time, instead of just feeling utterly shithouse, you'll also feel unbearably stupid and foolish.

But forgetting or ignoring the impact of pregnancy and abortion is the luxury some men have, and that's what makes it so infuriating that they also happen to be the ones who are predominantly making decisions about whether or not women are allowed to have them. For these cisgender men, pregnancy is a theoretical concept. They have no appreciation or understanding of the incredible intrusion it is upon one's body, nor do they understand how easily feelings about it can shift between happiness and despair. Even leaving aside for a moment the massive responsibility that comes later on with actually raising a child, the pregnancy itself carries many layers of trauma that cannot and should not just be dismissed as inconsequential.

As I write this, I'm about five weeks shy of giving birth. For almost three quarters of my pregnancy (thirty-two weeks to be precise), my mornings were spent bent over the toilet and vomiting bile. When I say 'bent over the toilet', what I really mean is that I was sitting on it in the normal fashion while spewing violently into the wastepaper bin. It turns out that pregnancy hormones will cause your morning dump to move from normal 'Gosh, can't my body produce interesting smells!' territory to 'I am literally carrying around the Bog of Eternal Stench in my bowels and now that I know this and have to smell the evidence of it, I will never stop puking ever again'.

Once the vomiting subsides, it isn't all tickety-boo prancing through meadows lit up by the glow of your pregnancy. No, what they don't tell you about morning sickness is that even when you stop vomiting, you can still spend the rest of the day feeling like you're *about* to vomit. This is most noticeable in the hours when you're awake, which will be three times longer than you'd like because the first trimester makes you bone-tired to the point where even walking a few hundred metres will leave you breathless and in need of a lie-down, and the third trimester brings with it bodies that need a million pillows to rest comfortably in beds that pregnancy insomnia prevents you from falling asleep in.

Do you know why you get so tired during your pregnancy? BECAUSE YOU'RE GROWING A FUCKING HUMAN IN YOUR UTERUS, AND IT'S FUCKING HARD WORK.

Leaving aside for a moment those who've gone through the whole experience and thus absorbed the post-birth hormones which cause them to forget how horrendous the whole thing was

(Mother Nature is a cruel mistress), do the people who speak blithely about babies and nurturing and pregnancy actually believe they have any fucking idea what they're talking about? For the most part, they seem to think that baby-growing is an external process that just happens to be attached to a woman's body. It's as if the only effect they think it has on us is that our stomachs protrude further out from our bodies (not too far out, though – pregnancy might be the only time in her life that a woman is permitted to have a round tummy, but she should still try not to be disgusting about it) and thus the only thing we really need to deal with is a shift in our perception of gravity.

This mythology around the relative ease of pregnancy has become especially clear to me since becoming happily 'with child'. When I compare this experience with both my previous pregnancies, the only thing that seems truly different to me is my own desire to greet what comes afterwards. I endured all of the same physical symptoms during my first pregnancy – the sickness, the dizziness, the soul-deep exhaustion. And while I ended the second one before those symptoms could appear, I didn't miss out on the hormones that have, with all three pregnancies, rendered me almost incapacitated by mood swings, anxiety and long stretches of being torn between wanting to weep and yet feeling completely unable to connect with my emotional self.

The wanting of a pregnancy and the projection of future life onto both the child and the you who will be charged with caring for it is what makes all of that stress and trauma bearable. It is a physical, emotional and mental strain to share your body with a developing foetus, and everyone capable of doing it should be granted the respect of being able to choose that course of action when and if they see fit. Because even when you want a child, it isn't all luminous cheeks and lustrous hair. Despite being very happy about the prospect of parenthood, there have been moments in this pregnancy where I've been unexpectedly overcome by the fear and anxiety of what this invasion means.

Sometime into the second trimester, I lay on the couch thinking about the foetal growth patterns I'd read about on a mobile pregnancy app I have on my phone. At sixteen weeks, it will be the size of an avocado. At eighteen weeks, the size of a capsicum. Out of nowhere, I was struck by the entirely unpleasant thought that I didn't *want* to have something the size of a capsicum lodged in my lower abdomen. Waves of panic started to wash over me. My skin became clammy. I felt like throwing up, but it wasn't because of the nausea that had become the backdrop of my days. I had a visceral sense of that *thing* floating around inside me, a lumpy creature that I would suddenly be able to feel and sense and yet be completely unable to separate myself from. It then occurred to me that this capsicum was in me already, but much smaller and even stranger-looking. I had seen it a few days earlier, stretching its arms and legs on an ultrasound screen. It was magical to witness, and I had wept. Later, JB and I grinned like fools and talked excitedly about how it had danced for us.

Lying on the couch that evening, the thought of that same thing wriggling around in me suddenly became horrifying. Any sense of connection I'd had to it seemed to disappear. The tiny being I had been thinking of with care and kindness, the thing that I had just days before felt such a rush of love for, had become foreign and alien. Somewhere inside, I heard a voice screaming to get it out of me. Gripped by anxiety, I imagined myself plunging a knife into my belly, forcing the thing that lived there to drain itself away from me and leave me in peace. Fortunately, there was still some semblance of a rational person operating in my brain who reassured me that these thoughts were not real and that they would pass. I focused all my energy on that rational voice. I've been in states of panic before, and I know that the light returns when the clouds have been blown away.

The claustrophobic feeling returned again at week twenty-three, except this time it didn't go away within a few minutes. It didn't even go away within a few days. Instead, I spent the next eight weeks consumed by anxiety and fear. As the capsicum grew bigger, it started to thrash around inside me like an eel in a bucket and reminded me how desperately out of control I felt. Every day started with me vomiting and each night saw me lying in the bath, thinking about killing myself.

Perhaps these examples shock you, but these temporary moments of insanity are far more common in people's pregnancies than you'd think. My guess is that women don't talk about them for all the same reasons we don't talk about other things that mark us as difficult, complicated miscreants – shame, fear, embarrassment and the mistaken belief that there's something wrong or broken about us. But think about it. Almost the only representation we have of pregnancy is a fantastical one built on Hollywood ideals and a distinct lack of medical insight. Pregnant women are rarely allowed to be anything other than grateful for the opportunity we've been given to become mothers. When the irrational side of pregnancy is explored, it's almost always in superficial ways. Women are shown having 'cute' meltdowns, or sending their partners out to fetch different food items so they can create incomprehensibly disgusting snacks (newsflash: I can only speak for myself, but I haven't had a single urge to eat ice-cream with a spoon fashioned from a pickle).

The birth itself is equally absurd in its depiction. We see stunning actresses whose body shapes (which in Hollywood typically means somewhere between an Australian size 4 and an 8) are unchanged but for the bowling ball nestled under their dress. Suddenly, a geyser bursts from between their legs. This is recognised in movie land to be the universal sign for 'Rush me to a hospital before this baby's born on our expensive-looking beige carpet!' From there, the excruciatingly long process of labour takes around twenty minutes with about two minutes of pushing tacked on at the end. And, voila – we have a baby. The newly anointed Vision of Motherhood dons her skinny jeans once more. Ain't pregnancy grand?

Of course, the reality is very different. We should know this, because most of our mothers have guilt-tripped us at least once in our lives with the news they laboured for hours and hours. My friend Ben Law's mother, Jenny, is so well known for talking about the damage her five kids did to her vagina that it's been immortalised in print, television and popular legend.

Pregnancy is a trial in a multitude of ways. The hormonal rollercoaster is horrendous. So is the puking, the gassiness, the exhaustion, the painful breasts, the extra chin hairs, the stretch marks, the bodily expansion, the sense of being taken over both physically and mentally, the extreme infantilisation some women suffer at the hands of the medical community. There is the fear that you will be the kind of terrible, irresponsible parent who feeds their child the wrong foods and doesn't pay close enough attention to whether or not they're sticking forks into electricity sockets. But even worse than the fear of being hopeless is the terror that you'll just be . . . uninterested. Because what happens if this baby comes along and, try as you might, you just can't bring yourself to care about it beyond ensuring it's clothed, fed and given a warm place to sleep? Generation after generation sees girls being indoctrinated from childhood into thinking that our primary purpose is to bring other children into the world. Failing to do so means failing to live properly and missing out on some vital part of human existence.

But what if motherhood just isn't for us? What if pregnancy is something some of us go through because we think we should or because we're pressured to or because we haven't properly thought about what comes afterwards? What if pregnancy is something some of us go through because we're told we have to, that we have no option, that to put ourselves first is to become a murderer and she-beast?

Abortion is not the act of a thoughtless, irresponsible woman with homicide on her mind and a cavalier attitude towards poor, innocent babies. Abortion is a choice that millions of women make every year because, astonishingly, we are more equipped than anybody else to know what's best for our bodies, our futures and our lives. Abortion is not the 'easy way out', as some anti-choice and anti-women banana brains like to claim. Rather, it is a procedure that all people capable of carrying a pregnancy should be supported to access both legislatively and socially. The state cannot and should not be able to force anyone to give their body over to medicine for any purpose – just as a person cannot be forced to donate a kidney to someone who will otherwise die, nor should a woman be forced to provide nine months of shared living space to a foetus she does not want to keep or care for.

This is why we need to keep fighting to take back complete control over our reproductive health rights. It isn't just for the women who are being criminalised because they had miscarriages, stillbirths and, yes, consciously chosen abortions. It isn't just for the women left to die because the archaic patriarchal views of their state decree that between their life and that of a weeks-old foetus, *they* are the expendable one. And it isn't just for the women all around the world and stretching all the way back through history who have sought out dangerous methods to end pregnancies they've determined to be detrimental to their own lives and health. All of these women are reasons to continue the battle to control our own reproductive systems – but the greatest reason of all is because *it is our unequivocal right to do so*.

This position is practical as well as philosophical. The people who suffer most as a result of anti-abortion legislation and limited maternal healthcare resources are women who are poor and/or living in remote areas with little access to medical facilities. Every year 47,000 women die worldwide as a result of unsafe abortions. Conversely, research shows that when you give women the ability to control the size of their families, the entire community benefits as a result. The most obvious explanation for this is that having fewer babies (especially in low income/healthcare areas) lowers a woman's risk of maternal mortality, which in turn prevents her children from losing their primary caregiver, thereby giving them a higher chance of staying healthy, clothed, fed and in school. Who'd have thunk it?

This is why movements like #ShoutYourAbortion (started by American feminists in response to government efforts to defund Planned Parenthood) – in which women openly and unashamedly share their abortion experiences on social media – are so important. Women are the ones who overwhelmingly experience pregnancy and abortion, and it's vital that we wrest back control of the narratives of both. We have been silent and compliant for too long. In many ways, it's an analogy for women's rights in their entirety. Don't speak too loudly lest they turn your microphone down again. Don't agitate for too much lest they take away what little we already have. Don't be too bolshy or they'll put us back in the cage. Don't talk about what your abortions actually meant to you because then you might not be able to have one at all.

Part of 'fighting like a girl' is owning your own choices and decisions. If you've had an abortion and you recognise that it was the best option for you at the time, own that choice. Be empowered by that choice. Tell anyone who disagrees with that choice that you don't fucking care what they think. I know this isn't always an easy thing to do, and there are some days when we don't have the strength to deal with people's hostility. But trust me – the more we stand up for ourselves and defend our rights, the easier it is to shrug off all that toxic noise.

It never occurred to me to keep my abortions a secret from anyone nor was I ever compelled to apologise for them. Part of that confidence came from growing up in a family where the notion of women's reproductive rights and control over their own bodies was sacrosanct. Part of it came from living in a state where no amount of public opposition or patriarchal bullshit had the power to suddenly render my choices illegal. This defiant stance about my own body means I'm often accused of being an unfeeling, evil, selfish murderess who, bizarrely, doesn't deserve to have children. I'm told, as so many women are, that I am a 'whore' who shouldn't have 'opened my legs' if I wasn't prepared to deal with the consequences of it. There's no shortage of irony in the fact that women are held responsible for whatever we allow into our bodies but denied any say over what we take out of them.

What I know is this: in a few weeks' time, if things go according to plan, I'll be meeting a baby I already love and whose future I can already see stretching out in glorious technicolour before me. This child and their future would not exist if I'd been forced to make a different decision when I was twenty-five. Fuck all those people with their placards and their judgment, their pathetic ideas of what we women should and shouldn't do with our bodies. As far as I'm concerned, I'm pro-life.

My life.

THE BELLE JAR

There is a mantra I repeat when things begin to seem too immense to process:

This too shall pass. And we will all be okay.

I began to say it sometime towards the end of 2012, when I went a little mad.

Frightening and disorienting as this madness was, it was familiar in that I had met it twice before. The first time was when I was twelve years old and struggling with the emotional disruption and change that comes from moving to an entirely different country. Madness introduced itself to me in my living room one afternoon and lingered by my side for a number of months. As no one else seemed to notice the stale weight of its presence or smell the metallic odour that seeped from the corners of its mouth, I tried my best to ignore it. But still it remained, whispering its threats into my ears and draping me in the cold, clammy sweat of the terrified. The world around me began to tilt and shift. *I have been abandoned in a boat,* I thought, *and I don't know how to navigate my way back to shore.*

The madness brought with it paranoia. I've always lived with the contradiction of being a calm and measured person who has a layer of irrational anxiety bubbling beneath the surface. I don't worry about locking doors or leaving ovens on (if anything, I'm too lax when it comes to real-life responsibilities), but since childhood, I've grappled with a particular form of catastrophic hypochondria. I say catastrophic, because I've never been scared of everyday illnesses. I rarely go to the doctor, choosing to deal with colds and sniffles the way everybody else does – by lying in bed moaning loudly about how miserable I am and insisting that eating Manuka honey out of the jar 'really does work'. With the exception of Nurofen Plus (one of the few things we can thank menstruation for providing access to) I barely take over-the-counter medication, let alone prescription drugs. In mid-2015, I broke my ankle while playing roller derby and refused to go to the sports clinic for twenty-four hours because I was sure it was just a sprain.

Catastrophic hypochondria is different. Someone with the kind of anxiety I have doesn't worry about being felled by a cold. Those things are small fry. Instead, we're convinced that life has something worse in store for us. By the age of six, I already felt this keenly. Every bruise was the harbinger of leukaemia, every sore elbow evidence of osteosarcoma. I'd run to my father, explaining each condition with comprehensive medical notes like, 'It hurts when I press here,' or 'I think this scrape might be getting gangrenous.'

'Well, don't press there then,' he'd sometimes reply. At other times, he'd make a show of looking carefully at whatever limb was concerning me then declare ominously, 'We'll have to cut it off then.'

His replies did little to address my anxiety, but knowing that he found them silly enough to make fun of (in a loving way) did bring momentary relief. Still, my fear that an imminent, debilitating death and/or condition await me have never really eased. In my life, I've diagnosed myself with having HIV, multiple sclerosis, motor neurone disease, brain cancer, possible blood clots and potential macular degeneration, to name just a few. I am currently concerned that the little squiggles and floaters brought out by light sensitivity are signs I might be going blind. Despite these things being completely normal, I'm still gripped by bouts of anxiety about what I'll do when I can no longer see. I sometimes catch myself in the act of testing my peripheral vision, checking the progress of two fingers as I move them slowly and deliberately from my ears to my nose. I'll bring a hand in close and assess the ridges that hide beneath its wispy blonde hair. So far, they've always appeared clearly and cleanly.

Still, I wait for the day they don't. This is one of my anxieties – waiting for my body to break down so it catches up to where I assume my mind already is.

At twelve, the madness came shortly after the ringing. One night, as I was getting ready for bed, a single note sounded in my left ear. It ran on a high frequency, piercing the silence with a steady, unrelenting drone. I assumed it would disappear soon enough, but it was instead joined by other notes. One by one they appeared, until an orchestra of ringing played inside my head. Days turned into weeks, but the noise just grew louder. Bedtimes were the worst. A quiet house cloaked in darkness only amplified the cacophony. I took to sleeping with a Discman beneath my pillow and deliberately grinding my teeth, both futile attempts to muffle the noise that was slowly pulling me further and further inside my head.

Around the same time, I developed an absurd and frankly disturbing fixation on religion. There's no way to write about this without sounding completely unhinged, so I'll just put it out there: I became convinced that the devil was trying to tempt me into handing over my soul, and that all I needed to do was give in to it. So profound was my paranoia about this that I had a panic attack one afternoon as it occurred to me the boy I had a crush on at school might actually be Satan in disguise. I began visiting the Catholic church near our house, and entered into discussions with a nun I met there about how I might convert to the faith. Harmless things filled me with terror – the sound of the creek running beyond the hedge outside our house, an accidental glimpse of something that looked like an upside-down cross, and what seemed to me to be the steady dismantling of an already jumbled mind.

My anxieties started to manifest in extreme expressions of obsessive-compulsive disorder (OCD). I favoured the classics: repetitive and specific numerical flicking of light switches, persistent hand washing done in a strict order (rub the soap on the palms then scrub each finger on my right hand four times, moving from thumb to pinkie and then moving across to repeat the method on my left hand before doing it three more times fully but in a forward-reverse-reverse-forward pattern), and repeated mantras. In my case, these mantras were prayers. I'd start with an Our Father and then do two iterations of a Hail Mary before cycling back to finish with another Our Father. It was the hand-washing equivalent of cleansing my soul, and I'd do it in the same pattern applied to my fingers. Forward-reverse-reverse-forward. The ritual had to follow this formation or else it became invalid, so even if I repeated it endlessly (which I sometimes did), it still needed to be done in basic fours. Anyone who suffers from OCD will be familiar with the power of counting, and I counted everything.

But all of this was happening deep, deep inside. If anyone around me noticed anything untoward, they kept it to themselves. This was also around the same time I developed anorexia and bulimia, two things that should be extremely difficult to hide but which end up being remarkably easy when cultivated in an environment that praises thinness and self-control in young women. Girls are trained to keep everything neatly tucked away and tidy, so much so that even our desperate cries for help become the whimpers of the politely inaudible. As a young woman sharing confessionals with other survivors of a girlish youth, I considered my experiences rare and unique, incorrectly assuming they made me the group's outlier. *I was an anorexic*, I'd offer solemnly. *I have bulimia.*

I viewed and spoke about eating disorders through the lens of a performatively horrified society that likes to pretend these maladies are an exception to the tapestry of girlhood and not one of the primary materials used in its creation. I thought it would shock people to hear I had spent years keeping intricate lists of my calorie consumption, that they'd be astonished by the fact I'd become so practised at purging that not only could I vomit with only the aid of my stomach muscles and not the stimulation of my gag reflex but that it was something I proudly considered a 'skill'. Now, when almost twenty-five years have passed since I first bent over a toilet and emptied myself of all I thought made me disgusting, I have a different reaction to hearing stories like these. *You too?*

A 2015 survey conducted by Girlguiding UK found that 58 percent of girls aged thirteen to twenty-one believed mental health in young women was a serious concern, 75 percent of respondents believed self-harming was a major health issue for people their age and 62 percent had known a girl who'd experienced a problem with her mental health.

And yet, the problem of poor mental health in girls is often overlooked or downplayed, dismissed as girls simply being dramatic or overwrought. The Girlguiding survey found that 82 percent of girls believed the adults around them 'didn't recognise the pressure they were under', a finding that seems to be supported by the lack of substantial discussion around the mental health challenges of women in general but particularly young women. It's strange that society can be fully aware of the ways in which girls can be hurt – after all, sexual violence, eating disorders, self-harm and poor self-esteem are hardly unheard of – and yet seemingly fail to understand how these various traumas are likely to chip away at the mental health of the girls harmed by them.

In terms of mental health, public conversations are still very much focused on how it transpires in young men. A friend of mine once confessed to me that she was secretly relieved to give birth to a boy because she was scared of the violence that might have greeted a girl. Her relief turned to anguish when someone else told her that the world holds damage for both girls and boys. With a girl, a parent worries that their daughter might be raped. With a boy, they worry he might kill himself. (To be fair, the person raising these dual concerns is enmeshed in trauma; they have worked for years in rape crisis centres and currently work with the survivors of gang-related sexual violence.)

But this isn't an entirely fair depiction either. Make no mistake: I think it's absolutely right and vital that we address the circumstances of suicide in young men because far too many boys are responding to feelings of anxiety and isolation by choosing to end their own lives. Of course this is devastating – how could anyone think otherwise?

What isn't often considered, though, are the rates at which suicide is attempted. According to the American Foundation for Suicide Prevention, while men (and white men in particular) are four times more likely than women to die by suicide, women are three times more likely to attempt it. There's some conjecture that this is because women choose less violent and immediate methods (in the US in particular, the suicide rate is boosted by having easy access to firearms – more than 60 percent of fatal gunshot wounds in America are deliberately self-inflicted, and that accounts for more than half of all deaths by suicide in that country).

We don't have to stop focusing on the high rates of suicide in men to also acknowledge that the urge to end one's life is something profoundly felt by and acted upon in women. Additionally, the ways in which suicide is conceived need to be broadened. An attempt on one's life isn't necessarily something undertaken in a single moment and with a single mode of choice. The girls and women who starve themselves and/or engage in endless cycles of binging and purging are practising a form of ongoing self-harm, and much of this is motivated by the desire to simply cease existing. So too are the girls and women who track their overwhelming feelings of pain and hopelessness by the cuts they notch into their arms, legs and torsos. These might not be suicide attempts in the way we typically understand them, but a good proportion of these people will profess to wrestling with the constant and terrifying feeling of either wanting to die or just wanting to go to sleep and never wake up.

I know what that feels like, because I've been there too. The mental distress and paranoia I felt at twelve didn't disappear, but I found a way to channel it into other forms of self-abuse. I practised the aforementioned cycle of starvation and purging. I wrote endless reams of text in my diaries about how useless and disgusting I was. I spent a solid decade from the age of thirteen feeling that I wasn't entitled to things like love, affection or even identification as a girl. Sadder still is that my belief in these things was characterised less by a sense of how deeply unfair that was and more by an inherent acceptance of it. Who was I to think I had the right to be treated like anything other than a repulsive freak? When my friends chattered about boyfriends or flirting, I listened with all the wonder of a person who's being given a rare and undeserved glimpse into the inner workings of a secret society. *You can look at these things*, I told myself, *but you can never have them.*

This acceptance of my own inadequacy was so profound that when I finally landed my first boyfriend at eighteen, I took to referring to him as 'my friend' when speaking with strangers or workmates who'd never met him. It wasn't to shield his privacy or to protect the fragility of our courtship from prying eyes. It was because I assumed people would think I was lying about it, and I believed this assumption to be fair and natural. Girls like me didn't have boyfriends or love or feminine identities, and it was embarrassing to act as if we did. So I lied about it to spare anyone from having to look at me with pity.

And still, no one seemed to know that anything was wrong – least of all me.

I knew that not everyone vomited up their food or chain-smoked cigarettes because it was a good way to remember to keep breathing, but I still thought it was normal that I did these things. This is one of the (many) terrible by-products of self-harm: the belief that it's not really all that damaging, because you only harm yourself enough either to leave no marks or make sure they're in places where only you can see them. You keep smiling for other people, laughing at their jokes, saying the right things and expressing the appropriate amount of excitement about life – and you do all of that because sometimes putting on a show is the only way to stop yourself from tumbling headfirst into the emptiness that seems to live inside you.

When I was twenty-one, I fell again.

I remember the moment clearly. I was lying in bed one night, trying to drift off to sleep, when a wave of adrenaline suddenly rushed through me. I sat bolt upright in the darkness and tried to focus on something – anything that would anchor me back to that point in space and time – but it was like trying to stem the flow of a river using nothing but your hands. I was overcome by a feeling of dread and terror so intense that all I could think of doing was fleeing: physically running out the front door and trying to escape it on foot. At the same time, I knew this would be pointless. The terror came from within me, and that meant it would be impossible to escape. I lay there in the dark and watched as it seeped from my pores. It grew in the room like a dark stain before snapping back and encasing me in a bubble of its own stench. I could bend its walls, but I couldn't break through them.

I stayed this way for months and months, bound by an invisible barrier that no one else could see but through which everything for me became muffled. It had the disconcerting effect of making it seem as if objects were both too close and yet also too far away, as if voices and sounds were fighting to be heard over persistent radio static, as if I was touching everything through gloves and tasting everything through plastic.

Fearing I would never get better, I went to see the university doctor. He was a nice chap and he was easy to talk to. I tried to explain to him how I was feeling, and he appeared sympathetic. It was as if reality only existed in a painting, I told him – or as if I did.

He asked me if I'd been experiencing anything unusual. Had the television or radio been talking to me, for example?

No, I replied. The television and radio hadn't been talking to me (but the thought they might soon start doing so began to plague me; even now, on anxious days, I might turn either or both on just to reassure myself that they're both working as normal).

Was I feeling suicidal? he asked.

I wasn't, I replied – although that wasn't strictly true. I didn't want to kill myself, but I was also sad and anxious and tired of being alive. I didn't want to die, but I was scared that I might spend the rest of my life tumbling around in an endless cycle of panic and fear. If you've never experienced anxiety, you might find it difficult to understand what that feels like. I can throw any number of clichés and similes at you: it's like trying to find your way out of a dark and dense forest, only to keep circling back to the same point you started from; it feels like being caught in a washing machine, disorientating and dizzy-making and like you're always on the precipice of drowning; it's like a carnival tent full of distorting mirrors, and you're too terrified to look into any of them because you're afraid your own reflection might assume a life of its own and start to mock you. It's like all of these things at once and that's an easy way to visualise it. But the simple and most universal truth is that anxiety just makes you feel incredibly, desperately alone.

I didn't want to kill myself. But I found myself frequently daydreaming about how nice it would be to lower myself into the ocean from the end of a jetty and just let the waves carry me out to sea. In my imagination, it would be less like dying and more like surrendering. I could give myself to the ocean, and everything would be okay. I could be salt and froth and calm and storm, but most of all I could finally be something that wasn't me.

I didn't tell the doctor any of this. All the advice and rhetoric around mental health tells us to reach out and 'let people know' how we're feeling, but such a thing is easier said than done. A large part of my anxiety at twenty-one stemmed from the fear that I might actually be on a downward spiral into madness, and giving voice to this fear would only hasten the possibility rather than alleviate it. How do you tell someone that you can't tell where your mind ends and your body begins, but you definitely know they're moving in completely different hemispheres?

I didn't know how to do that. And so, after reassuring him that I wasn't a risk to myself, this kind and well-intentioned doctor told me that I seemed to be experiencing some 'mild depression'. If I liked, he could prescribe me a half-dosage of Zoloft, but it was up to me. Did I want that?

I make careful mention of the compassionate nature of this doctor because I want to illustrate just how little understanding there is around mental health and the mental health of women in particular. At the age of twenty-one, it was possible for me to walk into a doctor's office and within roughly fifteen minutes be prescribed a reasonably major form of medication that I almost certainly didn't need. This isn't because the doctor was ambivalent about my health or cavalier about prescriptions. I'm not really into conspiracy theories about all doctors being in the pockets of Big Pharma (even though I acknowledge pharmaceutical companies are in the business of getting people hooked on drugs), so I don't think it was because this doctor saw me as a giant dollar sign. And above all, I don't think it was because he didn't care about my wellbeing.

I think it was easy to prescribe me drugs I didn't need because 'fixing' mental health is more complicated than people want to admit. It's a hard and often scary road. It has been hard and scary for me and I suspect that it will continue to take me down dark, forbidding paths for the rest of my life. I know this is true for a lot of girls and women – but again, we rarely talk about this because there's a lack of understanding about and perhaps even interest in the particular mental disturbances that afflict us. The ways in which we cope (which so often includes the ways in which we hurt ourselves) are more hidden and less immediate than some of the other methods used to tolerate mental illness. Addictions, self-loathing, solitude, irrationalities – these are our tools. And after all, aren't these the things women are supposed to be anyway? Quiet? Tremulous? Full of self-hatred? We have been imagined as irrational creatures from the very beginning, our pain and suffering dismissed as fanciful overreactions or desperate, pathetic grabs for attention we don't deserve and have done nothing of substance to earn. We are hysterical she-demons, governed by the mystical movements of the moon and therefore unknowable and dangerous to others. If history bothered to document our stories, there wouldn't be enough paper in the world to bear witness to all the women who've been imprisoned because our emotions proved too inconvenient for men to handle and too terrifying for them to ignore. Why should we expect anyone to care that we're hurting when the message we've received our entire lives is that hurt for us is not only inevitable but also somehow our fault?

I didn't take the Zoloft that day. My crutches have always been alcohol, Valium and cigarettes. These seem to me to be controllable substances in that the effects of them wear off reasonably quickly. I've had ecstasy twice in my life. The first time, I threw it up almost as soon as I swallowed it because I was suddenly gripped by fear of the unknown. The second, I began to panic almost as soon as the drug began to take effect. Anything that changes the chemistry of my body sparks my fight-or-flight response, which proves fairly incompatible with having an anxiety disorder.

With time and self-care, I eventually got better. That is to say, I didn't get any worse. Somehow, I figured out how to live in the world again. I spent the rest of my twenties dealing with a more muted form of sporadic angst. But then, as if on schedule, there it was again at thirty-two. Sitting at my desk one afternoon, I had a sudden panic attack. As I gasped for breath, I felt the all-too-familiar urge to run – not from the situation, but from myself. I wanted to break free of my skin and disappear to a place where thoughts don't exist, and any knowledge of the superficial self has been left far behind.

My particular battle with mental illness has always partially manifested itself in an existential crisis. When in its grip, I'm racked by an inability to understand how and why I am me.

I experience jags of disconcerting disassociation, unable to connect with the world as it happens around me but still aware enough to pretend that everything is fine. I find myself staring at the lines of my body, wondering where the limits of containment are. Could I begin to seep out of myself, becoming a half-person living between two states of being? Has it happened already? Like the two times before, the panic that rose up that day settled in to consume my life once again. I'd sit in the living room and feel suddenly overcome by terror about my state of existence. My skin would prickle and I'd gasp for breath. My body was nothing more than television static, crackling in and out of a reality I was no longer a part of.

I took to walking in the late-summer afternoons. I embarked on long stretches of pavement pounding throughout Edinburgh Gardens, listening to podcasts and musicals – anything that would keep me from delving into the dusty nooks and crannies of my mind. I sat under trees and counted my breaths until the sky began to turn the ghostly purple of dusk, and slowly I crawled my way back to sanity. My recovery this time took longer, much longer, but it happened. I had put my fractured self back together again, and although there were more chips than before and a handful of tiny pieces missing, I became something that once again resembled me.

I seek help from a number of different sources now, the most enjoyable of which are the long walks I take around my neighbourhood. I'll traipse for hours up and down the streets, admiring the flowers in people's gardens or marvelling at the rich, dense clouds that spread like mottled bruises across the Brunswick sky. I listen to audio books – novels that I've read before and loved, and to which I can get away with directing only half of my attention. The Harry Potter collection narrated by Stephen Fry is a favourite, as is the work of David Sedaris. I walk myself into the good kind of exhaustion, and it reminds me that life is just a matter of putting one foot in front of the other. It's a kind of mindfulness, although my teacher for that would tell me that distraction isn't the point. I've recently been meeting with her once a fortnight to discuss my impulse to run away from perfectly ordinary situations. She calls this my 'threat-brain'. She means that I, like most anxiety sufferers, ascribe danger to situations that realistically will not harm me but from which I feel I must escape. Instead of succumbing to threat-brain, she tells me just to notice it. Notice the feelings as they pass in and out of my mind, but don't give them any more weight than they need. Try to understand that they can't hurt me, even if they make me uncomfortable. Sit with them and be still. Above all, be kind to myself.

Sometimes, remembering to be kind to yourself is the hardest thing. One of my greatest strengths is also one of my most debilitating weaknesses, and that is my ability to maintain control over my life and emotions. I emerged from a childhood defined by eating disorders, emotional instability, obsessive-compulsive behaviour and little to no physical self-esteem. The world I live in is one that seeks to control women's physical and mental selves, to speak for us and to us as if we're children, constantly reminding us at every opportunity that we are unreliable witnesses to our own lives. Is it any wonder that I, and the millions and millions of girls like me who are made to feel so powerless, focus instead on asserting control every which way we can? Perhaps the most telling part of this tragedy is how adept we've become at doing these things in secret, viewing this secrecy as a necessary form of quiet resistance.

Three million Australians live with some form of anxiety and/or depression, and many of us are well practised in its concealment. Every time I speak openly about my own mental health issues, more friends come forward to reveal their ongoing struggles with crushing depression or anxiety. You'd think the knowledge that we're all in this together would provide some kind of comfort and relief. But as anyone who struggles with mental illness can attest, there is a deep loneliness in being tethered to the erratic whims of one's own mind.

I wonder sometimes if there's a freedom in madness. It can feel like I'm balancing precariously on a tightrope dividing two states of being. On my left lies calm serenity. On my right, the thing I fear most – being sucked into a hole of rushing noise that makes no sense, the cacophony of a million thoughts crashing into each other at high speed. But if a decision could be made to at last surrender to it, to give up and allow myself to fall east to what sometimes seems the inevitable conclusion, might I find that it wouldn't involve hurtling to the ground in a bloody mess but floating instead to a less frightening dreamscape? If there were a way to switch off, would I?

And yet, this is what I keep circling back to: that there is so much to live for. There is the man who lies next to me at night, who feels content enough in the secret world of intimacy we've created together to provide safety for me there too. There is the life we made together, our wondrous, impossibly beautiful baby, whose daily achievements manage to be both simple and magnificent. There are sunsets streaming through bedroom windows that look out over well-worn tram lines, the smell of jasmine on spring evenings, and the taste of real butter melted on fruit toast.

There is evidence that I have survived this before; that I will go on surviving.

There is love. There is love. There is love.

Maybe the Cheshire cat was right. Maybe we are all a little mad. And if we are all in this together, then none of us are truly alone. That means me. But it also means you.

Across these pages, I reach out to you, dear one whose heart feels so alone.

This too shall pass.

And we will all be okay.

—8—

WOMEN AGAINST FEMINISM

Sometime in early 2014, a movement began to spread across the internet in the form of a hashtag meme. Women, most of them young, white and conventionally pretty, started posting photographs of themselves holding up placards that began with the phrase *I don't need feminism because . . .*

The posts were collated under the hashtag #womenagainstfeminism, with explanations ranging from the absurd (*I don't need feminism because I don't want to politicise my gender*) to the defensive (*I don't need feminism because I'm not a manipulative idiot playing victim*), from the reassuring (*I don't need feminism because I respect men and refuse to demonise them and blame them for my problems*) to the grossly offensive (*I don't need feminism because REAL feminism is about equal opportunities and respect for women. NOT abortions, free birth control and the ability to walk around like a shameless slut while damning the male population for being born!*). I'd have thought advocating for respect for women included not referring to them as shameless sluts, but that's just me.

I may be a screeching, self-styled victim with a severe case of the misandries, but I have to wonder where women like this get their information. Heavens, there are barely enough hours in the day for all the ritual demonising of men required to maintain membership of the Coven of Feminist Witches, let alone traipsing all over the place trying to score free birth control. As it is, feminists can only just about manage one or two abortions a week, which is a modern miracle when you think about it, considering it's a well-known fact we're all far too unattractive for any man to ever want to sleep with us. Isn't that why we're so angry all the time?

Personally, I like the contributions made by American blogger Rebecca Brink. Donning a series of wigs, Brink photographs herself in similar poses holding beautifully satirical interpretations of the various philosophies of the Women Against Feminism. Her statements reflect the confusing lack of awareness displayed by these women towards feminism as a whole and its various aims, not least of which is that the male problems seemingly being ignored by the radical separatist lesbian overlords are actually caused by the construction of patriarchy, not the dismantling of it.

Despite the endless evidence of its use and purpose to their lives, there are a multitude of reasons why women choose not to identify with the feminist movement. I'll go into some of those reasons a little bit later, but I want to start with one of Brink's examples, which I consider to be the most obvious, and the most pressing.

I don't need feminism because I want boys to like me.

A lot of shade is thrown at girls and young women who don't identify as feminists. Every time a celebrity says something silly about gender inequality, or claims to be Not A Feminist because 'I love men!', another think piece pops up to ponder with furrowed brow and admonishing tone all the reasons why young women might be letting the side down. I've probably written a few of them myself.

But the truth is our political identities are so intricately entwined with our emotional and physical identities that it's impossible to look at feminist engagement without acknowledging the ways women are punished for it in an already punishing world. Women are told we're meant to be beautiful, compliant, sexual but not slutty, thin, small, cutesy and, above all, willing to prop up the structures of power that keeps patriarchy firmly in place. Feminism is a challenge to all of this, and it's perceived as a monumental threat by the people who benefit from and/or feel safe in an environment that relies on entrenched gender inequality.

But why would any woman invest in a system that requires her compliance to survive? Well, movements for social justice have always faced a backlash. For some, the backlash can be too intense. Feminism attacks patriarchy, which is a brave act against a system that has ensured it maintains access to the best tools, the most effective weapons and the privilege of being able to constantly shift its own goalposts. It requires a lot of emotional resilience to be able to stand up to the legacy of centuries of structural inequality, and I fully understand why some women are either too scared, too bruised or simply too exhausted to maintain the energy for it – particularly when intersectionality dictates that significant numbers of women are also battling oppression on a multitude of sides, whether its racism, ableism, homophobia, transphobia or classism.

No one with any real understanding of the complexities of feminist activism and intersectional oppression could truly begrudge a single woman these feelings of identity ambivalence, because staying strong in the face of such overwhelming opposition can be a fucking hard slog. Unless you're a cis, white, heterosexual man whose minimal expressions of solidarity with women always nets you the maximum number of pats on the head, maintaining faith in the feminist identity can feel like pushing shit uphill while having more giant buckets of shit fired at you from a cannon constructed entirely out of shit.

But how does this backlash manifest itself?

Its most basic and recognisable execution comes courtesy of the way feminists are de-feminised. Part of patriarchy's *modus operandi* has always been to keep women tethered to a constructed idea of femininity and therefore distracted from fighting for their own political and social equality. Confusion is also a key component here, with the changing whims of fashion and how they tie into capitalist goals (in this case, the essentialist goals of keeping all members of a community dissatisfied and thus always striving to first keep up with the Joneses and then outstrip them) meaning that what is considered 'feminine' and attractive is subject to constant change.

At any given time in history, women have been told to be either fat, thin, plump, short, tall, sexually adventurous, sexually prudish, brunette, blond, fecund, scrawny etc. etc. etc. (It's imperative also to note that western colonialism and imperialism have also resulted in racist ideologies which have almost constantly enforced one other 'must have' item in a woman's arsenal – white skin. To the white women like myself who are reading this book and who haven't started doing this already, please make it a point to continuously examine and interrogate the ways you experience privilege despite being subjected to other forms of discrimination and oppressive ideologies.)

So it's not just about creating a completely arbitrary set of ideals and convincing women we're nothing unless we adhere to them – it's also about being consistently misleading about the longevity of these ideals so that we're kept in a perpetual state of self-loathing and gendered competition.

This is capitalism at its finest – telling women we're rubbish so that we can keep working towards perfection. Conform to this system and everything from magazines, TV talk shows and the zeitgeist will call you 'empowered', which is just a fancy way of saying you're a chill woman who's happy to 'embrace her femininity' because it just makes you feel healthier/sexier/cleaner/more womanly.

Feminists, on the other hand, have very rarely been referred to by the mainstream as positive examples of empowered woman-hood. Calling yourself a feminist in 1972 inspired pretty much exactly the same public response as claiming that title in 1997, and neither were especially different from the disdain heaped on turn of the century suffragettes and modern day tidal wavers. For more than a century, women have led political campaigns which secured among other things the rights of women to vote, to run for political office, to not lose our jobs once we were married, to not be raped by our husbands in those same marriages and to (at least legislatively) be paid the same amount of money for the same work. Yet despite these extraordinary achievements, feminism is still dismissed by both men AND women as a hate-based movement run by fringe-dwelling lesbians who want to destroy everything that's good and wholesome about the world. I entered the words 'feminists are' in Google, and the first three predictive responses that came up were 'feminists are ugly', 'feminists are sexist' and 'feminists are stupid'.

There's an oldish joke which goes something a little like this.

Do women become feminists because they're ugly, or do they become ugly because they're feminists?

This is just one of the many hysterical 'funnies' told about women who demonstrate any kind of belief in our own fundamental right to liberation. When you live in a world where your primary value is bestowed based on how willing you are to appease the notion of 'femininity', you're also expected to maintain a sort of silent vacancy about the multitude of microaggressions and humiliations that go along with that. So it is that feminists – us outspoken banshees who stalk the streets in terrifying gangs with our ludicrous calls for 'equality' – are ritually and aggressively dismissed as aberrations of the feminine code. Opponents attempt to strip feminists of our womanhood (which is interchangeable with our humanity) by rendering us sexless, repulsive, foul. Because if a woman cannot be endorsed favourably by the male gaze as something desirable, what's the point of her at all?

Still, while it's up to every woman to identify as she sees fit I do question the motivations of those who so overtly declare themselves to be anti-feminist. I'd say this is because they almost certainly recognise the differences and particular ways that women *can* behave in order to gain very limited power and approval from men, even if they aren't quite aware of just how much that can be traced back to socialisation.

For me, feminism isn't just about gender equality as an end goal, because that implies that the structures we live under currently are the correct ones and the only problem with them is that women do not experience equity beneath them. I disagree. I am in favour of radically reimagining what our societies should look like, including the ways in which masculine ideas of power and leadership are absorbed as natural and normal. Of course, gender equality is important, but for me feminism is also about liberating women from the expectation that we behave in a certain kind of way in order to be taken seriously or given any kind of power at all, however nominal it might be.

Sure, feminists have to deal with asinine attacks from angry, threatened men whose go-to response is always to dehumanise and degrade us, but they aren't the only people standing in our way. I might frequently be called fat, ugly, angry, sexless, slutty (figure that double standard out!) and just pissed off because other women are prettier than me, but I expect to be called all these things. What I cannot tolerate are the men who try to claim some kind of feminist allegiance (and consider themselves heroes for doing so) while lecturing women on how we're setting back the fight for gender equality. Give me a dollar for every man who begins a sentence with 'As someone who's always been in favour of women's rights . . .' and ends it with '. . . you are doing more harm for women than good' and I will use the proceeds to buy a very expensive yacht on which I can live while sailing the vast ocean of male tears that stretches on for eternity.

For a start, no feminist I know gives one iota of a fuck about the problems any man has with how we conduct our own movement. And for another thing, fuck off. I have encountered so many boring, faux feminist men who do nothing but criticise the feminists who make them feel uncomfortable, and it's becoming infinitely clear to me what their real problem is: they're too fond of congratulating themselves for being a Super Right-On Guy and have enjoyed too much adulation from grateful feminists in the past. Faced with this new reality of feminist activism and anger, they feel uncomfortable and targeted. They don't like it. It's angry. It makes them feel picked on. All of a sudden, they can't rely on being rewarded just for turning up. And instead of sitting down for a moment and thinking about what that means, most of them lash out and use the very same paternalistic methods they claim to hate to chide women for being troublemakers and children.

It doesn't matter which way you slice it or how much one advocates for 'gender equality' – women are always expected to be nice. And unless a man has truly had to come to terms with the ways he benefits from privilege and has been willing to do the work of engaging with that, no amount of pretensions to feminism will change the fact he still feels ever so slightly more comfortable when a woman stays quiet and listens to what he has to say.

How does this tie into Women Against Feminism? Because it all comes back to the same thing – women capitulating to the system in order to be given some notion of power within it. Rather than run the risk of pissing off the patriarchy and dealing with all the whiny, angry and hostile fallout of that, it's easier for them to position themselves as foot soldiers and wardens. Women are of course free to disagree wildly over the politics of feminism and its aims, but there's nothing more depressing than watching them join forces with men to slut shame other women, ridicule their bodies or, as I once saw happen in the misogynist shitshow of a Facebook events page, enthusiastically laugh along at a joke that implies the most intelligent part of a woman is the semen she spits out when a man ejaculates in her mouth. *Look at me, boys! I'll laugh hardest and loudest when you make degrading jokes about women because I'm super chill about that stuff! Love me!*

But amidst all the frustration and head-desking over the hatred these women display for their own kind, I've realised there are three key things that encourage women to set themselves against a movement invested in their liberation and equality. Understanding these might just be the key to figuring out how to work together.

1. RETRIBUTION

The mechanics of internalised misogyny are complicated, but they're largely driven by fear of retribution. Feminism is perceived as a threat by some people, and the only recourse they have is to threaten it right back. For the girls and women who experience these threats on an ongoing basis, it's understandable that they'd want to minimise exposure to them.

Look at me, for example. I am a reasonably prominent feminist. This means I daily receive messages calling me fat, bitter, ugly, unrapeable (yes, that happens), angry, stupid, opportunistic and – in a bizarre stretch of logic – hypocritical for being paid to write about women's rights. I don't get these messages because there's something special about me that incites the rage of men who would otherwise never dream of calling a woman a 'pig-faced slut who's just angry that attractive white men don't want her' (thanks, anonymous man on Twitter!). I get these messages because I'm a feminist, I talk about feminism publicly in a way that doesn't position men and their feelings front and centre, and I'm unapologetic about that.

So of course other women see the way feminists like me are responded to and think twice about joining our ranks. Who would willingly sign up to being called a pig-faced slut every day?

Sometimes, anti-feminism isn't about women being unable to 'think for themselves', as the argument goes. It's about an unconscious battle for self-preservation. Being a feminist isn't easy – but being an outspoken one can be even more difficult.

2. NEGOTIATION

That urge for self-preservation is very strong, and we see how it manifests as negotiation all the time. Consider the women who join in victim-blaming narratives, reasoning that if V hadn't done X then Y wouldn't have happened. That's just 'common sense', and therefore women who willingly engage in X are 'asking for it' and can't be surprised when Y happens. You know, like those danger-tempting women who walk down the street at night-time in come hither skirts as if they have some kind of wacky right to not be raped. *I'm not saying she deserved it . . . but *I* would never be that stupid.*

This impulse to negotiate is atrocious. It's the worst and most ignorant kind of victim blaming, and it only contributes to the narrative of men's violence against women as something shadowy and external – a reality that women are at risk of creating through provocation and therefore responsible for avoiding. But while women who victim blame are infuriating people acting in repugnant ways, it's also true that many women consent to the limiting of their behaviour as a means of negotiating their own safety. The fact that none of this works is by the by. It is too easy for them to believe that blaming other women for the violence they experience will offer them some kind of protection. They can't talk about why this might not be true because it makes them a target for male rage and indignation, so instead they consent to participating in the removal of responsibility from male perpetrators in order to carve out a small slice of symbolic power within those structures.

But negotiation is not power. It's compromise, and it never works in women's favour.

3. WILFUL, SELFISH IGNORANCE

Feminism argues that women are people too, and all people with privilege are susceptible to the kind of selfishness that keeps them indifferent to the struggles of others. Or, to put that another way, some women are just mean-spirited and awful and they don't give a shit about anyone but themselves. These are the women who think that feminism is meaningless because they don't personally have any problems and claim never to have experienced any form of sexism. (LOL, whatever, love. Give me some of the pills you're taking, because I could do with a nice trip to fantasy land.)

If you're not forcing yourself to routinely interrogate the benefits you enjoy in society, it's all too easy to tell yourself that other people are inventing their disadvantages. So people born into financial independence tell themselves that poor people need to work harder; people born into the relative utopia of Australia argue that refugees fleeing war-torn countries are 'jumping the queue'; and some women favoured by the world's preference for compliant, conservative 'traditionalists' understand and enjoy the benefit they think they get from being an ardent supporter of the status quo. Who cares about the grievances of angry, bitter women when your own situation is relatively comfortable?

But part of feminism's core mission statement (at least as I see it) is to advocate for a world in which all women, not just some, are given equal opportunities and respect. That some women don't yet understand this is a shame, but they may one day come to this realisation. That some women do but simply don't care is an outrage.

What does all this mean for the Women Against Feminism 'movement'? I expect it will flare briefly and then disappear into irrelevancy. Firstly, it boasts a fundamental misunderstanding of feminism from the outset, and seems instead designed to support the conservative ideals that harm women rather than help them. But secondly, it's presenting absolutely nothing new. This is just another caterwaul from the backlash that's always attempted to push back against feminism's success. As frustrating as this backlash might be, it's also never managed to do any kind of long-term harm to feminism. It's little more than a high-pitched tantrum, a tedious annoyance far more than a serious threat. And if a woman wants to take pride in being anti-feminist, the only kind of emotional energy I can bother expending on her is pity. Whatever power she thinks she's gaining by being a cheerleader for the patriarchy is totally illusory because it will always be connected to men's approval. Even within the Women Against Feminism movement, the women themselves are secondary leaders to the men who congratulate them for keeping order in the house of Status Quo. What else can we do but feel sad for them and hope that one day they see the light?

The good news is that, unlike these wannabe Stepford Wives, feminists don't need the approval of men to justify our existence.

Whatever backlash they send our way will be met with resistance ten times harder, smarter and more determined. We'll never give up fighting for all women to be treated with dignity and liberated from patriarchal oppression.

Even the ones who don't believe it exists.

—9—

MAN-HATER

In the fifteen or so years that I've been actively feministing, I've never tired of being asked whether or not I hate men. When I say I've never tired of it, I am of course lying. If I could summarise my experience of the anti-feminist backlash into one tedious, repetitive interaction, it would be thus: 'Do you hate men? Wait, let me rephrase that. *Why* do you hate men?'

Although my care factor for whether or not men think I hate them hovers somewhere just below zero – and I will teach you how to adjust your scale similarly – the blatant lack of self-awareness on display when this question is asked (and asked and asked and asked, repeatedly, on and on into infinity) still manages to astonish me. Here's a sample of some of the things that have been said to me by men distressed by the thought that feminism might not be a political movement that advocates for gender equality, but just a club for ugly chicks to hate on blokes:

Misandrist. Man-hater. Feminazi boner killer. Joyless harpy, jealous of the prettier girls. Dumb fat cow. Ugly femmo.

Sour-faced wrinkled bitch who's only angry about rape because no one would ever rape her. Wants to kill all men, but only because no man would ever touch her. Hope you like living alone, bitch, because no one's every going to want to put up with an ugly, angry cunt like you. Lose some weight, you fat heifer. Clemmy's growing a moustache, she must be transitioning. She's been drinking so many men's tears she's turning into one. Did the doctor build that vagina for you, bitch? That bitch is as ugly as a dead dog on the side of the road. I bet no one's even pierced your virgin smelly arsehole until you cried, you ugly cunt. Fix your teeth, fix your face, go on a diet, get over your fucking victim complex, stop being such an angry, irrational cunt all the time. Are you a sociopath? You have major mental health issues. You're a sick, twisted individual. You bathe in men's tears? Do you bathe in the tears of Tom Meagher? You must have loved the Paris bombings – think of all those murdered boys and men whose tears you can bathe in now. You're a cunt. I hope you get raped by someone with AIDS. I hope you get raped by a pack of Muslims. Fuck you, you fucking man-hating dyke.

Do feminists hate men? When you consider the level of hostility women are subjected to just for standing up for ourselves, surely the better query is *why do so many men seem to hate women so fiercely, so aggressively, so violently and so passionately?*

As pertinent as this question might be, it's rarely asked in response to the knee-jerk paranoia around feminism and what it supposedly means. Instead, feminists and non-feminists (or, as I call them, dickwads) alike funnel endless reams of energy into debating the utterly pointless question of whether or not feminists are required by law to hate all men, as if answering this will reveal the secret key to unlocking *real* gender equality. In actual fact, this boring, trivial fixation is nothing more than an effective means of constantly diverting any attention away from feminism's success (potential or actual) and directing it towards feeding society's obsession with placating men at all times. That misogynists (both the out and proud ones and the ones still hiding in the closet) are able to effortlessly wave away the comprehensive evidence feminists have for women's oppression in the world is a feat in and of itself. That they manage to do it while also elevating themselves and the violation of their *feelings* as a more legitimate and unconscionable form of oppression is nothing short of remarkable.

Oh, you think that domestic violence is a terrible scourge, do you? You think it's an outrage that almost two women in this country are murdered weekly by aggrieved partners or ex-partners, and that the all-too-common response to this is, 'Well, why didn't she leave?' instead of 'Why did he kill her?' You think it's astonishing how few people know that the most dangerous time for a woman in a situation of intimate partner violence is the period immediately after leaving? You think we should be horrified that one woman is hospitalised every three hours in Australia as a result of gendered violence? You think we should be outraged that Aboriginal women are eighty times more likely to make up these numbers? You think we should shine a light on misogyny and take a united stand against abuse? You think we should do that instead of perpetuating it by insisting that sexist jokes are hilarious, that there's no link between the way society views women and the way society discards them, that perpetrators of violence couldn't possibly be influenced by the world they live in, a world that shits on women regularly and valorises the strong, heroic man who sits at the top of the food chain? *Why don't you care about the men who are victimised too, you misandrist bitch?*

Oh, you think that girls and women shouldn't be blamed for their own sexual assaults, as if they have the right to exist peacefully in their own skin without having to give up something, like their autonomy or dignity or fucking right to free agency? You think girls should be allowed to wear what they want, as if it's somehow men's responsibility to control themselves around women instead of women's responsibility to fend off temptation? You think women should be allowed to sleep with one man, and this freedom doesn't mean they have an obligation to sleep with his friends? You think we should consider it cause for major concern that one in five girls over the age of fifteen will experience sexual violence in her lifetime? You think girls of colour shouldn't be excluded from the protection all adults should afford to all children, that they shouldn't be described as 'fast tailed' or having 'dressed older'? You think women with intellectual disabilities should expect to be treated with dignity and sexual respect? That we should be utterly disgusted to sit with the knowledge that over 90 percent of them have been subjected to some form of sexual violence? You think that the sexual assault of girls and women shouldn't be treated as some kind of unfortunate by-product of being alive, but the symptom of a diseased society which views women's bodies as expendable commodities to be used, thrown away and then blamed for being on display in the first place? You think men should be held to a higher standard than that? *Well, answer me this, feminazi: why do you paint all men as rapists?*

You think that women shouldn't be ridiculed for speaking openly about their experiences in the world? You think that people should actually have to listen to women when they speak and be open to the possibility of learning something? You think women might have something of value and insight to say about what sexism looks like and how it presents itself? You don't think that we can just rely on men to be able to define sexism for us and insist that their interpretation of our experience is the correct one? You think that most men have no idea what sexism feels like, that most of them think it's the same as them getting upset over being 'lumped in' with the Really Bad Men – you know, the ones who girls and women have a responsibility to always, constantly and vigilantly protect themselves from but are also never allowed to talk about because that might make other men, the good men, feel bad? Wait a minute, you think sexism actually exists in the western world and isn't just the province of those backward countries where women are really oppressed? Countries where really oppressed women understand and experience *real oppression*, like men telling them what they should and shouldn't wear in order to avoid being exploited and assaulted, where men occupy the majority of positions of power, where the voices of men are amplified while the voices of women are silenced, where women are killed by men all the time – you know, the kind of oppression women in the west apparently don't experience at all, and yet show no appreciation for being spared? You know, like the kind of oppressive behaviour that can be blamed solely on brown men and that allows white, western men to feel safe and insulated from having to engage with their own patriarchal complicity and criminal behaviour? You actually think that we should listen to women when they speak about this stuff instead of just laughing at them or telling them to get over it or calling them vile, abusive names until they understand that their oppression is made up because men here are nice and women would be wise to remember that? *You should see what we could do to you if we wanted to, you ungrateful cunt.*

You think the elevation of men's stories, voices and experiences over women's is a bit uneven, do you? You think it's telling that the vast majority of people elected to govern are men, despite the fact that communities which demonstrate strong representation of women in leadership roles have been proven to create healthier, better communities overall? You think the prevalence of white, middle- to upper-class, cis-het men in positions drafting and passing legislation isn't just unfair but damaging, as if the input of the swathes of people who exist outside of this category might have something relevant to say about how society should conduct itself? You want to see more funding directed towards art created by women, towards books written by women of colour, towards films featuring trans characters played by trans people, towards columns helmed by disabled women, more stories more art more voices more music by more women of all identities? *Why do you want to silence men?*

LOL, you think the gender pay gap is 'real'? You think women should receive equal pay for equal work, even though there's a possibility they might later leave in order to take on the necessary and thankless task of providing humans for the next generation? You think that companies should be forced to absorb that cost, because research has shown that letting women exit the workplace forever is bad for the economy while retaining them makes good financial sense? You don't think that's a waste of money? What do you know about money? You think issues like superannuation and retirement are key feminist concerns because women over the age of sixty-five are one of the fastest-growing groups represented in statistics on homelessness? You think women actually deserve to be paid the same as men, instead of being paid less and also being lumped with the majority of the world's unpaid domestic and reproductive labour? *Stop blaming men for not being good enough at your jobs.*

Wow. I can't believe you hate men so much! I feel sorry for you. This isn't what real feminism should look like.

∎

You know what? Some women do hate men. They have good reason to. They might have been raped and beaten and downtrodden and abused, and they have reached their breaking point. They might have lived a nightmare you can't even conceive of. To these women, men might represent the enemy because the role they have played in these women's lives – a role that might involve sexual abuse, exploitation, emotional manipulation and perhaps even attempts to kill them – has consistently shown themselves to be exactly that. If these women hate men, who is anyone to blame them?

Other women may not hate men, but just marginally despise them. They have good reason to as well. They might have been undermined and devalued their entire lives. They might have been told their womanhood makes them inherently weaker than men and been forced to sit and endure quietly as their freedom contracted in correlation with the inverse expansion of the boys around them. They might have been told, 'Do this,' and given no explanation for why such drudgery should become their respons-ibility aside from 'because it's women's work'. These women might have wondered why their brothers were allowed to stay out late and roam the streets while they were kept indoors because 'it's not safe for you'. Later they might wonder why, if safety was such an important consideration for girls, they never heard their parents talk to brothers about not hurting women. These women watched as the boys around them ascended to thrones built of privilege, and it made them sick to realise these boys believed they'd earned their coronations.

Still others may not hate or despise men at all. They might love men. And they might be able to do this while recognising the extraordinary advantages that men in general (particularly the white, middle-class, cis-het ones) enjoy over everyone else, often in tandem with the denial that these advantages exist at all. These women who love men – the women who enjoy the presence of their husbands, fathers, brothers, sons, cousins, friends, colleagues, the man who serves them coffee at their local, the Uber driver they spoke to last night – might also express frustration and anger over the times men do not treat them with the same level of respect. They might rant when a man tells them to 'lighten up' when they complain about sexist commentary. They might fume when a man tells them that instead of complaining about street harassment and 'tarring all men with the same brush', they should be flattered by it because 'it's a compliment'. These women who love and adore the men in their lives and recognise the potential for goodness that exists in all men might still feel like crying sometimes, because for all the love they offer the world's men, the hate those men are capable of offering back can be heartbreaking and soul-destroying.

Instead of berating feminists for being misandrists, perhaps these men should start taking responsibility for the abominable, destructive and dehumanising treatment of women throughout all of history up to and including the present day. Because here's the thing: at a broad sweep, men have given us countless reasons to hate them. They have certainly provided ample evidence of their hatred for us, and the violence they inflict has more physical, cultural and economic power behind it than women subjugated by a patriarchal system could ever hope to replicate.

Despite all this, most of us don't hate men. Most of us still engage with men on a substantial level, choosing to befriend them, marry them, create families with them, become mothers to them. We choose to love them. But we are allowed to love ourselves as well. Yet when we engage in this radical act of self-love, unashamedly, openly and fearlessly, we are asked, 'Why do you hate men?'

Why do we hate men?

Again, the better question to ask is: why do men hate us, and why do they hate us so much?

■

Very few people seem to find anything offensive about the presumption that feminism is a cover for 'misandry'. The stereotype of the man-hating, ball-breaking scold is so deeply entrenched in cultural ideology that identifying feminists as such is typically absorbed as par for the course. Those women who do take umbrage at this representation (and if you are one of them, I fervently hope that this book will inspire you to let go of those concerns) are met with the same response given to all women who complain about how society or individuals depict them as objects of ridicule. They're told to get over it, to lighten up, to learn to take a joke. They're also told that they brought it on themselves, that being a feminist in this day and age is automatically synonymous with man-hating, that if they truly cared about equality they'd call themselves a humanist (which, by the way, is an existing ideology with a definition that has nothing to do with gender or equality at all) or the even more meaningless 'egalitarian'. 'Outspoken' feminists – by which I mean feminists who dare to speak about their politics in any way, shape or form – incite the anger of people deathly afraid of women's power, and whose only recourse against it is to try to nullify it by using the threat of male exclusion.

This is standard procedure. It's seen as perfectly acceptable to accuse a woman of misandry and admonish her for the supposedly gargantuan crime of man-hating. This stereotype is used to control women, because – as I've already mentioned – one of the worst things a woman can do is to consciously opt out of the apparently great privilege of enthusiastically sucking on patriarchy's dick. Man-hating = bad.

But what happens when similar discussions of misogyny or even garden-variety sexism are raised? What happens when a woman criticises the actions of one man or a group of men, and connects these actions with the gender inequality that thrives in broader society? If you guessed that a dozen or so men would pop up to clarify that, actually, *not all men* are like this and that must be specified before the feminist discussion goes any further then DING DING DING! Congratulations! You win a prize! It is a cushioned band to protect your noggin from all the head-desking you must do.

'Not all men' has become the notorious battle cry some men (see what I did there?) bellow whenever women start speaking about the impact misogyny has on our lives. It's become a running joke on my Facebook page, with regular commenters often taking informal bets to see how long it takes for a variation on the 'not all men' theme to pop up on posts about domestic violence, sexual assault or just basic male entitlement. I've found that the theme of these comments can be separated into three basic categories.

The Super Right-On Male Feminist Ally: Is totally here for women's rights and equality and totally wants every woman to know just how here he is for them. He's so here for them that it upsets him to be associated with those other guys. Instead of turning his Super Right-On attention to schooling those bad boys on their behaviour, he thinks it's more important to get women to acknowledge just how much of an ally he is. And if they refuse to do that, how can he in good conscience continue to support them?

Typical comment: 'Those men disgust me, but I'm disappointed that you don't acknowledge that not all men are like this. How are we supposed to be allies if you lump us in with the bad guys?'

What you should say: 'If you think the post isn't about you, then it's not about you. But if your allegiance is conditional on being flattered and showered with gratitude, then you weren't really an ally to begin with.'

The Feminism is Dangerous and that's Why It's Dying Whiplash Prophet: Is very concerned with letting you know how irrelevant and outdated he finds your views. In fact, he's so concerned with letting you know how irrelevant you are that he'll devote multiple hours to the theme, using whatever medium he can to yell at you that men are tired of being demonised and subjugated by the feminist agenda. This guy is deeply aggrieved by the thought men are being stereotyped unfairly, and will defend that stance by building a Straw Feminist and attempting to set her alight.

Typical comment: 'This is why feminism is such a joke now, because you act as if all men are criminals. In fact, 99 percent of men are good guys, but you don't care about that. Feminists are just angry because they're ugly.'

What you should say: 'Can you cite your source for the statistical claim that 99 percent of men are good? Please note that "my butt" is not considered a peer-reviewed journal.'

The Fuck All Feminazis Guy: Hates feminists because his wife left him and/or beautiful women don't want to date him. Claims this is because he isn't rich, ripped and willing to treat them like an arsehole. Cannot conceive of the fact that it might actually be because he is a terrifying, sad individual who quite obviously has a problem seeing women as human-being people. Fuck All Feminazis Guy thinks men are genuinely enslaved by an all-powerful matriarchy. He blames feminism and the family courts for male suicide rates. Refuses to be labelled a misogynist because he insists no one loves women more than he does.

Typical comment: 'Fat fugly feminazi cunt, do you bathe in the tears of all the men who killed themselves this week? Fuck you, not all men are the bastards you make them out to be, you dumb slut.'

What you should say: Nothing. Block and delete them. These men don't deserve your time, and their hatred of women is legitimately terrifying. (Of course, if you're like me you never do what anyone tells you, so if you have to respond, do it with a meme. I like the one of Dawson Leary crying, but kittens sometimes work too.)

We can laugh about these guys (particularly the last one) and we should. In fact, a note on that: women should direct more of their laughter at men, primarily because men can be so ridiculous and they also get so upset when women laugh at them. Ever had a man tell you to relax and take a joke? Ever had him tell you you're overreacting when you object to something sexist he's said or behave as if you're being hysterical and unreasonable because you told him something was offensive? And have you ever hesitated over calling out a man on his rank, sexist humour because you didn't want to have the inevitable interaction which involved him laughing at you and telling you to stop being so sensitive?

Of course you have – you're a woman. But compare that attitude to the way men behave when we laugh at them in return. Oh my good giddy aunt, you'd think we'd poured a jar of fire ants all over their junk. The way they *erupt* into a volcano of rage is hysterically funny in and of itself. It's almost as if they haven't spent their entire lives being conditioned to think of themselves as a foolish waste of space who lacks the proper objectivity to understand how ridiculous they are. It's almost as if they haven't been shamed and gaslit into absorbing ridicule as part and parcel of simply existing. Why . . . it's almost as if they've been raised to believe they're worthy of some kind of respect!

I've started joking about men more often and more deliberately on social media now just to watch as they stumble over themselves to lecture me on how offensive I'm being and how disgustingly sexist I am. At the end of 2015, I sent out a deliberately provocative tweet that said, *I'm not sexist or anything, but men just aren't funny*. Of course, this is the kind of thing women hear all the time. When we argue that maybe, probably, perhaps, possibly this isn't strictly true, usually in relation to the lack of women on comedy bills or supposed-to-be-funny panel shows, we're told that if women *were* funnier, we would get more gigs as funny-makers. That's how the world works, you see. It's a meritocracy. And if it's a meritocracy (which it definitely, definitely is except for in the millions of cases when it isn't), then we can hardly blame all the white, middle-class, mostly middle-aged, cis-het men for just being better at everything.

So I tweeted out a variation on an argument women hear all the time and I kid you not, within about three seconds there were ten men gnashing to get their gobs around the bait. One of them said he was a Feminist (with a capital F) and followed my work, but he had found this tweet 'extremely disappointing' (I guess he can't follow my work too closely, because most of my tweets are considered extremely disappointing to one man or another). A handful more swiftly rattled off tweets of their own about things women couldn't do as well as men and that was nice because then it felt like just an ordinary day instead of another Clem Wants To Make A Point On Twitter festivus. Another guy just started tweeting the names of famous male comedians at me alongside a hashtag, as if maybe I'd just woken up that day with temporary amnesia and imagined I might be living in a world where women weren't constantly reminded of men's Great Achievements. *Oh!* I was supposed to think to myself. *Billy Connolly! Of course, I forgot about him. Well, I guess that settles the matter. CASE CLOSED.*

Rather than dissuade me, that little experiment just further convinced me that women should laugh at men frequently and often and even more so when it makes them mad. Don't let anyone tell you this is an example of 'reverse sexism', or some other made-up thing that doesn't exist but which once again makes privileged men out to be the most victimised group in society. Laughing at the men who grow irate whenever women assert themselves isn't bullying, nor is it a blanket dismissal of men the world over. To borrow an olden day phrase, it is what it is. Pointedly, the 'is' of this is highlighting how absurd and ridiculous some men can be when their power is challenged even slightly. If they have even a shred of the self-awareness that they claim to, they might just use it as a teachable moment for how it feels to live in a world where your opinions and hurt are routinely dismissed as 'humourless oversensitivity'.

But here's where we need to get serious. Because while those Not All Men types may be parodies of outrage in and of themselves, they also have a lot of power. They have a lot of power because women have been trained since birth to coddle men's feelings and to regulate our behaviour so as not to appear too intrusive or domineering. We are taught to shrink ourselves so that we take up as little space as possible, but we are also told to sacrifice the little space we do have – and to do so joyfully – to men and their voices.

For feminism to work, apparently we need to be appealing to men. We need to be nice to them. We need to make them feel like it's a non-threatening movement that will take all of their interests and needs into account and hold their hand as we transition into an equality that will in no way disadvantage or even moderately disrupt their current privilege. Unfortunately, a lot of women take this message to heart because doing anything contrary to it presents as almost frightening. This is why, despite the stereotypes of separatism and misandry that are so repeatedly levelled at feminist activists and workers, so many women bend over backwards to try to be as accommodating as possible to men's sensitivities. These women believe, with the best of intentions, that we are better served by stroking men's egos than by issuing some straight talk to them.

No. Feminism is not obligated to provide equal space at the top for men to lead us. That idea is completely ludicrous. It isn't our duty as women to set a better example so that we can confidently advocate for equality without fear of being accused of hypocrisy. Resisting the urge to allocate time, money, resources and space to ensuring men are given authority in the feminist project isn't 'silencing' them – it's a deliberately political act that reasserts the rights of women to lead ourselves in a world that would still prefer we toddled off to the parlour after supper so the men could smoke in peace.

Let's ignore for a moment the fact that the world beyond feminist institutions (and often even within them) does little to nothing to prioritise inclusivity of anyone who occupies a marginalised identity. This 'inclusivity' that's expected of us – the inclusivity that's in fact *demanded* of us if we want to demonstrate the true spirit of 'equality' – is little more than replicated patriarchy. Consider the reasoning. We need men to speak if we want anyone to take feminism seriously. We need men to speak to other men if we want them to listen to our message. We need men to speak if we want to show that we're not out to subjugate them all and install a matriarchy.

Really? We want to dismantle a patriarchal system which values men's voices over women's and prioritises them in almost every sphere that's given value in the world, but if we want our movement to be successful in this venture we need to elevate men to the head of it?

None of that makes sense!

Men's voices are considered to be fundamentally more authoritative than women's – this is one of the core expressions of patriarchy and has been throughout all of history. So how is it remotely challenging that perception to insist that men's voices are the only ones that will be heard on feminism?

Additionally, feminism and the treatment of women has always been constructed differently by men as a group than it has been by women. In our society, a man is able to consider himself a feminist (indeed, he'll often be promoted by himself and numerous others as a feminist deserving of praise) simply because he says he won't tolerate violence against women. But how does that same man react when a woman discusses sexual violence with him? Let's say she argues that women should be able to walk wherever they want, whenever they want and trust that if something 'bad' does happen to them, the public and police response won't be to issue warnings to women about modifying their behaviour. Is his reaction to listen to her input, acknowledge her experience and agree that, of course, she's absolutely right – the emphasis should always be on a zero-tolerance approach to criminal activity and a blanket support for human-being women people? Or, as my own experience suggests, does he react by telling her that she's wrong? That everyone has a responsibility to take care of themselves and make wise choices, that this isn't victim blaming, it's just common sense, that there are Bad People out there and we don't always know who they are and how dare she or any woman tell him, a man, that he isn't allowed to advise his daughters or wife or sister or friends that they need to take more care on the streets?

There are exceptions, of course. But in the vast majority of cases, when men speak to other men about feminism and gender equality, it is through the prism of protection and paternalism.

Men, we mustn't do this. Men, we need to take care of our women better. Men, we need to make a pledge to always be Stand-Up Guys. Very rarely will you hear these conversations being framed in ways that incorporate women as anything other than objects requiring masculine defence.

When this tendency towards paternalism is critiqued by women, it is us who bear the brunt of the resulting anger. Why aren't you being more supportive of men? Men are just trying to help. You'll never win men over if you keep telling them what they're doing wrong. You'll never get men onside if you keep being mean to them. Don't you dare tell me that I don't care about women. And then, the best one of all: *You're everything that's wrong with feminism today.*

If you're still uncertain about the subtle ways in which this paternalism is enforced, consider the different ways men and women are treated when either group advocates vengeance for victims of domestic violence. Men are allowed to say things like, 'I would beat the shit out of any man who was a wife beater,' or, 'Those bastard men who rape women are pigs and they ought to be castrated and then shot.' Pop culture's cup runneth over with stories of men banding together to 'teach' other men a lesson, while women have been conditioned to find this kind of vigilante behaviour attractive. This starring role of Woman Protector is almost exclusively assigned to men, and as reward for their efforts they receive standing ovations and showers of bouquets.

What happens when women say these things or act in similar ways? When women talk about protecting ourselves against violence? When women reference the steps we take just to walk to our cars at night? When we talk about what should be done with rapists and wife beaters and misogynists, or indulge in fantasies of what we might like to do to them? What happens when women stand in front of men and say, 'This is what our lives look like and this is why the world is so fucked up. If you care about that in the slightest, you'll stop telling me and other women what to do and you'll start listening to what we think YOU can do to help make the world a better place'?

Wow. Fighting violence with violence, hey? That sounds a bit hypocritical. Shouldn't we be arguing that *all* violence is bad, not just violence against women? Violence is never tolerable. Also, Not All Men are like that. I insist that you acknowledge Not All Men behave in this way before you make that argument, otherwise I'll have no choice but to ignore everything you say and write you off as a man-hater.

Men cannot change the world FOR women, because men have no concept of what it's like to live in the world AS women. They don't know what it feels like to have their specifically gendered experiences either immediately discounted or assessed (unconsciously or deliberately) as exaggerated. They don't know the trauma that accumulates from hearing constant commentary about all the ways in which they're weak, how they inherently lack merit, how they possess less business acumen, how they cannot help but be overly emotional and irrational, how they could succeed just as well as the other side if they tried hard enough, how they're all their own worst enemies and how in fact it's other men who disadvantage men the most. Men cannot understand how infuriating it is to have circumstances of safety be reduced to behavioural change not in perpetrators but in victims. Even those opposed to victim-blaming attitudes can't really appreciate the impact that being exposed to them has, especially when opposition to these ideas is often met with abuse and ridicule.

How can men possibly hope to change the world in all the ways that women need when half the time they don't even realise we're living on two different planes of the same dimension? We are the only ones equipped to lead the feminist fight because we are in possession of knowledge that can only be gleaned from experience. Surrendering control of our liberation to the same men who benefit from us being denied it isn't just a dangerous exercise in irony – it's a guaranteed way to ensure nothing truly changes.

Women are being killed on a weekly basis by men who hate them so much but want desperately to control them. We're raped, violated, abused, pushed around, undermined, ridiculed, mocked, beaten, bullied and degraded. And to make matters worse, we're told that our complaints about these things are overwrought, hysterical and defamatory.

Suck it up, princess, the world isn't fair. Get over it, it's just a joke. A good cock up ya will sort you out.

And still they ask: Why do you hate men?

—10—

HATE MALE

'It's really a Shame that a man wasted Sperm on a low life Cunt like you! Should've masturbated into the toilet!'

This was tweeted at me sometime in the early months of 2016 by a fellow using an obvious nom de plume. It's fairly typical of the kinds of love letters men send me on the internet, right down to the questionable command of grammar and random capitalisation. It was also written late at night, which makes sense when you realise it's part of the ritual he and his ilk need to prompt the sad, sweaty erections that precipitate the good old-fashioned hate-wanks that characterise the entirety of their interaction with women.

You might expect that being sent something like this would deeply wound me or at the very least hurt my feelings, but it mostly just amused me. Does Mr Anonymous think sperm is in such short supply that men are seriously required to pick and choose where they expend it lest they be guilty of endangering the species? Just think of all the other things my father could have done with his precious deposits if he hadn't wasted it on a low life Cunt like me! He might have created some edgy art (it was the eighties, after all) or used it to fertilise a tree. Perhaps he could have ejaculated into an envelope and sent it to an unsuspecting lass alongside a note calling her a 'fat-arsed whore who can't get laid', coincidentally pre-empting Twitter in the process. So many opportunities to really honour his ball boys, and he wastes them on making a wretched life like mine.

What a Shame!

Of course, I'm not meant to laugh at this. No, I'm meant to read it and feel humiliated and small. I'm meant to think of myself as a dirty, rank piece of shit whose lack of value is so profound that even a puff of jizz shot into a toilet represents more of an accomplishment than the entirety of my sad, sorry existence.

Reader, it doesn't work. As I've said on numerous occasions, there are only so many times you can be called an ugly cum-dumster whose twelve-inch vibrator probably doesn't even touch the sides of her gaping cunt (actual marriage proposal sent to me by nos235@yahoo.com – I said yes, obviously). All the hateful slurs, the misogynist attempts to undermine you, the furiously violent descriptions of what they'd like to see done to you (to save you the time of wondering, I'll just tell you that it always comes back to rape and/or mutilation) . . . after a while, it all becomes white noise. Angry white noise, sure, but white noise nonetheless.

This doesn't make the onslaught of it any less annoying. As much as I can genuinely, hand on heart, say that I do not care whether TruthSword45 and his cartoon avatar finds me repulsive or not, I do resent the tedious waste of time involved in having to read his nonsense at all. I get it, TruthSword – you think I'm a grunting hog with daddy issues who's only angry about rape because it'll never happen to me. I invite you to count the fucks I give in the field in which I store my fucks where there also happens to be no fucks left because the field is made entirely out of concrete and actually doesn't even exist.

Listen, I've been the target of hostile online abuse for the better part of a decade. Long before we constructed lives for ourselves on social media, I was reading emails from men obsessed with musing about the state of my genitals, the instability of my mental health and the apparently deep and traumatising lack of attention I'd received from men my entire life, starting with my father. One of the first articles I ever wrote for a mainstream newspaper audience involved me disclosing the fact that not only had I had two abortions, I also felt no guilt or regret over them.

To say this didn't go down well with the conservative News Ltd Sunday paper readership would be an understatement. *A Current Affair* even tried to do a story about it, which tells you all you need to know about the general public sentiment. I chose to ignore the requests for contact from ACA's producers, largely because I'd actually rather wear a thermal suit made entirely out of soiled nappies than have that appearance on my résumé.

But this was my first taste of the kind of hostility that greets women who speak their truth, particularly to a mass audience. Abortion is legal in South Australia (where I was living at the time), and it's provided for free through the public health system. In other words, I hadn't done anything other than exercise my rights to access reproductive health care in a state that does not provide limitations on the number of allowable procedures. From a purely emotionless standpoint, this was no different to the time I had a potentially cancerous mole cut out of my right arm, except that skin cancer probably would have been easier to deal with than an unwanted baby.

After my abortion piece was published in the *Sunday Mail*, I was inundated with hundreds – and I mean *hundreds* – of emails and online comments about how disgusting and inhuman I was. Anything you can think of, I was called it. Slut, whore, ugly cunt who needs to learn how to keep her legs closed, selfish, irresponsible, stupid, murderer, baby-killing sow, slag and so on and so on. A guy wondered how someone as ugly as me could have found one man willing to fuck me, let alone two of them. Another agreed, stating I was 'uglier than a dead dog on the side of the road' and the very fact I'd had sex at all was a miracle.

People hear that a woman's had an abortion, and they become giddy over the permission they feel they've been granted to degrade and humiliate her sexually. I knew this was what would happen when I wrote that piece, but I didn't anticipate just how torrential the hate would be. I didn't know that, years later, I'd still be receiving messages about it from Men's Rights Losers all over the world, or that my apparent nickname at News Ltd in Sydney would be 'Cankles McBabystopper' (a term coined by the blogger Tim Blair, whose multiple paid *Daily Telegraph* blog posts about me include one titled 'Transitioning', where he uses a close-up photograph of the hair on my upper lip to ponder whether I might be turning into a man).

The fact is, women who put themselves out there have always been subjected to abuse. The intensity of that abuse has been compounded by the sheer magnitude of the online space, but it all spawns from the same motivation: to shame us into silence so that we scurry back to our little lives, leaving men to dominate and control all the power that remains. If we complain about the excessive cruelty used against us, we're accused of being 'too sensitive'. We can't take the heat. We crumble at the first sign of opposition. We want to be treated like children. We're babies who need to be taken care of. We need to toughen up, be more like men. Learn to roll with the punches, understand that everyone gets joshed and riled and we shouldn't expect special treatment just because we're delicate little baby girls who want to be given everything for free.

Allow me to tell you about the time I ruined a man's life.

It was November 2015. Some guy had come to my Facebook page to tell me I would 'jibber less with a cock in my mouth', which was a new and imaginative pick-up line that I had not heard before.

I was disturbed by his comment not because it upset me, but because his avatar showed him photographed with his kids. This isn't unusual; despite popular argument, men with children aren't immune from holding repulsive attitudes towards women, nor does their paternity stop them from contacting those women in an attempt to harass them. Misogynists have to come from somewhere after all, and parental conditioning is usually a pretty good start. Unfortunately, the existence of children (particularly daughters) is often used to discount men's capacity to be sexist. The theory is that being the lord and master of girls you've created somehow makes you more invested in the freedom and liberation of girls everywhere. Apart from that being patently untrue, it's also pretty gross thinking. Girls don't become humans just because they're related to you, and plenty of men see their daughters and wives as subordinate to them. Still, the argument that 'he can't be sexist because look, he owns a few women' is still trotted out as if that somehow settles the matter. (See: Tony 'one woman in the cabinet' Abbott.)

Part of my tactic in fighting the abuse of women online has always been to signal boost it for the benefit of people who either don't know what it's really like or insist that women lie about how prolific and violent it can be. It's reasonably effective, especially because it often results in even more abuse being directed my way. (Seriously – these guys need to get a new strategist; they kick so many own goals.) With that in mind, I screencapped this guy's comment and wrote a separate post about it to demonstrate that yes, actually, men with children and wives and sisters and mothers can also be gross, misogynist pigs.

In response, a young man named Michael Nolan popped by to add his two cents.

'Slut,' he wrote.

Now, on the scale of abuse I normally receive, this doesn't really rate much of a mention. As far as its capacity to cause an ouchy, it had about as much impact as the guy who contacted me yesterday to let me know I am a 'stupid bad person'. Still, the casual arrogance of it annoyed me. This was a post that put on full display the kind of man I'm often told I'm making up or exaggerating. I had his photo, an example of his violent attitude towards women and evidence that he was raising children – but none of that mattered to a bro like Nolan. It was just another one of those jokes that women are expected to suck up and swallow without complaint so we don't inconvenience the dudes who confuse being asked not to abuse us with being grievously oppressed. Nolan seemed to feel completely entitled to compound the intent of that humiliation by spitting 'slut' at me, just so that I and other cunt-whore-bitches like me would be reminded of what position of relevancy we occupy in the world.

Unfortunately for Nolan, he had his workplace publicly listed on his Facebook page (which also happened to be chock-full of incredibly racist 'jokes'). I sent a message containing some choice screencaps to his employer. It wasn't long before I heard back from the serviced apartment group at which he was a supervising manager. They first told me they were looking into it and then, presumably fearful of the bad publicity that might come from letting it slide, made the decision to terminate his contract.

I posted a follow-up with this information, and that's when the shit storm really started. The next few days saw me facing a relentless tide of abuse from people, most of them men, calling me a whore, a slut, a dumb cunt, a fat bitch who needs to get laid, a bitch who should kill herself and, in one particularly memorable moment, a woman who needed to be shot in the face and put in a grave.

If Lewis' Law states that the comments beneath any article about feminism justifies feminism's existence, then Ford's Law asserts that the abuse received after exposing abuse proves how very prevalent this problem is.

But funnily enough, the circumstances of Nolan's life began to twist and turn according to what my detractors wanted to believe about feminist retribution. Not only had I ruined a man's life, I had done so *just before Christmas*, leaving him, his wife and all of their children destitute, homeless and without any presents from Santa. That Nolan was unmarried and childless is apparently irrelevant, as was the fact that he really didn't seem to care about losing his job nor did he ever participate in the frenzy that occurred afterwards. Nope – an entire life had been manufactured for him in which he had not only done nothing wrong but was now a hard-working husband and father being punished by an evil, scheming (fat) feminist intent on destroying the fabric of society.

Even now, when months have passed, I still receive regular online comments from men outraged by my actions. 'Slut,' they write to me. 'You just try and fucking get me fired!' They tell me I'm thin-skinned, that I can't handle 'bad words' and that, in addition to all my other faults, I'm stamping out free speech and 'silencing' people. Because being allowed to call someone a 'cunt-faced ginger' on the internet without them fighting back is what freedom's all about, apparently. Quick, somebody raise the barricades. There are some angry men out there and they have some songs they need to sing.

Still, why did I choose to retaliate against Nolan in particular? As I've pointed out, 'slut' is hardly the worst thing I've ever been called. It wasn't even the worst message I'd received that week. That would be the email I received saying (and I quote verbatim): 'You deserve to be gangraped by a pack of aids infested niggers. Die, fucking bitch.'

The answer is simple. I did it because I'm sick and tired of men abusing women online and continuing to get away with it. Fuck all those entitled, bullying misogynists who act like the world fucking belongs to them and they can do whatever they like without consequences. I can withstand their boring tantrums (as tedious as they are) but I'm angry about how many women they manage to bully into silence. They think it's their right to retaliate against any woman who disagrees with them or challenges them in any way, and their preferred methods always involve dehumanisation and degradation. They think they're untouchable, because until now very few people have ever held them accountable for their behaviour. Instead, they're coddled and protected, their actions defended as 'harmless fun' or 'just a little mistake'. Women are expected to absorb their hostility without complaint, to let it diminish and shrink us all so we can ensure they never have to answer to anything.

And if we refuse to do all this, to cop their rape and murder threats on the chin because 'they're just words, get the sand out of your box', then we're demonising them and punishing them unfairly. It's worse than violent harassment – it's *misandry*.

I cannot tell you how many times I've been admonished for putting the abuse of men on display for the world to see. How often I've been told off for 'humiliating them' or 'bullying them', simply because I insist on showing everyone else the words they're so proud to send me when they assume I'll keep it 'our little secret'. People have told me that this kind of retaliation makes me 'just as bad if not worse' than the men who get off on degrading me with their words and detailed descriptions. Really? I'm 'just as bad' as someone who tells me I need to have my 'virgin smelly anal passage pierced by a mammoth cock', because I took their courageously written words and broadcast them to a much bigger audience? That I might actually be even worse than them, because *my* actions could result in them losing their job or being publicly humiliated, and I need to be more responsible than that?

When women complain about the abuse we receive, we're told to 'get over it' or 'harden up', two pieces of advice that completely miss the irony of the fact that the most thin-skinned, sensitive and retaliatory people online are white men aged between fifteen and thirty-five. You only need to read any of the comments on a post gently making fun of people who think 'misandry' actually exists to see that. After the Nolan incident happened, an extremely irate man tweeted at me (very seriously, I might add) that I wouldn't stop until I had succeeded in having all men in the world fired from their jobs.

I replied, 'I won't stop until all men are fired . . . into the sun!'

To highlight just how incapable some men seem to be at reading humour when it's directed at them, this response was shared around as apparent 'proof' that I not only wanted to see an end to all male employment, but that I actually wanted to catapult them directly into the blazing ball of fire the earth rotates around. A young chap even contacted me a few months after this to argue with me about how much I supposedly hate men.

'You said you wanted to fire them all into the sun!' he exclaimed.

'Do you think it's possible that I might have been joking?' I replied, with far more patience than I usually possess.

'But you said it,' he answered, as if this settled the matter.

And in the minds of boys and men like him, I guess it does. They can 'joke' about rape, abuse, violence, sending women back to the kitchen, fucking women up, beating the shit out of us, telling us with their fists to know our place and whatever other reprehensible horrors you can conjure up in your mind, and these are nothing but festive japes. But a woman jokes about building a cannon in the desert to blast the world's men into the atmosphere and this is A VERY SERIOUS CRIME THAT MUST BE TAKEN VERY SERIOUSLY.

Chaos ensues.

Once again, women are expected to absorb the brunt of the hate sent our way because nothing we do in response – even when it's directly following the advice of those people who love to tell women what to do – is ever acceptable.

Here's how a typical interaction with the defenders and perpetrators of online abuse goes.

'Just block and delete them like a grown-up!'

blocks and deletes

'Oh, so you're censoring people now? What, can't you handle debate?'

attempts to engage in a meaningful discussion, explaining why harassment is unacceptable

'Get over it, it's just a word. I get called words all the time and I don't cry like a baby!'

loses temper, resorts to name-calling and/or sarcasm

'I should have known you'd resort to ad hominem attacks. You feminists are all the same: you can't even defend your position without becoming abusive!'

This is doubly frustrating considering the majority of these conversations take place in online spaces with crude mechanisms for dealing with interactions like these. Facebook, the platform I use most frequently, is shockingly bad when it comes to responding to abuse. Time after time, posts featuring women's bruised and bloodied faces have been declared 'not in violation' of the site's community standards, as have the countless posts joking about rape and intimate partner homicide or comments calling for women to be tortured.

In mid-2015, hundreds of girls and women in South Australia had their private photographs stolen and shared online without their consent. The social media team at Channel Seven's morning 'news' program *Sunrise* (which look, let's be honest, is the televisual equivalent of a drophole toilet in a country town famed for its racism) linked to the story with a caption asking, 'When will girls learn?' In protest, I posted a near-topless photograph of myself with extensive commentary condemning this kind of victim-blaming bullshit. Across my chest, I had scrawled #getfuckedsunrise.

The post went bonkers almost immediately. To date, it has been shared over 700,000 times. That night though, astonishment quickly turned to discomfort as I began to be inundated with private messages and public comments from men, most of them hostile. Some demanded I send them nude photographs, and then called me names like 'fat whore' and 'slag' when I either ignored them or told them to fuck off. Others dropped by uninvited to talk about my 'saggy tits' and how, as one man put it, they'd 'seen better on a pit bull'. I was called an attention seeker and an idiot, told that I was irresponsible for encouraging girls to behave 'like sluts'. One man publicly requested that I 'sit on a butcher knife' so that I could 'never reproduce'. Another privately messaged to say he was going to come to my house and rape me.

All of that, just because I posted a photograph with commentary protesting the idea that women sacrifice our right to be treated with respect the moment we share an intimate image of ourselves with someone we've been led to believe we can trust.

Despite reporting most of these comments and messages, none of them were considered to violate the (extremely lax) community standards at Facebook HQ. If I wanted to, I was told I could block the users, but that was about it. Deciding this was inadequate, I instead began the laborious process of screencapping as much as possible, posting everything I could to show just how viciously some men react to the sight of a woman standing up for herself and other women. Unfortunately, men like that don't like having their words put on display for everyone else to see. They don't like being publicly associated with their vile misogyny, because it makes it that much harder for them to claim the title of Good Guy. So, despite frequently being among the many who mock women for being 'unable to handle' the onslaught of abuse online, they started reporting the posts.

And this was where Facebook suddenly drew the line. Not only did they remove the multiple posts I'd made, they also slapped me with a thirty-day ban. To be clear, all I had done was post *images* of the messages and comments sent to me that had been declared fine by Facebook's standards. But while it was evidently acceptable for these men to send these messages in the first place, it suddenly became an act of hostility for me to make an example of them.

What can be concluded from this? That misogynist abuse, whether it happens in the online world or not, is considered the responsibility of women to handle quietly, timidly and without any sudden movements or retaliation lest men be unfairly embarrassed. The people who baulk at the thought of men being forced to adjust their behaviour have absolutely no problem advocating for solutions which involve women removing ourselves from public life entirely. Basically, it isn't fair to demand that men change behaviour that's ultimately harmless, and if women don't like this we should just get off the internet.

But listen. I didn't force Michael Nolan to violate his company's social media policy by writing the word 'Slut' on the Facebook wall of a woman he'd never met. In fact, I've never invited anyone to invade my little corner of the internet and bombard me with the weight of their frustrated masculinity. I don't seek men out to conduct Facebook or Twitter drive-by shootings, turning up unannounced to call them names, query their mental health or cast aspersions on the relationships they have with their mothers. All I have ever done is exercise my right to post on a page attributed to my name on a publicly accessible website, and defend myself against an onslaught of attacks.

But the fact of my existence is still so enraging to some men that they can't help but persistently, incessantly harass me in the hope that they might one day be successful in getting me to shut up shop. And in keeping with most executions of abuse or violence against women, the responsibility for their behaviour falls to me. I'm making them do this with my outspoken views. I'm encouraging their abuse by being such an angry feminist. I'm making it worse by fighting back. Just ignore it and they'll go away. Grow up. Stop being so *sensitive*.

Listen, I have been a human-being woman person for approximately thirty-five years now and at least ten of those traverses around the sun have been since the internet became widely accessible. I've been called every name you can think of, often multiple times in a day. Men call me names on my Twitter account, on Facebook, via my email address, on the radio, at public speaking events and sometimes even through letters forwarded on to my home address. I've amassed such a huge scrapbook of abuse that I actually present a comedy lecture on it, so ridiculous and laughable is most of it. Those inclined to pen such prose draw on every anti-feminist and anti-woman slur that's been made available to them through the gross collective imagination of the misogynists at large, and I haven't retreated yet. I can *handle* pretty much anything they throw at me. What I can't handle is their hypocrisy – because do you know who crumbles quicker than you can say 'whiny man baby who loves the sound of his own voice'? Dudebros. If I had a dollar for every time a man complained that I was 'bullying' him just because I shared an example of his gendered, abusive name-calling, I could build my own fucking social media site and install an automatic no-join policy for all the douchelords who think misandry is really A Thing.

If I couldn't 'handle' it, I would have retreated into private life a long time ago. But I'm still here. I'm still writing, still speaking and still refusing to be the kind of woman that makes men like this feel comfortably in charge. They hate it and they retaliate viciously, but all of that just proves how much power I actually have over them. Much like the gaping cavern of my gigantic cunt, they can't touch the sides of me. Beyond using them as an example to others of what fear does to people, I never think about them. I don't care whether or not they like me or agree with me, whether they feel personally victimised by my views or what they think of my body, face or sexuality. And judging by how furiously they react to even the remotest slight or gentle joke had at their expense, I also know that they're the ones wrapped in thin skin, breaking at the slightest provocation, yelling fiercely about their rights and humanity.

There is an obvious conclusion to be drawn from this, and that is the boys and men who feel most entitled to ridicule everyone they enjoy power over cannot handle it when that spotlight is turned on themselves. This is their perception of oppression: being laughed at on the internet.

This fear of being laughed at is what we can use to win against them. As hard as it might sometimes be to summon cheer in the face of their toxic bilge, laugh loudly and laugh often. Don't give them your earnest energy or sensitivity, because they don't respect that. In fact, they get off on mocking it and stomping all over it. They don't care about the issues you care about, so they feel no obligation to treat your emotions about them with any shred of respect. Attempting to engage with them seriously or convince them of your position only ends up making you feel more frustrated and upset. Trust me, I know – I tried this approach for years.

Instead, treat them like the boggarts they are, and use that knowledge to destroy them. For those people unfamiliar with the world of Harry Potter, a boggart is a spirit that lives in dark and dusty places and whose power comes from taking on the appearance of the thing a person fears most. This is a fairly apt description for the losers who troll women on the internet, because underneath all their bravado lies little more than a glorified black hole of rage and dust mites. The only way to defeat a boggart is to cast the Ridikulus spell – you summon the spectre of your fear either dressed in something ridiculous or cast in an absurd situation, and the resulting howls of laughter progressively weaken it until it explodes.

Online trolls are the boggarts of the internet, and laughter kills them. So laugh. Laugh and watch them wilt. They'll fight back, of course. But the more they shrink before us, the more strength you'll have to go on fighting. That's what all of us need to do – we need to fight back and take the space that belongs to us, no matter how angry it makes these men feel and no matter how viciously they try to tear us down.

For too long, women have been subjected to the rage of men as a means of keeping us quiet and compliant. Our bodies, sexuality, physicality, behaviour and temperaments have all been stolen and distorted to try to humiliate us into silence. We are punished for acting out, tormented for speaking up and ridiculed for fighting back. The abuse we suffer online is just the latest iteration of this, and it can be overwhelming in its intensity.

But the good news is that we *are* winning against it. More and more women are finding the strength to push back. More of us are laughing at the sad little troglodytes who think their pathetic insults can still make us cry into our pillows. We're not letting misogynist rage consume us to the point of mass silencing anymore, but are shouting back into the hurricane without fear. Women are standing in solidarity with one another against the onslaught of this abuse, and simply bearing witness to that encourages more of us to join the line. These words that have been used to cut us, wound us and destroy us have suddenly lost the power they once had, and the men who've wielded them are going to have to accept the dawning of a new era.

Because out there, on that vast ocean of male tears, the tide is turning. Women are finally captaining the ship.

Men can either get on the boat, or they can drown.

— 11 —

DICKTIONARY

Fellow feminists, it's true what people say: feminism *is* a dirty word. But contrary to popular opinion, this isn't because of the way feminists look or the things they say or even the way they say them. Feminism is a dirty word because, no matter how much they might try to argue otherwise, the concept of gender equality is still so deeply horrifying to a lot of people that they feel entitled to lash out at feminists using all the tools a gender unequal world has given them. If the weight of history and power instructs women to behave in particular ways so that the patriarchy can maintain its foundational support, it stands to reason that any challenges to this status quo are reacted to swiftly and mercilessly.

So how is this done? Well, in a society built on thousands of years of patriarchy, the shortest path to punishment for the people who threaten this structure is to metaphorically criminalise the ways in which they fail to live up to its standards. For women, this presents as a deliberate and hostile undermining of our worth by reducing even further the limited currency we're given in the world. The system works by controlling our value. Our bank balances rise and fall based on how fuckable we are, how polite, how docile, how deferential, how eager to please and how willing we are to pretend that this state of affairs isn't just normal but actually desirable – and all of that happens before we even take into account the value meted out arbitrarily according to our skin colour, size, physical ability, race, biological sex and economic status.

Luckily for patriarchy and the people privileged by it, history is pretty much wall to wall full of women who conform to this bullshit. This isn't because they're stupid or because they necessarily enjoy being perceived as second-class citizens who lack any real comparative merit to men. It isn't because women are okay with being essentially hunted creatures whose survival depends on figuring out ways to avoid the male violence and sexual oppression that exists everywhere but most often in their domestic environments. And it certainly isn't because patriarchy, when stripped of all its illusions and negotiated benefits, makes women happy. How could anyone truly be happy being considered and treated as if the mere fact of your biology not only makes you weaker but also content to focus inwards rather than outwards?

In fact, women's conformity to patriarchal power is partly due to the false (yet oh so insidious) ideas of 'normal human behaviour and evolutionary biology', and partly due to survival. In regard to the first, the status quo takes the view that men and women are different, there's no point questioning it, we bring different strengths to the table, I like being treated like a woman, I don't want to change a tyre, maths is hard! It succeeds by convincing men and women alike that while these gendered 'skills' might be different, they're equally valued – as if women should happily accept being denied the same economic, sexual and social freedom as men (while being expected to satisfy the ego of the ever-present male gaze) because we might have a car door opened for us, gain a few free dinners and have some blowhard promise to 'treat us like a queen'.

That this argument usually refuses to address the measure of value that these supposedly gendered traits are accorded is a fact not lost on feminists. That 'free ride' that women supposedly get at the expense of hard-working men? It's fucking conditional, friend. We already know that the women who try but fail to fulfil their part of the contract are subjected to ridicule and judgment. But the women who actively go out of their way to burn the whole thing down are treated as public enemy number one.

Patriarchy is a controlling force which succeeds by implementing a series of rigid rules and regulations for women's behaviour, and feminists have always been the loose cannons who threaten to sink the ship. No one can predict what we'll do or what kind of womanhood we'll occupy. We might not wear make-up! We might have hairy armpits! We might fuck other women, but not in a way where men are invited to watch! We might even be mean to men! We might have opinions that men don't like! We might we might we might we might OH MY GOD WHAT MIGHT WE DO?!

Worst of all, we might convince other women to turn their backs on the whole thing. To step out of line and reject these age-old, bullshit mechanisms of control and realise their own power. And where would the men who enjoy patriarchy be then? Fucked, I'd say, and not in the way they've come to believe is their right.

This is what it largely boils down to: the power of men to fuck whom they like, when they like, and have the object of their fucking express gratitude for the selection. What happens when a culture that relies on women believing the only power we have is to be chosen by a man for mating suddenly encounters women who don't want a bar of that? It doubles down on reinforcing the importance of that narrative. So it seems that the only (legal) recourse mainstream society has against the scourge of boiler-suit-wearing, clod-thumping anarchist man-women who've risen up to destroy civilisation is to persistently remind us how repulsive we are and how unqualified for masculine desire.

Although this might hurt initially – hey, we've all been raised in a gender-unequal world and it takes a lot to break those invisible chains – it soon becomes apparent how hilarious it is. I mean, come on! It takes an extraordinary amount of arrogance and stupidity to think that the same people who oppose the sexual objectification of women would be even remotely upset at the thought that bog-standard men were denying us the privilege of being sexually objectified. Oh no, my scary opinions made the angry man not want to do sex to me – WHATEVER WILL I DO?

Every time a man calls me a name, I feel more justified in my belief that I'm on the right path. Because if that man wasn't so afraid of what my distilled rage might achieve, why else would he care so much? If it isn't the desperate fear of losing their grip on power that prompts men to deploy every tactic they can to try to silence feminists, what is it? And if feminists are really an irrelevant throwback to the 1970s that 'normal' people have moved on from, why bother paying any attention to us at all? Why not just let us have at it in our supposedly small online echo chambers, slowly suffocating ourselves in semantic arguments, patchouli oil and the dreamcatchers we've woven from our own pubic hair?

If it's really true that no one's listening, why are they all so intent on making us shut up?

Ah, but see – people *are* listening. And that makes us dangerous. We must be stopped! And the easiest way some (most) ordinary Joes have conceived of doing that is with the liberal application of a paint-by-numbers list of insults. I've taken the liberty of collating some of them for you here.

Not only will you know what to expect, but you'll have ample time to practise not laughing as some irate neckbeard with spittle pooled in the corners of his mouth yells that you're a 'fucking ugly virgin lesbian with a gaping cunt the size of a small shipping container'. (That's MISTER fucking ugly virgin lesbian to you.)

Here, in no particular order, some wah-wah words you can work on getting over.

Feminazi: Feminists advocate for the liberation of women from patriarchal dominance. Feminism is literally defined as a movement that seeks political, economic and social equality between the sexes. Feminists protest rape culture and argue for a world in which both women and men can be unshackled from the gender stereotypes that underpin violence. Feminists have never started any wars, launched any missiles, imprisoned any dissenters or tried to eradicate an entire race. I'm a little rusty on history, but I'm also pretty sure that feminism didn't invade Poland and then attempt to establish a fascist empire across all of Europe.

On the other hand, feminists have devoted a lot of time and energy over the decades to winning the vote for women; fighting for reproductive healthcare access and rights; challenging work-places to institute equal pay for equal work; building refuges for women and children escaping violence; protesting governments that turned a blind eye to the practice of child marriages; agitating to be represented in political governance; pushing for the rights of women to own property and live independently, and; marching for the rights of young men not to be conscripted and sent off to battle. So yes, given all that, I can see perfectly how it correlates with Nazism, a genocidal political ideology that sought to eradicate an entire race from the world and establish a Third Reich based on white power.

FeminISISt: I'm called a feminISISt or feminISISist about once a week. In terms of logic, it's really no different from being called a 'feminazi' – it's just that the conspiracy theorists banging it out on their keyboards are a smidge more racist. I guess the accusation being levelled here is that feminists want to kill all men and then install a caliphate. Which, I don't know, maybe some of us do. It's a broad movement.

The thing is, you can waste time getting offended or upset at being likened to a fundamentalist terrorist or you can laugh it off. Let's face it, only a massive toolbag with a bale of hay where his brain's supposed to be would think that either of these words had the capacity to seriously wound anyone.

Bitch: Bitch is one of the most standard go-to insults used against women regardless of whether or not they consider themselves a feminist. While most people don't literally think of 'female dog' when they call someone a bitch, that meaning and everything associated with it is buried in there all the same. A bitch is a woman who doesn't play nicely – a bestial horror who can suddenly turn on you and bare her teeth in an aggressive manner. But the word 'bitch' has been employed to denigrate women so routinely that arguably it's been sanitised to some degree. It's barely even considered a swear word anymore, and it's acceptable to use it as a noun, a verb or an adjective. Women are bitches. Women bitch about other women. Women are bitchy.

On the rare occasions 'bitch' is used to describe men, it's with the intent of emasculating them. Men are told to 'stop whining and acting like a little bitch' – the implication being that they're humiliating themselves by behaving like women possessed with weak and pathetic anger. At the heart of this is the idea that women are not only incapable of disagreeing or asserting ourselves in a strong and/or convincing manner, but that our very existence is one that needs to be tempered and rendered accommodating in order to earn us a conditional entrance ticket to the broader hallways of life.

As commonplace as it may be, 'bitch' is still covertly used to put women in our place. But when someone calls you a bitch because you had the nerve to exist on your own terms rather than theirs, you can really only feel sorry for them given all the unique challenges they're facing. I mean, fancy making it all the way to adulthood when you still possess the social skills of a toddler who's three hours overdue for a nap and doesn't have their favourite teddy bear. This kind of behaviour is excusable in a two-year-old but, honestly, some of these man-babies really need to grow up.

Fat: If you're a feminist, accept right now that you will frequently be called fat regardless of your shape. This is because the world is full of literal walking arsebags whose genetic material somehow managed to survive the gross ineptitude that otherwise characterises their life and make it not just past uterine implantation, but bafflingly sent them all the way through the birth canal and into what we know as 'life'. These people have an imagination so limited and colourless that they actually believe 'fat [insert other insult]' is some kind of sick Wildean burn.

'Fat' is probably one of the most asinine and predictable insults ever conceived, yet it's remarkably effective at scaring women into silence. The 'why' of that is easy. We live in a society that is deeply fat-phobic, and doubly so when you invite misogyny into the mix. Poor body image is at staggeringly high levels in women, particularly young women. We are instructed to be afraid of fat and all that it's supposed to represent. In women especially, 'fatness' is treated almost like a shameful, contagious disease.

A woman who is fat bears the visual, physical evidence of one of two possible personality maladies. The first is her inability to adhere and/or conform to social notions of attractiveness, a failure which is further reinforced by ideas of greediness, laziness and gluttony. But the second is considered to be a threat rather than mere ineptitude. A woman may have become fat *despite* the cultural pressures which demand that she minimise and reduce her body, and she may choose to remain that way because of sheer indifference to them. To wit: she may be fat while giving zero fucks what men have to say about it.

If fuckability is manufactured as femininity's primary goal, the label 'fat' only serves to strip women of any value and worth they might otherwise have. So it is that calling a woman fat has become easy shorthand for calling her disgusting, repulsive, a space stealer, foul, inhuman, unwanted. It is to suggest to her that her body is unfuckable and therefore her life and everything she stands for is utterly pointless.

But what does it really mean, when you break it down? Why is it that women of such varying shapes and sizes can be dismissed with that one word, whether or not it's factually applicable or not? The simple explanation, as always, is that the person calling you fat is a fucking twit who lacks the intellectual capacity to argue against your political ideas and so tries to deride you by telling you that you're too fat to fuck. Boohoo. I've taken to agreeing with men who call me fat. 'Yes, I am the fattest person in the world,' I say, 'and I am going to sit on you until you suffocate and then I will eat you.' It works a charm.

Hairy: In addition to being thin, women (particularly in the west) are expected to maintain the illusion of hairlessness. Any sign that puberty might have bestowed upon us a spray of fuzz beneath our arms or a thatch of fur between our legs has to be eliminated immediately. Waxing, shaving, plucking, electrolysis – women have to fork out precious financial resources just to achieve what is then laughably passed off as a 'natural' state.

For men and women similarly invested in maintaining patriarchal notions of gender performance, hair on women seems to be oddly terrifying. It's been a long time since I was afraid of going out in public with three-day-old stubble on my legs, but I know there are still far too many girls and women who feel crippled by the anxiety of hair. I used to be one of them. When I was twenty-seven, I took a guy home one night in the dead of a New York winter. I liked him, and was excited to have him in my house. We took our clothes off and he pointed at my hibernation armpits, sneering, 'You should shave those, that's disgusting.' I wish I'd had the confidence then to kick him out, but I just sat there mortified and ashamed. Then, humiliatingly, I tried to make it up to him by giving him a BJ.

NEVER AGAIN.

Newsflash. Women grow hair. It is not unnatural. It is not unclean. It is not offensive. And it certainly isn't anyone else's goddamn business. Who the hell cares if you have hair or don't have hair or sometimes have hair or can't grow much hair or grow so much hair that you occasionally even cultivate it into beautiful sculptures of horticultural majesty?

Answer: dickheads. Dickheads are literally the only people who care about whether or not women have hair on their bodies.

Lesbian: The only thing more terrifying than a hairy fat bitch who men don't want to fuck is a hairy fat bitch who doesn't even want those men to want to fuck her. How can he control her if she doesn't even feel sad at not being objectified by him? In most mainstream popular culture, lesbians are only acceptable if they: a) conform to mainstream codes of feminine beauty, and b) are totally cool with men watching and maybe even joining in. Other lesbians are just, like, gross and stuff.

Lesbians are a little difficult to navigate for a society invested in male dominance. If we are so fervently sold on the idea that not only is it natural for men to be in control but natural for women to want to be controlled by them, then applying the lesbian tag to 'difficult' women remains an effective way to shame them.

Why does this fear of a realistic vision of lesbianism exist? It comes down to the fear of superfluity. If we can live independently, make our own money and maintain functional, satisfying sexual relationships with other women, where does that leave men? If women are expected to aspire to men's sexual approval – and we absolutely are – then consciously existing outside of that contract is like a form of social heresy.

But here's what it comes down to: women who assert our own right to self-determination pose a threat to men's power. And if misogynists weren't so dim and so obsessed with trying to shut women up, they would realise there is a deep and intense irony in trying to insult feminists by accusing us of not needing men. Like . . . no shit, dingus.

Ugly: When it comes to shutting down a woman's voice, her detractors have very selective vision. Not even the most objectively attractive women in the world are immune from the tag of 'ugly' if they dare to say something that someone (usually a man) doesn't like. It is used to invalidate a woman's contributions, and works on the premise that women only become entitled to interact with other people (again, usually men) when we can demonstrate support for the toll of womanhood. Or, to paraphrase the writer Erin McKean, to embrace the idea of beauty as the rent women must pay in order to live in the world as a legitimate human being and not merely as a thing that can be ignored or pushed aside once its words become inconvenient.

It is necessary to keep repeating this, because perhaps repetition will convince the unconvinced of how insidious this feeling is: the pinnacle of women's value is placed not just in her beauty, but in her willingness to work eagerly towards that beauty.

In a patriarchy, it isn't enough simply to be aesthetically attractive; a woman must also show commitment to the idea of what it means to be attractive. She must be polite and deferential when necessary. She must be agreeable. She mustn't inspire feelings of anger or resentment, or challenge the status quo. And above all, she mustn't threaten masculine power. Women who do these things aren't just fat bitches. They aren't just hairy monsters. They aren't just recast as desexualised lesbians (which is a completely ludicrous premise in the first place). They're also slapped with one of the most definitive labels you can apply to a woman to disenfranchise her opinions and right to speak: they are ugly, and to be ugly means they serve no purpose to men.

I can't remember the first time I was called ugly, but I can remember the last. It was today. I was called it numerous times by numerous different men, all of whom are so obviously enraged by my refusal to concede ground to them that they've reached for the one word they believe will destroy me. *That'll show her!* you can almost hear them thinking. *She'll think twice before being such a loud-mouthed shrew again!*

BRB, laughing myself into a coma.

We have to stop being afraid of the term 'ugly'. Feminism is about so much more than fighting for the rights of women everywhere to feel beautiful. Beauty is such an arbitrary state, and for women especially it has become an unnecessary trap. If we're aiming to liberate women, we would find more success in doing away with notions of beauty and ugliness altogether. It's fine to want to be pretty – but it's also fine not to care about it at all. Because in exactly the same way that there is nothing wrong with being fat or hairy or a lesbian, there is nothing wrong with not being considered traditionally attractive.

We are not all beautiful snowflakes. But that's okay, because we're so much more than that. We're smart, passionate, angry, funny, complex, flawed, brilliant human beings who are not only more than the sum of our parts but better than the sum of how we make other people's parts feel.

The people who call you ugly are afraid of you and they are afraid of how much you don't need them. And that's why you keep talking anyway.

Slut/whore: Sigh. Raise your hand if you've ever been called one of these and raise both hands if you've been given the double whammy. I'll wait for everyone reading this to pick up their books from the floor, because I guarantee you've just dropped them.

'Slut' and 'whore' are used so interchangeably that they may as well patch them together into a single portmanteau word. A slutwhore or a whoreslut. Mix up the letters of slutwhore and you can spell 'worthluse', which is pretty close to 'worthless', and is essentially what you're being labelled every time an angry troglodyte decides to try to take you down a peg or two because you're not attracted to the way his knuckles drag along the ground. All you need to know about being called a whoreslut is that it has absolutely nothing to do with you and everything to do with the intense terror some men have about the impending collapse of the patriarchy.

Let's unpack what all this means. According to popular theory, sluts and whores are women who have no respect for themselves. They have no respect for themselves because they've engaged in consensual sex with thousands and thousands of men in the past, or maybe even just one man or maybe, astonishingly, no men at all. See, even though A Slut is understood to be a woman who fucks a lot, the extreme diversity of women it's used against – virgins, single women, married women, grandmothers, daughters, bosses, lesbians, sex workers, adolescents, employees and so on and so forth – indicates it's not really about sex at all (not that any of us should care about that anyway).

What's really being thrown down when someone calls a woman a slut or a whore is that she deserves to be fucked as if she's nothing. She deserves to be degraded, violated and humiliated, because she's worth nothing. She is worthluse.

Raise your hand if you've ever been called a slut or a whore for the sex you've had. And raise your other hand if you've ever been called a slut or a whore for rejecting a man's request for sex or even just attention.

I'll just wait while you pick up the book again.

Frigid: Usually used in connection with slut, which is just too hilarious even to bother with. What a bunch of oxymorons.

Bitter: Applied on its own or in tandem with one of the other charming epithets listed above, 'bitter' is supposed to mark women (and feminists especially) as something toxic and unreasonable. There are myriad reasons we're said to be bitter, but once again they all boil down to the supposed depression we feel at being excluded from the male gaze and its associated approval. Here is a list of just some of the reasons why men have said I'm bitter:

Because I'm old and haggard.

Because I'm fat.

Because I'm ugly.

Because men don't want to sleep with me.

Because I'm jealous of the younger, thinner, prettier women who men do want to sleep with.

Because I'm stupid.

Because I have toxic ideas and they're poisoning me from the inside out.

Because feminism is a disease.

It's a curious thing, trying to label someone's opposition to patriarchy as a simple case of bitterness. Never forget that women are expected to accept the supporting roles handed out to us. Instead of aiming for liberation, we're supposed to find happiness by aspiring to the good opinion of men and propping up the structures of power that benefit them. So it doesn't really matter how young, thin and pretty we are. What matters is how willing we are to maintain the illusion that these are the most important things we can be, as judged by a male gaze. If we refuse to be compliant within this power dynamic, we are 'bitter' – as if the acidic fault lies with us for wanting to be thought of as equal rather than a grateful doormat happy to receive a fucking.

But the bitter fruit doesn't care how it tastes to others. If I can make a chauvinist sick up in his mouth at least once a day because he doesn't like what I have to say, I consider that a personal achievement. Bitter is the new black, babes.

Mentally unstable: Modern women who are labelled crazy for valuing and asserting themselves as autonomous human beings join a long tradition of similarly scorned women punished throughout history. In Salem, they burned women as witches when we did things that contradicted the social order and destabilised its power. Over the centuries, women have been institutionalised and subjected to the most horrendous treatment for such 'crimes' as becoming pregnant outside of wedlock; having sex before marriage; having sex outside of marriage; enjoying sex; being depressed; wanting to live independently; being lesbians; being transgender; living in an era where no-fault divorce didn't exist but having husbands who automatically possessed power of attorney and wanted to marry someone else; being women's liberationists – the list goes on and on.

In Patrick Hamilton's 1938 play *Gas Light*, Bella Manningham is subjected to constant psychological abuse by her husband, Jack. He flirts with the servants, disappears at odd times and insists she's imagining it when she tells him the gas light grows dimmer each evening. In fact, Jack is responsible for the fluctuations of the gas light and is aware of it – but it serves what turns out to be his criminal leanings to have Bella believe she's going mad.

Hamilton's play gave rise to the term 'gaslighting', which is a helpful way of pointing out when someone's reasonable perception of events is being deliberately undermined by someone else in order to convince the first person that their behaviour is unsound. Feminists are constantly subjected to attempts to gaslight, from anti-feminist family members, friends and partners and beyond to the broader media and cultural narrative which benefits by painting feminism as irrational and extreme.

And none of this is new. Women have long been accused of 'being hysterical' when it comes to having a political viewpoint that challenges the status quo. Calling a woman 'crazy' isn't a logical argument by any stretch of the imagination, but it's been settled on as an easy way to dismiss the validity of what she's saying. Because any woman who looks around at the structures of power in society and finds them flickering like the gaslights is OBVIOUSLY imagining things and is thus clearly unstable.

But listen – you are not unstable or crazy. You may have issues with depression and anxiety (present), you may have clinically diagnosed issues with mental health, you may wake up some days filled with searing rage that cannot be quelled (goodness knows I do) – but you're not unstable or crazy. The world you live in is real. The way you see it is real. And no one else can define your experience of it, especially not the people for whom those injustices and inequalities are theoretical.

Your experience of living as a woman in this world isn't a product of your imagination and it isn't invisible. I see it too. And so does she, and so does she, and so does she, and so does she.

Little girl: I'm thirty-five years old. I have lived independently for seventeen years. I earn my own money, pay my own bills, cook my own food and fight my own battles. Yet I've lost count of the number of times older men (and some older women, particularly those of a conservative and mildly self-hating bent) spit the word 'child' at me. This is usually accompanied by accusations of being immature, nasty, silly and selfish – a naughty little girl running amok in a world of Serious Adults who would like nothing more than to sit her in a time-out and make her apologise for her harridan ways.

There is a sense, too, that this chiding relates to the inability of so-called argumentative women to 'wake up to the real world' (which is yet another phrase we hear repeatedly). 'Adults' are supposed to have learned that the world isn't always fair and that we don't always get what we want. Children throw tantrums when they don't get what they want. Children need to be disciplined. Children need to realise that the world doesn't owe them anything. Children need to grow up.

But it's no coincidence that it is men who most often berate the women whose behaviour they find disagreeable as 'immature little girls'. The world is predisposed to valuing men's words, actions and deeds. From birth, boys are praised as courageous, strong, tough, bolshy, adventurous, heroic, rambunctious and rough 'n' tumble. Boys who like to play outside, to explore, to get dirty, to build things, to run freely, to use a loud voice, to use sticks as swords, to pretend at being pirates and cowboys and police officers and firefighters – these kinds of boys are referred to as being 'typical'.

Girls, on the other hand, are praised for a much narrower scope of perceived qualities, most notably the ones that involve being pretty, sweet, cute, gentle, diminutive, deferential, kind, thoughtful and helpful. From the moment we're born until the moment we die, girls and women are told what not to do – don't take risks, don't be bossy, don't be too loud, don't get dirty, don't open your legs, don't put your hands in there, don't speak up for yourself, don't be disagreeable, don't backchat, don't provoke the boys, don't eat too much, don't wear revealing clothes, don't get tattoos, don't swear, don't drink too much, don't be rude, don't reject compliments, don't make men feel bad for liking you, don't be too independent, don't be intimidating, don't be a know-it-all. When referring to girls, 'typical' usually means frivolous, appearance-obsessed, delicate, slight and prone to whining.

Am I a little girl? Technically speaking, I'm actually closer to menopause than I am to puberty. I have crow's feet around my eyes and increasingly more whiskers sprouting on my chin. But what does age, experience and the occasionally depressing reality of biology have to do with anything? I am a woman who advocates for liberation in a world that dehumanises, abuses and degrades girls and women on a regular basis. I do all of this without keeping my voice in check, without deferring to male opinion and certainly without asking for permission to speak. And this, in the eyes of gender equality's opponents, makes me

nothing more than a loud-mouthed toddler who has fundamentally misunderstood how the world works.

In desperate need of a root: This is a lovely little observation
offered to me on a regular basis by men who, for the most
part, I wouldn't touch even with a ten-foot pole that was
attached to a cast-iron robot casing in which I could sit while
swaddled in a hazmat suit and a giant, oversized condom. For
international readers, a 'root' is charming Australian slang for
sexual intercourse. Specifically, heterosexual intercourse involving
the penetration of a vagina with a penis. You might know this
sentiment as 'needs a good dick up her' or 'in need of a good
dicking', or perhaps something even less imaginative that involves
being an angry woman who wants cock.

See, feminists aren't driven to despair by the consequences of
misogyny and violence. We aren't enraged by the lack of political
representation, the condescending language used to ridicule and
mock us, the legislation installed by all-male committees to curtail
our reproductive freedoms or the number of women beaten, raped
and murdered every minute of every day. No, we've just been
driven bonkers by the absence of wang in our lives (and beds).
Clearly, what we need is a series of erect cis-het dicks to come
along and cure us of our political beliefs and agitation.

There's another term for this kind of mentality. It's called
corrective rape, and it's routinely employed against women, men,
trans and gender non-conforming people around the world. It's
used as a weapon against sexual expressions and what's perceived
to be unacceptable behaviour. Corrective rape is the heteronormative attempt to punish transgressors by reasserting the rightful
dominance of the heterosexual, cisgender man.

The men who call for difficult women to be fucked into submission might not be actually going out and forcing themselves on and into them. But even joking about it supports an attitude that not-so-subtly suggests that they would be within their rights to – that it is only their benevolence and 'decency' which keeps them from doing so, not awareness of the lack of dominion they have over women's bodies. 'Get a dick up ya' isn't just variously used as an insult or a threat. It's also used as a reminder (sometimes an unconscious one) of the bodily autonomy and power gifted to men as a courtesy and denied to women as a rule. It's a way of saying that women are nothing, and that we'll stay that way until a man comes along and makes us something.

Man-hater/Misandrist: This is one of my favourites, and a good thing too because I probably get called some variation of a misandrist or man-hater at least a few times a day. I think one of things I like about it is that it's underpinned by a layer of astonishment – as if it's not only reprehensible that a woman could have anything remotely close to feelings of ambivalence towards men, but that such a thing could be possible at all. But then there's the nonsensical bent to it. After all, if a woman truly hated men (and presumably knew it), what possible emotional harm could it do to point it out to her?

That's not the point though, is it? When men call me a man-hater or a misandrist, what they're really saying is that there's something wrong with me and the way I refuse to soothe their egos and flatter them with my positive attention. Such an accusation is supposed to make me feel embarrassed and ashamed, because heaven forbid a woman be held in low esteem by a man. But it becomes much easier to ignore the inherent accusation there when you realise the term 'man-hater' isn't really about women hating men at all – it's about women acting outside of the bounds of respectable femininity in a way that adversely challenges men so much that, ironically, they can only respond by hating women. Trust me on this: anyone who calls you a misandrist or a man-hater is either a closet misogynist themselves or invested in perpetuating the patriarchal dominance of men.

This all stems from the basic fear that women's cavalier rejection of men (both in body and thought) will destabilise men's power and dominance. When a woman behaves in a way that indicates she doesn't need a man or his approval (and this can be as simple as refusing to change her opinion to accommodate his, or indicating that she doesn't care what he thinks), the fact of whether or not she likes men in general is irrelevant. She's behaved in a way that makes a single man feel uncomfortable or intimidated or strange or maybe just even dismissed, and the only recourse he believes he has – indeed, the only one he's been conditioned to have – is to make it her problem and her failure. Oh, she disagrees with me or says something that makes me feel as if she might have a life outside of wanting to flatter me and secure my good opinion? She's just another fucking feminazi man-hater, mate.

There was a time when I took special pains to reassure men of my like for them. My speeches and articles were peppered with caveats about how wonderful men were. I wanted everyone to know that of course I loved men. I had a brother and a father and male friends who I just adored! *See?* I was telling them. *You don't need to be scared of me! I'm not here to threaten your masculinity or make you feel bad!*

Vomit.

Because what purpose does that serve? Why does every conversation have to begin with reassuring the men in the room that you think they're more fabulous than the time Cleopatra packed a box full of bees and discovered it could be used as a vibrator? It's such a condescending expectation and a complete waste of energy. All the evangelising in the world about men's natural brilliance won't convince the people who are determined to view feminists as a threat, and trying will only frustrate you further. So let them believe that you hate men if they want to. I promise you it doesn't hurt. It makes no difference to you or your message, and it frees up all this precious time to focus on the message at hand – women's liberation from the prison of gender inequality.

Besides – and this is really important – 'misandry' is not in any way, shape or form comparable to misogyny. It can't be, because that would assume we live in a world where the treatment of men and women is unilaterally equal. It isn't. Women do not have the political, social or economic power to cause any kind of lasting damage to men as a whole.

On the other hand, misogyny *does* have the power to brutalise and harm women, and it employs that power with sustained and terrifying regularity. Every day, women are raped, beaten, trafficked, enslaved and, devastatingly, murdered. In an overwhelming majority of cases, these things are done to them by men. And this isn't a problem which discriminates based on geographical location or race, despite what casual racists and misogynists would like to believe.

Meanwhile, the more casual forms of misogyny are treated either like funny japes or the consequence of women's own silly behaviour. Men are being funny when they humiliate women for being old or fat or ugly, and they're being deadly serious when they urge women to 'take more care' after a bloke decides that having a drink with a woman entitles him to fuck her.

Misogyny kills women. In Australia, it's currently killing women at a rate of roughly 1.5 women per week. Misandry just hurts men's feelings.

Why, then, do so many people seem more outraged by the latter than the former? Why are Facebook memes depicting women tied up and beaten passed off as clever comedy by the men who post them, while the women who criticise those men or simply express their displeasure are accused of being hysterical man-haters determined to paint all men as violent closet rapists? Why, when women are the ones perpetually ridiculed, abused, harmed, humiliated and degraded, are we also the ones expected to apologise for being 'too angry' about it?

I refuse to offer reassurances and caveats about men anymore. It's a waste of time, and it's an insult in a world that privileges these same men in almost every single aspect. I talk about liberating women from the kind of inequality which sees us raped, killed, forced into giving birth, paid less, beaten, humiliated and subjugated, and tries to pass these things off as a seemingly unavoidable part of human nature, perpetrated by no one in particular. If people need to call me a man-hater to justify maintaining that fiction, so be it. I'll just be over here actually doing something about the wretched state of the world, and fighting for the rights of all women to walk freely within it.

■

I can tell you for days on end to laugh at this dross and you would agree with me, but that doesn't stop it from being intrusive, enraging and occasionally upsetting. I know we're joking around here, but don't feel bad if there are still days where you feel so intimidated by the thought of Captain Neckbeard screaming at you that you vow to hide your feminist light under a bushel and never speak of equal rights again.

THIS IS NORMAL.

Take a look around at the feminist guard. Sure, we're battle-scarred now, full of piss and vinegar and an arsenal of wisecracks. But we've all been there. We've all ingested the bullshit dredged up by the patriarchal backlash and decided that the only way around it is to pre-empt revelations of our feminism with disclaimers. Like, 'Oh, but I'm not really like a *feminist*-feminist,' or, 'But don't worry, I totally love men still.'

Something I've learned along the way is that exposure to abuse in an already hostile world really is a feminist's best friend. Trust me on this – the more you hear harsh words used against you, the more immune you become to them and the more ridiculous they seem. It's just impossible to be personally wounded by the phrase 'slutbag cum dumpster' when you're hearing it for the fiftieth time. Don't get me wrong – it's absolutely offensive on a macro level. I find it terribly upsetting that men still use this kind of sexually punitive language to try to put women in their place. But on a personal level, it no longer has the power to weaken me.

It's a bit like how words begin to sound meaningless when you repeat them over and over. Try it now – chant 'fork' for a minute.

Fork fork fork fork fork fork fork fork fork fork fork fork fork fork fork fork fork fork fork fork fork fork fork fork fork fork fork fork fork fork fork fork fork fork fork fork fork fork fork fork fork fork fork fork fork fork fork fork fork fork fork fork fork fork fork fork fork fork fork fork fork fork fork fork fork fork fork fork fork fork fork fork fork fork fork fork fork fork fork fork

fork fork fork fork fork fork fork fork fork fork fork fork fork fork fork fork fork fork fork fork fork fork fork fork fork fork fork fork fork fork fork fork fork fork fork fork fork fork fork fork fork fork fork fork fork fork fork fork fork fork fork fork fork fork fork fork fork fork fork fork fork fork fork.

I guarantee that it'll take less than twenty seconds before you suddenly have no idea what a fork is or why it's supposed to sound like that. Look at the word on the page – doesn't it look weird to you? What the fuck is a fork anyway?

If you want to be open about your feminism, you're going to get a backlash. It's just the way things are. But you are fucking stronger than crumbling under its weight. Women have been subjugated since the dawn of time and we have survived. We have survived despite the odds never being in our favour. We can handle a few snotty words thrown at us by the pathetic, scared little men who truly believe that it's possible to destroy us by calling us fat angry slutwhore ugly hairy immature misandrist bitches who are just crying out for a dick to shut us up.

I mean, we've been hearing this shit for centuries. If they're really all as creative and visionary as they seem to believe, they could come up with something original instead of remaining such an intellectually bereft bag of soggy dickblisters.

Now THAT'S an insult.

–12–

THE GOOD GUYS

In 2015, I celebrated International Women's Day by taking part in an all-day feminist event at the Sydney Opera House. All About Women is steadily becoming a staple on the Opera House's events calendar. Over the last few years, it's gathered incredible women together from both inside and outside Australia to discuss issues of gender equality, leadership, feminism and even, in the case of Leymah Gbowee, to relate how the women of Liberia (tired as they were of male leaders' impotence and foot-dragging) organised themselves to end the Second Liberian Civil War. If there's ever a place to experience Imposter Syndrome, it's in the Opera House's green room during All About Women. This is why I normally just hide in the corner drinking wine, sweating into clothes that are distinctly less glamorous than what everyone else is wearing and hoping I don't make a mess of myself.

On this particular day in 2015, I had both listened to and spoken on a number of panels discussing a broad range of issues.

My head was full of vibrant conversations about men's violence against women, how feminism needs to move beyond seeking equality for white corporate women with white corporate men, the necessity to fight for radical liberation for all women – women of colour, Aboriginal women, disabled women, trans women, Muslim women and every other woman who has been historically sidelined by the feminist movement – and how new technology was creating previously unthought-of spaces that mobilised both collective organising and resistance to the ever-present backlash. In a session called 'Mother Courage', the 2015 Australian of the Year, Rosie Batty, sat in conversation with feminist writer Tara Moss and discussed openly the institutional and social dismissiveness of men's violence against women that had led to her ex-husband murdering her young son right in front of her.

On my last panel of the day, we spoke about the layered invisibility of women in pop culture, and how this artificial reflection of the world's diversity succeeds in diminishing not just our voices and engagement, but reducing even the minimal space we feel we're entitled to occupy. My co-panellists and I talked about the importance of women's anger, and how it has been pathologised as 'hysterical' and 'irrational'. It was the best kind of dialogue – robust and vigorous, and held between people who almost certainly did not agree with each other all of the time but who could at least find common ground in the isolation felt by women within the wider world.

And yet, after all this refreshing focus on liberation and structural oppression, and with three intelligent, competent and experienced women on stage, the very first question to come from the audience queried why feminism doesn't spend more time and energy on engaging male 'champions' and providing space for them to speak about feminism. Why, this woman asked, had that morning's session titled 'How to Be a Feminist', not included a single man on it?

Wait a minute, what?

Make more space for men to be leaders in the feminist movement? Lady, feminism has far too many women it needs to make space for and include in public discourse before it starts worrying about whether or not men are being denied room at the top.

Besides, men are already *everywhere* in modern feminist discourse. If we have to fold in on ourselves any more than we already have just to create additional space for them, we'll be forced to amputate all our limbs. Men are the looming shadow in the room, the invisible spectre that dictates women's discussions and dominates mainstream feminist concern. Women have been instructed so often to worry about what the men will think about every single thing we do or say, every move we make and every thought we think, if we have to start practising feminism like this then we might as well just rebrand it 'society' and be done with it. Instead of being brazen, unapologetic activists fighting for liberation, all too many women have now learned to pepper their politics with caveats, sentiments designed to reassure people that feminism is really a rather gentle kind of philosophy – a group of nice women doing nice things who would like equality if that's okay with everyone else but who most definitely don't pose a threat to the general order of things.

In its quest to be palatable and welcoming, mainstream feminism has become too conciliatory in its aims. You'll no doubt have been at a public talk or discussion about women's rights and heard reassurances that, of course, we are not talking about ALL

MEN! That of course the men in THIS ROOM are good, decent ones who care fiercely about women's rights. That most men are wonderful human beings who wouldn't lift a finger against a woman and who certainly never, ever participate in or benefit from the structures which oppress us.

Because Not All Men, right? I mean, we'd hate to make them feel bad.

On the other hand, if men are genuine allies to women – if they are genuinely invested in our liberation and equality – why should they feel entitled to any kind of acknowledgment or reward? More to the point, why do we feel constantly pressured to give it to them?

This is a challenging prospect for some people. The roots of patriarchy run very, very deep. Some feminists fear that if we don't mollycoddle sympathetic men, they'll throw a tantrum and go home. But doesn't this urge to placate and flatter simply replicate the same power dynamics that underpin our oppression in the first place? Consider the language we use for men who pay even the vaguest lip service to women's liberation. We call them Ambassadors. Champions of Change. Everyday Heroes. We congratulate them for wearing white ribbons and for talking about employing more women. For *talking* about it.

But who's doing the actual work? Women, that's who. And we are never praised for it. We aren't celebrated as Good and Decent people. We aren't heralded widely by our communities. There are no ambassadorships handed to us or titles bestowed like Champion and Hero. When Charlie Pickering writes the occasional article about how bad violence against women is and publishes it on Mamamia (a website read almost exclusively by women who are likely to agree that domestic violence is A Bad

Thing), he gets 50,000 Facebook shares and a thousand women squealing about what an incredible person he is. When a woman does the same thing, she can expect to field dozens or hundreds or sometimes even thousands of comments labelling her anything from a man-hater to a fucking fat whore of a bitch who needs to be shut up by having one cock shoved in her cunt and another one whacked in her mouth.

(A note on Charlie Pickering: it is worth mentioning that a 2015 viral video from his show *The Weekly* which featured a mono-logue on rape culture and an accompanying song performed by three very talented women, neither mentioned any of the feminists who had been raising awareness about that issue for years nor acknowledged that the segment had been devised and pushed for by one of the show's female writers, comedian Cal Wilson. Instead, Pickering was festooned with accolades and praise and called an 'amazing ally', because this is precisely what happens when men lazily co-opt women's work on gender equality and casually, without thought or even recognition that there might be anything wrong with this, pass it off as their own.)

Speaking of men who put in minimal effort where women's rights are concerned, let's talk about programs like White Ribbon and Champions of Change. Once upon a time, I was full of praise for these movements. I couldn't say enough good things about Andrew O'Keefe (who I still love from afar) and his role as a White Ribbon ambassador. 'Look at these wonderful men talking about violence!' I thought to myself. 'Aren't they fantastic?' I saw it not only as my duty to let everyone know how fantastic they were, but my privilege to be able to discuss them in such glowing terms.

I was first disabused of this notion when I was invited to speak at a training day being held for workers in the women's health sector. I was delivering the opening address, which included a few paragraphs about the importance of programs like White Ribbon and praise for the 'exceptional' work I thought they performed. I still cringe when I remember the response from this roomful of frontline service providers; they were exceptionally polite and gentle as they shared with me their concerns that organisations like White Ribbon were very good at receiving large amounts of funding and public attention and not especially good at actually *doing* anything. These were people working directly with survivors and current victims of domestic violence and trying to do the best they could in drastically underfunded organisations. They were mostly women (because women, as we know, perform the vast majority of underpaid carer roles and domestic violence work absolutely falls under this banner), and their work was and is almost completely unrecognised in comparison to the empty gestures of 'ambassadorships' and 'champion' labels.

To be clear, no one enters the women's health sector for the glory. But it is infuriating to watch people continue to do this hard and brutal work only to have the public support they desperately need be diverted to flashier places like the White Ribbon Foundation. This is an organisation that appears more invested in raising awareness for its own brand than tangibly opposing men's violence against women. It has no problem enlisting public representatives with demonstrable records of sexism against women (e.g. Tony Abbott, who is on record as stating it would 'be folly to expect that women will ever dominate or even approach equal representation in a large number of areas simply because their aptitudes, abilities and interests are different for physiological reasons', a view that seemed evident in his establishment of a government cabinet that contained only one woman) or aligning with other organisations that employ men who *definitely* have track records of violence against women (e.g. radio station Triple M, with whom White Ribbon partnered in late 2015 despite the fact it employs in on-air positions both Matty Johns, a former NRL footballer involved in a team-related pack sex incident which left a nineteen-year-old woman suicidal and suffering from ongoing PTSD, and Wayne Carey, a former AFL football player whose conduct towards women is well known – in 1996, he pleaded guilty to grabbing a woman's breasts outside a nightclub and declaring, 'Why don't you go and get a bigger set of tits?' He was later charged with assaulting police officers in Miami after his then-girlfriend Kate Nielson alleged he had smashed a wine glass in her face (she later dropped the charges).

A friend of mine, a man who formerly supported White Ribbon, recently told me that only about 40 percent of surveyed ambassadors identify as feminists. Oh sure, they're happy to boast the title of 'Ambassador', a title that allows them to claim the status of Good Guy Who Cares About Women, but they don't consider it important to align themselves with the movement that advocates for equality between the sexes.

But that doesn't matter, because being associated with White Ribbon has become a shorthand way for people to tell themselves (and everyone else) that they're making a difference. This isn't always a duplicitous gesture. For some individuals, it's just a matter of being a little ignorant about the fact that there are other organisations they can team with to achieve more. This doesn't make them terrible people. They have at least expressed an interest in figuring out how to change the world for the better. Unfortunately, they've been convinced that their engagement with the issue stops when they put that white ribbon on and take their pledge, and further empowered by a wider society that reassures them this is enough.

Because why should they do more? They don't have to. Literally no force or movement in society with any discernible power is trying to make men do any more than this. The equality illusion is exactly that – equality is conceived as something metaphorical rather than tangible. Equality is currently interpreted by most of society as a commitment rather than an action. Frustratingly, the only commitment required from men is in them just saying they support equality for women, even while they continue to enjoy the specific benefits granted to them under a patriarchal system.

What happens when a woman suggests that equality means more than this? That equality might actually mean men sacrificing a good chunk of their power so that women might achieve parity with them? Anarchy! Men can't give anything up! That's unfair! That's the OPPOSITE of equality, people losing something! How does that even work? It's not really equality, is it, if someone comes out worse? That's the problem with feminism – you don't want equality, you want superiority! Misaaaaaaaandry!

This tedious, shrieking response to any discussion that attempts to frame equality as something more than just a word men and women say means feminists end up feeling pressured to scrap this 'cruel, mean-spirited, unequal, misandrist' approach and go back to the one which achieves nothing and gets us nowhere – the one which involves men being able to just say they support equality and enjoy all of the resulting accolades and praise, but which doesn't result in them losing their edge in the workplace, their financial supremacy, opportunities for promotion, speaking rights, leadership roles, position as unspoken head of the family unit, right to talk to or touch women whenever they feel like it and greater domination of the overall physical, emotional and mental space that we occupy as human beings.

Here's a ribbon. Pin it on. Don't worry, we won't ask you to think about anything beyond that because we know you're a Good Bloke.

And that's just the individuals. When we look at the corporate engagement with programs like White Ribbon, it's even more depressing. In fact, lending support to White Ribbon has become an easy way for the organisations that are still overwhelmingly dominated by men and male thinking to mitigate the role they play in perpetuating damage done to women. Get your all-male board of directors to stand up there on 25 November with a white ribbon pinned to their lapel and it doesn't matter what happens during the rest of the year – you are White Ribbon-affiliated, and that means you are Agents of Change.

In 2015, Western Australia Police tweeted out their support for White Ribbon, asserting their commitment to a future in which women don't experience violence. This is fairly comical, given their record on the treatment of Aboriginal women. Earlier in the year, police in Port Hedland imprisoned a twenty-three-year-old Aboriginal woman (named in the press as 'Ms Dhu') for the shocking crime of a couple of unpaid fines. They did little to secure proper medical attention for her as she went into septic shock in front of them (one officer later testified that they thought she was faking it) and she died.

She died.

She died.

She died.

This is the same police force which has been in the press for issuing an astronomical fine to an Aboriginal woman living in poverty who was caught shoplifting tampons from her local supermarket. But sure, they're totes into helping chicks out because white ribbons look great on their uniforms.

Those who can't interpret the punishment of a poor woman for stealing sanitary products as a form of violence are among the majority who don't understand that the broad complexity of violence is compounded against those who also suffer the oppression of racial inequality, poverty, ableism, homophobia, transphobia and mental illness. But again, having even a minimal understanding of what constitutes violence is irrelevant to the White Ribbon equation.

All the sporting codes in the country make a big show of supporting the White Ribbon foundation. They trot out their ribbons and pledges on 25 November and then spend the rest of the year allowing men facing charges of sexual assault and/or domestic abuse to continue playing and being paid. When people question them on this, their supporters come out in rabid support, yelling, 'Innocent until proven guilty! Should he not be allowed to work and earn a wage?!' As if it's going to economically ruin a football player to be suspended from playing a few games. Meanwhile, sporting forums and Facebook groups are filled with comments casting judgment on the women involved. They're star-fuckers and footy sluts. They're lying. They wanted it and then they changed their minds later. They were mad because he just wanted a fuck and didn't want to go out with them. They're making it up to get revenge. They're ruining a man's life.

Eddie McGuire can get on radio and make hilarious 'jokes' about drowning a female colleague, but it's not like he really *means* it. Danny Frawley and James Brayshaw can enthusiastically go along with him but it's all just playful 'banter', right? Stop getting your knickers in a twist! If women can't handle the rough and tumble nature of the footy field, they should bugger off!

Oh, but don't worry, they're all Good Guys. He's a Good Guy, he's a Good Guy and he's a Good Guy. It doesn't matter that they tell sexist jokes and tell women to get back into the kitchen, to stop overreacting, to be less irrational, are you sad, love, just because you can't get a root? You need a good root, if you weren't so ugly maybe you could get a root, I'd throw you a root but even I'm not that generous, you just need a good dick up ya, I bet you'd jibber less if you had a cock in your mouth, you big fucking lesbian dyke, man-hater, fuck you, you fat bitch, dog, whore, slut, cunt, *you are nothing.*

This is just the tip of the iceberg when it comes to the discrepancy between what White Ribbon claims to represent and what it actually does. Unfortunately, most of the women's health sector workers that I speak with on a regular basis are too afraid to say any of this publicly because they're scared their organisation's already paltry funding will be further cut.

This was just one of the many things I realised that day, after I presented my naive thoughts to a roomful of people infinitely more qualified than I to discuss these issues but who responded to my inexperience with kindness and patience. I accepted their invitation to stay for the remainder of the training, and I learned more in those two hours than I had in years of reading newspaper articles and participating in 'this is what I think' conversations with similarly unenlightened people. Even now, one of the reasons I love being invited to work with women's health organisations is because of the sheer wealth of knowledge I encounter. It has been my great privilege to absorb information from women like Ada Conroy, who works not only for an organisation helping domestic violence victims and survivors but who moonlights as a men's behavioural change therapist, and Diana Labiris, who flicked a floodlight on in my brain simply by asking me to think of what it meant that almost all of the people behind the thankless organisation, catering and clean-ups of the White Ribbon morning teas that are designed to celebrate men's contributions to the cause are women.

I know now why that is. It's because women do the work. We always have. It is usually done without complaint or protestation, because most girls are conditioned from birth to accept that unpaid domestic labour is our natural responsibility. White Ribbon is supposed to be an organisation where men speak to other men about violence prevention – but it's women who send out the invitations, plan the food, type up the name tags, wait at the door to greet arriving guests and then sit and listen as corporate suits are applauded for being Good Guys.

Do men really need to be acknowledged for doing the right thing? Do they even realise they're taking credit for work that women have performed more tirelessly and with greater risk to their health and wellbeing? Do men need to be revered and admired, their egos stroked with the palms of a thousand tired hands?

Or is it that women believe men need to have these things in order to continue caring about us – that this is the negotiated trade we must make to get them even nominally interested in helping disrupt the violence we suffer at the hands of their brothers?

To the men who may be reading this: I am not interested in placating you, nor do I care if feminism makes you personally uncomfortable. It should make you uncomfortable, and if you are genuinely interested in becoming part of a better world, you will take that discomfort and use it to find a better way. Women are being killed in ridiculous numbers. Sexism is rife across every level of society. You may not be personally responsible for any of this, but you are also not targeted by the aggression of it. This isn't about your feelings. So stop expecting women to preface their anger and activism with disclaimers that, of course, it's not about YOU.

Because it is. It's about you because it's about patriarchy, and even the kindest, nicest, most supportive and decent man benefits from this structure in ways that women just don't. Men have to be proactive in recognising that and fighting against it, and that requires effort and commitment. It's not enough to just turn up.

YOU have to do the work.

But why are you being so mean to me? you might be thinking. Why are you making me feel like this is all my fault?

Listen up, son, because I want to work with you on this. You have to get over this idea that when feminists talk about men's violence against women (which is more broadly about the dominion of men as a whole over women) that we are talking about you personally. No matter how vulnerable and defensive these conversations might make you feel, no one is actually coming around to your house and screaming through the windows, 'Tyler, you fucking abusive bag of shit, get your arse out here now and answer to your crimes!' If you are feeling sensitive, it is because the last decade of feminism has regrettably made a concerted effort to bring issues of gender inequality to the fore by steadily removing almost all mention of men's complicity. Of course you're feeling antsy at being thrust into the spotlight now – haven't you always been told that most men are wonderful, brilliant creatures who would never do anything terrible to a woman? Having been reassured that this is not really about you at all, it must be difficult to sit there and listen while angry, misandrist feminazis like myself point a finger in your direction. That's not fair! You're a good person!

But are you? I mean, really? I'm just going to throw this out there because, as far as provocative truth bombs go, it's been ticking away for too long: this universal male decency we keep hearing about is largely a myth.

Sure, most men might not be bad. You're probably not bad. But it takes more than 'not being bad' to be 'actually good'.

■

Whenever conversation is raised about patriarchy, violence and the lack of equality that still permeates our society, I find myself inundated with messages or comments from men offended by the discussion of male-perpetrated violence. Most men, they take ostentatious pains to remind me, are 'decent', so why do I insist on tarring all of them with the same brush? It's not fair and it's not true. If I want their ongoing support, I had jolly well better start being nicer to them.

Leaving aside the arrogance it requires to listen to a conversation about the gendered violence suffered by women and make it about your hurt feelings (not to mention the privilege in knowing you can just walk away from social justice without really being affected), I'd like to know where the evidence is for this so-called decency. Is it in the number of men who stand by while sexist jokes are made because 'it's meant to be funny'? Is it drawn from those folks who want women to know that even though they're not saying it's our fault, we shouldn't have been drinking so much? Is it found in the proportions of dudes who talk about how it's women's own incompetency that's holding us back from sitting in positions of power or being paid equal wages for equal work? Is it in the number of men who wax lyrical about how 'ugly' women are when we express a robust opinion, or dare to not pluck and preen their bodies in a way that 'all' men find pleasing (a supposedly universal revulsion made slightly inconvenient by the number of men who are either indifferent to hair or actively turned on by it)?

Are these men really 'good'? Or is their supposed decency constructed entirely around the fact they've never beaten a woman and they won't let anyone say anything nasty about their mothers? How can we really know?

The truth is, all it takes to be hailed as a 'decent bloke' is to take an each-way bet at doing nothing – nothing to perpetuate oppression, sure, but also nothing to stop it. As if the privilege of this complacency weren't bad enough, some of these 'decent blokes' want to be rewarded for their lack of action, an expectation that not-so-subtly reveals the very same entitlement that serves to perpetuate gender inequality. Translated, what they're really saying is, 'Praise me, because I have refrained from behaving in a way both you and I know I could get away with if I wanted to. Please may I have my cookie now? Actually, just give it to me.'

Have you heard the joke about the male feminist who walked into a bar? It was because it was set so low.

There's a scene at the end of the wonderful film *Made in Dagenham* where this very concept is explored. Written by William Ivory, the film is one of those classic British feel-good productions where an oppressed class rises up against their superiors and fights for justice. In this instance, it depicts the fight for equal pay conducted by female sewing machinists at Dagenham's Ford factory in the late 1960s. Led by Rita O'Grady (played to perfection by Sally Hawkins), the women's protest against gender discrimination becomes so big and powerful that it leads to the creation of the UK's Equal Pay Act 1970. As the movement gains momentum, their struggle finds itself undermined by some of the male union heavyweights. On her way to speak to a vote that would force the union to back them, Rita is confronted by her husband, Eddie. He's trying to stop her from going, and decides to use the bargaining chip of what a Great Guy he is. Eddie reminds Rita that, unlike many of the other husbands, he isn't at the pub every night getting drunk or out 'screwin' other women'. ''Ere,' he says, 'I've never once raised me hand to you. Or the kids!'

When I watched this movie for the first time, my heart sank in this moment. I felt sure that Rita was going to capitulate to Eddie, and go back to the role of the dutiful wife. My heart was ready to break at the thought of her returning to her kitchen while her colleagues went on without her to force the union to take them seriously. How many women have sacrificed their dreams and political ambitions in similar situations – because they've been reminded of the positions they are supposed to fill instead and weren't supported enough to break out of them?

Not Rita, though. I should have known better than to doubt her! She takes one look at Eddie and hisses, 'Christ. You're a saint now, is that what you're tellin' me, Eddie? You're a bleedin' saint? 'Cause you give us an even break?'

'What are you saying?' he responds, astonished that this hasn't worked out as he (and I) thought it would.

Rita goes in for the kill.

'That's as it should be!' she explodes. 'Jesus, Eddie! What do you think this strike's all been about, eh? Oh yeah. Actually, you're right. You don't go on the drink, do ya? You don't gamble, you join in with the kids, you don't knock us about. Oh, lucky me! For Christ's sake, Eddie, that's as it should be! You try and understand that.'

Rita delivers her final blow.

'Rights, not privileges,' she says. 'It's that easy. It really bloody is.'

And it really bloody is.

In many ways, Eddie represents the challenge facing many men who otherwise consider themselves to be decent blokes. Eddie *was* a nice man. In Rita's community, he was the kind of husband a woman would be considered lucky to have. But that's only because the bar for all the others was set so exceptionally low that all Eddie needed to do to be considered a prize catch was not have an alcohol problem, be a womaniser or beat his wife and kids. Should he or any man expect a medal for such basic decency? And what does it say about the perceived domain of masculinity if this kind of decency makes you the exception to the rule?

Too many of us labour under the assumption that being good is simply a matter of being not bad. It says a lot about those of us who are privileged (and as a middle-class, cisgender, employed white woman, I include myself in those ranks) that we have made it so easy to frame decency as being merely the opposite of active discrimination. Am I a good person to people of colour simply because I don't attend KKK meetings or burn crosses on my front lawn? Am I an active ally to Aboriginal people because I don't use hate speech to describe them or dress up in blackface for costume parties? Am I a friend to trans people just because I 'let' trans women use 'my' bathroom and I sobbed after watching *Boys Don't Cry*? Are disabled people less discriminated against in my presence just because I don't call them cripples or spastics and I thought Stella Young was a genius?

Of course not. Not purposefully contributing to the oppression felt by people already marginalised by the system doesn't make me a champion of human rights. I might not be actively making things worse for another human being, but that doesn't mean I'm doing anything to make things better. What it might mean is that I maintain a conscious neutrality on the social circumstances which make their lives harder while enjoying the benefits that come my way simply because those systems are designed in my favour. My privilege in these areas affords me the luxury of remaining impartial if I choose while allowing me to feel secretly smug about what a wonderful, accommodating person I am.

It took me some time to learn this (because society is not generally overly concerned with the top levels of hierarchy having to learn anything about why their power is so undeserved), but unpacking privilege is a lifelong process. It can't be done in a day. White people, for example, don't get to read an article about racism, nod our heads and then suddenly decide our personal growth work is done. Until we live in a world where racial discrimination is eradicated, even well-meaning white people like myself will always be guilty of committing micro-aggressions and making mistakes. Arguing against that reality isn't only disingenuous, it creates further harm for the people who have to endure the sting of racism every day. The best we can do is to commit to learning from, listening to and signal boosting the work of people for whom racist oppression is a reality. Not the white people who think it's our right to decide what is and isn't racist, a ranking system that's usually based on the attitudes, jokes, beliefs and prejudices many of us not only don't want to have to sacrifice but want to be further protected from having to feel bad about.

The same is true for gender inequality. Men who refrain from doing the wrong thing are no more or less than just that. They are not heroes just because they don't behave like misogynist pricks. If a man doesn't beat his family or cheat on his wife but still laughs at sexist jokes or stands by while they're happening, is he really a great promoter of equal rights? Or is he just a normal person making his own way down the river of life and causing no great ripples either way?

There are two lessons that are vital for us to learn if we have any hope of overcoming the sinkhole of action that lives inside the Making Sure Men's Feelings Aren't Hurt By Feminism movement.

First, we are under no obligation to reward men for being basically okay. Feminism is the fight to bring about gender equality and equity for all, not the battle to gain equality for women as long as men are okay with that. It will not be won by replicating the same patterns of patriarchy that, among other things, sees men taking credit for women's work, having to work half as hard to be praised twice as much and being automatically inserted into positions of leadership simply because we are still battling the deeply ingrained social conditioning that makes everyone instinctively believe men are just better placed to wield authority. No one deserves a medal because they managed to resist being a certified fuck-knuckle *even though – and maybe especially because – they could if they wanted to but they didn't*. We need to reposition men's opposition to violence, sexism and gender inequality as the norm, not keep acting as if it's some kind of mind-blowing display of sacrificial kindness.

Secondly, we have to start being okay with saying that. I know it's difficult, but men aren't children or dogs. They don't get a cookie because they did the right thing. Not giving them a reward is not the same as swearing at them or throwing a bucket of shit at their head, even though some of them might act as if it is. We have to resist the urge to respond to basic decency by treating it as if it's some kind of enormously magnanimous gesture. It isn't. There shouldn't be anything astonishing about a man who doesn't degrade women, hurt them or treat them as somehow less than him. As Rita O'Grady says, *that's as it should be*. You don't get a fucking ribbon just for turning up to a morning tea, especially not when women's reward for doing so much more than that is to gratefully scoop up the crumbs you leave behind.

Rights, not privileges, Eddie. It's that easy. It really bloody is.

WHEN WILL YOU LEARN?

In the early hours of 22 September 2012, a young woman walking home from a night out with her friends stops to talk for a few moments with a man unknown to her. Perhaps made uncomfortable by his demeanour, she feigns needing to make a phone call. She places a call to her brother in Ireland and resumes her journey home. Moments later, as she turns down a side street, she is dragged into an alleyway by the same man. She is raped and strangled. Her body is left there while her assailant goes to pick up his car. She is wrestled into the boot, driven to a lonely patch of ground fifty kilometres north-west of where she died and buried in a shallow grave. She lies there for seven days before she is found.

The woman's name was Jill Meagher. Two days after police recovered her body, 30,000 people marched down Sydney Road in Brunswick – the road where Jill Meagher had encountered her attacker – to protest men's violence against women. It was a watershed moment, pricking the nation's conscience and precipitating greater discussion of the trauma and abuse visited on women daily. It was also perhaps the first time I noticed widespread use of the phrase 'rape culture' in the Australian media; that term has subsequently been absorbed into the Australian vernacular.

It seemed to be the start of some kind of change.

I remember that week vividly. The public's distress over the disappearance of this 'beautiful, radiant' Irish girl was palpable. Her husband's grief, compounded by the fact that he was initially under suspicion (because it is almost always the husband or the boyfriend or the man known to the woman who is responsible for her destruction), trickled down on a city already made grey by a winter that had spilled over into spring. In a twist so cruel it would seem overwrought in a crime novel, it would later emerge that a worried Tom Meagher had tried to telephone his missing wife at the exact moment she was being killed just a few streets away.

That week exemplified some of the more potent elements of rape culture, particularly the propensity to place the onus of prevention and responsibility onto its potential victims. On a Facebook page set up to help find Jill, one man wrote the following:

She was obviously at a bar/club, left there in the early hours of the morning, obviously partially pissed/drunk, and she 'lead someone on' [sic] and the consequences followed her. If she is going to flirt with someone, make sure that you go through with it because someone is obviously pissed off with her . . . in my opinion, it's now old news, she met with foul play as a result of her actions inside the pub/bar OR as I mentioned before . . . ask the husband.

As repugnant as these views are, I expect nothing less from the bottom-feeding troglodytes who belch their way up through the bile of humanity's most pointless specimens to make sure their Very Important Opinions about how women should and shouldn't behave are heard. Of course this man thinks women and our wily, flirty underpants areas are responsible for the violence enacted against us, because this man is made entirely out of garbage, and his skull is filled with the garbage water that ferments and drips out of the bag's corners onto your bare toes and makes you gag. Leaving aside for a moment the dazzling lack of understanding about consent contained in the line, 'If she is going to flirt with someone, make sure that you go through with it because someone is obviously pissed off with her', this guy is not especially unique. He is a classic victim blamer, refusing to address how violence and entitlement manifest to expressly excuse perpetrators while further criminalising women who simply want to be treated like autonomous human beings. He is probably married and has daughters, and he uses this fact to establish himself as some kind of common sense expert and champion for women's rights.

Garbage Man is a problem, but mainly insomuch as he's reflective of a broader narrative that gets played out over and over again and reinforced by those in positions of relative authority. Only a couple of days after Jill went missing, Neil Mitchell – who, for reasons still unclear to me, is a well-known and seemingly respected talkback radio host on Melbourne's 3AW – expressed on air the hope that she had been 'off partying somewhere, [because] judging from her Facebook page she likes a good party'. That it's become de rigueur for journalists to rummage around on private Facebook pages in order to pad out already distressing stories is problematic enough – that Mitchell found it necessary to comment on what kind of lifestyle Jill may or may not have enjoyed in what was at the time a speculative story about her probable abduction simply beggars belief.

Shortly afterwards, Melbourne's *Herald Sun* newspaper ran a long, unnecessarily dramatised piece by their resident crime writer, Andrew Rule. Rule spent approximately a thousand words painting a picture of a beautiful, naive young woman who simply should have known *better* than to walk down the dark, forebidding corridor of Hope Street when she could have taken an alternative, longer route that Rule – who does not live in the area and does not regularly use its streets – determined to be safer and more sensible. Waggling his finger at the silly, thoughtless girl who'd gone and got herself missing, he wrote:

> Police believe the stretch of Hope St from Sydney Rd west across the railway line is Jill's usual route home to their apartment. We all have our favourite routes, from habit rather than logic. But for a stranger looking around in daylight, there seems no obvious reason why a young woman would choose to walk this way home late at night . . . There are better spots for a young woman to be walking alone after a night out drinking with workmates, ending in Sydney Rd after starting in the city.

This kind of tongue-clucking, finger-wagging attitude isn't uncommon, particularly when it comes to women who wander too far from the path of 'common sense' and 'get themselves in trouble'. As a society, we need catch little more than a whiff of the Harmed Woman before people fall over themselves to declare what it is she and her short skirt did wrong and how future women can take sensible precautions to avoid falling into the same arbitrary, in-no-way-shape-or-form-connected-to-actual-perpet-rators-or-social-attitudes kind of stinky mess. You know, just in case we were in any danger of forgetting that sexual assault and violence is something women just stumble into because our silly lady-brains weren't paying an appropriate amount of attention.

You know the drill. Don't walk alone at night. Don't wear revealing clothes. Don't drink too much. In fact, don't drink at all. Don't talk to strange men, but don't ignore men who are probably just trying to have a conversation with you – can't a man even have a *conversation* with a woman these days without being accused of being a rapist, how dare you unfairly malign ALL MEN with your paranoia and man-hating, don't you know that 99 percent of men are good and decent and would never harm a woman? What do you mean, you let him walk you home? What were you thinking? Don't you know how dangerous that is? You girls have to learn how to take better care of yourselves, you can't just go walking around with strange men, it's not safe, you never know what might happen, you'll give them the wrong idea. What do you mean, you won't let me walk you home? But I'm just trying to get you home safely, I'm not a threat to you, how dare you make me feel like I might be a threat to you! You know, you're the reason why men are giving up on even trying to be polite to women anymore, because look what happens when we try to do the decent and right thing: we just get treated like there's something wrong with us. That's the problem with feminism, it makes all men out to be rapists. What do you mean, you invited him in for a drink? Don't you know what kind of message that sends? Ladies, when will you learn? If you don't want any trouble, don't invite it into your house! Of course something happened – what did you expect?

Later, people would argue that the unrelenting, horrified public attention Jill received was a classic example of Missing White Woman syndrome. There's truth to this; pretty white girls from nice middle-class backgrounds are absolutely valued more highly than those other women more likely to be targeted by violence. Women of colour, sex workers, trans women, poor women, drug-addicted women, old women, fat women, ugly women – these women don't play so well on the cover of a newspaper or as headlining stories on the nightly news. I would never begrudge anyone, particularly a woman from any of those demographics, feeling angry over how disappearances like Jill's reinforce the hierarchy of value that women occupy in the eyes of society.

But there were other things that contributed to the force with which Jill was thrust into people's minds. She worked for the ABC, which made her one of the media's own. She lived in the inner city, alongside numerous other young women who were accustomed to walking home by themselves at night after drinking on nearby Sydney Road. And, perhaps most significantly, her disappearance and subsequent discovery took place over a single, neat week that was punctuated by intermittent developments. The planting of her handbag in a laneway off Hope Street. The release of CCTV footage showing a 'person of interest' talking to Jill outside a bridal store near her turn-off. The news that a man fitting the same description had tried to rape a Dutch backpacker months before. Cafes and bars buzzed with theories about what it could all mean, while enjoying the sense of narrative power that came from being armchair detectives. Amid all of this, a basic and gross human contradiction revealed itself. There was the visceral hope that Jill would be found alive. There was the horrible frisson of depraved excitement that she might not.

It was grey and rainy the morning news broke that the man from the CCTV footage had led police to where he'd taken Jill's body. I cried when my boyfriend told me, but it wasn't just for the way she had been killed. It was also for the way she'd been discarded, as if she were a fast food wrapper tossed out a car window onto the highway, the occupants suddenly considering themselves too good to have to deal with the detritus of treats they'd excitedly demolished only moments before. He had raped her, brutalised her and strangled her to death because her unwillingness to speak with him and 'be nice' had made him mad. He had done all of those things to her, and then that fucking bastard had driven her far away from where she belonged and just dumped her in a hole on the side of the road.

■

The rape and murder of Jill Meagher mobilised a new wave of discussions in Everyday Australia about the impact of men's violence against women, particularly when rape was a factor. It wasn't dissimilar to the grief and outrage felt over the 1986 murder of Anita Cobby, a young nurse abducted on her way home from work by five young men who then spent a number of hours gang-raping, torturing and mutilating her before finally leaving her to die in a paddock.

In 1986, phrases like 'rape culture' had no traction in suburban Australia, but the concept of the Lurking Monster certainly did. Girls were taught (as they always have been) to fear strange men – the things they could do to us were worse than anything our fevered minds could conjure up. Modern history is full of the terrifying stories of young girls and women like Jill and Anita, snatched from the streets by depraved men intent on inflicting punishment and violence on them. Ebony Simpson, Janine Balding, Sophie Collombet, Stephanie Scott – they all linger as the ghostly evidence of what can happen if we fail to take proper care.

The problem with this account is that it only tells a tiny fraction of the story. In the grand, sweeping narrative of women's experience of violence, our 'worst nightmare' forms but a footnote. A convenient ghost story, sure – but, like most ghost stories, predicated on our own creeping sense of fear and the unknown. The truth is that men's sexual violence against women is found far less frequently in the dark and shadowy alleyways of popular nightmare than in the quiet, mundane streets of suburbia. It suits the cultural narrative (dominated as it is by masculine ideology) to imagine something so brutal as rape occupying a form of Hollywood cinematography, but the reality is quite different. Friends, acquaintances, boyfriends, family members: these are the men who statistically pose the biggest threat to girls and women, and it is the stories of these men that are whispered between us, confessed over bottles of wine and shared around as proof of membership to a club nobody ever wanted to join.

But here's the thing about rape culture. Like the devil, the greatest trick it ever pulled was in convincing the world it doesn't exist. It doesn't matter how many rooms and houses and buildings and cathedrals can be filled to bursting with the hauntings of abused women, how many names can be thrown into the fire around which all women are invited to chant their truths, how many scars (both physical and emotional) can be brandished to show the depth of all of these wounds – none of that matters in a world in which all that is required to discredit a woman's entire being is to point at her and yell: LIAR.

'Yeah, where's your proof?'

'That doesn't sound right to me.'

'I don't find that very believable.'

'It probably didn't happen like that.'

'Regretting it after the fact doesn't make it rape.'

One of the most heartbreaking things I've learned as a woman is how little people (even other women, conditioned as we've all been to bend towards patriarchy and prop up the rape culture it cultivates) are prepared to believe women when we offer testimony about our lives. Stand up and tell a story about your own lived experience and then wait for the inevitable dissenting interruption from someone who wasn't there and who knows absolutely nothing about you beyond the fact you're challenging their comfortable notion of the world. Despite the overwhelming evidence (both statistical and anecdotal) that's available on the prevalence of sexual violence, it is still far easier for people to believe that women are lying or exaggerating or misinterpreting a situation than it is for them to believe that Ordinary Men could be capable of such things. In the consciousness of broader society, people are far more horrified by the idea men could be impugned with such mystifying accusations than they are the fact that women are subjected to such abuse every day.

Of course, this is also vehemently denied. Most people will swear black and blue that they condemn rape, that all rapists should be locked up, given a taste of their own medicine, hounded until the end of time, executed, beaten to a bloody pulp and so on and so forth until all possible variations of revenge fantasy have been exhausted. But this is a fate only suitable for the concept of the rapist they've constructed in their minds – the rapist who acts like Adrian Bayley, who snatches poor, innocent white girls off the street, stealing them from their husbands and families and robbing the world of their gentle smiles. What happens when he looks more like their favourite sports star, or the local football hero? Their son? Their brother? Their friend?

Suddenly, things get a little murky. These men who look like our brothers, friends, sons, colleagues, and teammates – men like that don't *rape* women, for crying out loud. We know them! We josh about with them, we drink with them, talk with them on the internet. Sure, they make the odd ribald joke, but who hasn't done that? No, they couldn't possibly be responsible for something as heinous and horrifying as sexual assault. *She must be lying.*

No matter how much evidence is offered to the contrary about the profiles of generic rapists and their wholly generic lives, this narrative keeps reiterating itself time and time again. And the violated bodies of girls and women keep piling up, just another set of notches scratched into the bedposts of a world that doesn't give a shit.

■

I used to think I wanted to be a lawyer when I left school, until I realised I actually just wanted to play one on TV. Discovering this somewhat lessened the sting of missing out on the necessary marks to study law at university, a relief that was starkly magnified once I met some of the people who'd actually got in and heard about torts (not a fancy cake, as I had hoped).

Since becoming a feminist writer, the distance between me and the law (or those who practise it at least) seems only to have widened further. I now find myself fielding angry emails or subtweets from defence lawyers in particular who cannot abide how ignorant I am when it comes to How The Law Actually Works.

'Clementine,' they'll write to me witheringly, 'there is no conspiracy taking place here. What you are witnessing is merely the proper and full execution of the law. White Male Magistrate #7,098,283 is simply interpreting the law as it has been written, and you cannot blame him for doing so. A suspended sentence of [insert paltry number of months or years] for this sex crime is not the equivalent of a slap on the wrist, because the threat of jail is actually very scary. Stop writing about things you don't understand. Sincerely, Annoyed Male Defence Lawyer #5097.'

I find this hyper-defensive argument interesting, because it implies that what is essentially little more than a social doctrine has been written by a power higher than ourselves – that it is infallible and constant and not at all influenced by cultural ideas or practices. I mean, it's almost as if the law hasn't been crafted and passed down throughout the years by a group made up predominantly of white men from privileged backgrounds and for whom violence against women is largely a theoretical quandary.

This citation of the law as some kind of incontrovertible celestial ruling is particularly galling when you see how it helps to prop up the foundations of a very much man-made rape culture. If you're paying any kind of attention at all, you'll know that society overwhelmingly directs the responsibility for rape prevention towards women. These are the social 'laws' that women are instructed to follow if we want to participate in general life. We're reminded frequently to 'take care of ourselves'. To not drink too much, dress sensibly and not behave unwisely with strange men. Our bodies are positioned as some kind of external piece of equipment that, without proper care and attention, can be stolen or broken into after we've been careless enough to leave them discarded or unlocked somewhere. Stranger-rape still dominates most of the conversation around rape prevention, despite it posing the least likely risk to women's bodily safety. Because of this, the majority of victims and the factors which lead to their abuse are ignored.

Our current strategy of expecting women to be responsible for preventing rape ignores two fundamental issues: how rape is both a gendered crime and an act of casual dehumanisation. But more so, it shifts the emphasis from legislative and law enforcement bodies to actually end sexual violence (or at least establish zero tolerance policies around it) to that of 'social law' – i.e. the need for women to self-regulate so that we don't disrupt the status quo.

In 2013, American political analyst Zerlina Maxwell earned the damnation of the Fox News audience when she appeared on the show *Hannity* to discuss whether or not women should be armed in order to protect themselves from sexual assault. Maxwell, a rape survivor, made the daring suggestion that women shouldn't be directed to do anything when it comes to sexual violence. Instead, she argued that we need to start telling men not to rape people.

As Maxwell so succinctly told host Sean Hannity, 'You're talking about this as if it's some faceless, nameless criminal, when a lot of times it's someone you know and trust. If you train men not to grow up to become rapists, you prevent rape.'

Cue predictable outrage and, ironically, an onslaught of threats against Maxwell that included rape. Because there is nothing more frightening to a society intent on demonising women's behaviour than even the merest hint that men's behaviour might be in need of regulation.

Here is the uncomfortable truth that remains conspicuously absent from most mainstream discussions about rape prevention: rape is a gendered crime almost always committed by men. Figures released by the Victorian Crime Statistic Agency show that in the fiscal year of 2011/2012, 78 percent of juvenile and 90 percent of adult victims of sexual assault were women, while 95 percent of juvenile offenders and adult offenders were men.

This isn't to say that all men are potential rapists (although the culture of rape apology certainly paints them that way when it perpetuates the idea that men have sexual needs that can be triggered by women's behaviour), nor does it deny that men can be victims themselves. It's merely to state the obvious: that rape is a crime almost solely perpetrated by men and almost solely experienced by women.

But perhaps it's easier for men to absolve themselves of responsibility for caring about these numbers because, unless they're in a high risk group for incarceration, the threat of rape isn't something they're taught to live with. And if they don't feel like rape is something they'll ever perpetrate, then it's easy to imagine it has nothing to do with them at all. The fears and threats to women therefore become our problem alone to solve, far away from any space in which men might have to hear about it and thus be unfairly maligned or implicated.

Again, this comes back to the way a form of social law is practised around sexual assault in place of an effective public and judicial legislation that places the onus of blame onto perpetrators. Why can't we mount an effective campaign that puts men front and centre as both the cause *and* the solution? Because here's another stat to add to those cited above. When Canada ran its 'Don't Be That Guy' campaign, a visual project directing men to alter their behaviour by shifting the responsibility of rape and sexual assault prevention onto them, reported incidents of sexual assault dropped by 10 percent. This is a significant difference when you consider the fact that one in five girls over the age of fifteen will report being sexually assaulted in their lifetime.

Still, it's very difficult to have straightforward conversations about rape culture, particularly in a society that relies on victim blaming to avoid looking to closely at patriarchal dominance. In Australia, this is particularly evident in the way rape culture is covered up in the sporting community. In the AFL's recent history, more than thirty-six footballers have faced charges of sexual assault (and that doesn't take into account the fact that, despite my general pessimism, we have actually moved forward enough as a society that women report rape and sexual assault now at a rate that was unheard of as recently as twenty years ago).

To date, not a single one of these players has been found guilty.

Now, I'm not suggesting that allegations are automatically fact. Of course everyone's entitled to a presumption of innocence, and false charges for rape do exist (although at essentially the same rate as any other crime, which is roughly 2 percent). I'm also not suggesting that a footballer can never be falsely accused of a sex crime. But it seems pretty suspicious to me that a culture which a) admits to fostering entitlement and privilege among young men, and b) does this while simultaneously demonstrating *overwhelming* evidence of its disdain towards young women would not have *a single situation* in which one of these young men was guilty of violating precisely the kind of person who holds the least value within their community. Not a single one?

There are eighteen teams in the AFL. Twenty-two players are selected for each game. That means there is a minimum of

396 players across the board each year, operating in a professional and social environment that treats them like heroes and works furiously hard to clean up the messes they leave behind so that the precious team machine isn't affected. This is the same league that heavily penalises players for taking recreational drugs or attacking another player on field, but gives 'indefinite suspensions' lasting a single game for players who beat their girlfriends. (Consider, for example, the suspension in 2009 of Adelaide Crows player Nathan Bock. Bock admitted to assaulting his girlfriend at a nightclub and was given a suspension that management stated would last indefinitely. He was back on the field one week later. The next year, Bock was drafted to the Gold Coast Suns and given a massive pay rise.)

So: 396 players every year in a hyper-masculinised culture of entitlement sitting on top of an already existing culture in which one-fifth of all women are sexually assaulted. Women are a fundamental part of the fan base that attends AFL games, accounting for approximately 40 percent of members and attendees. At any given game, the stadium will be packed with thousands of them. Thousands of women, and one-fifth of all of them have been sexually assaulted. Statistically, it will have been by somebody they know well or someone who moves in the same circles as them.

Now look at all those thousands of men: the players, the fans, the umpires, the coaches, the management team, the media. There's a lot of them, right? Zoom out even further and look at all the men you know, the ones you know from school, your work, your sports club, the pub you go to on a Saturday night, the mates you chat with in online forums, the blokes who fix your car, who catch your train in the morning, who call their mothers on Mother's Day, who walk past you on the street on their way to doing normal, everyday things. Men with families, friends, colleagues, siblings, children – people who'd swear to the heavens that they were all Decent and Good and would never do anything to harm a woman at all and how dare you even *suggest* that, there's literally nothing in the world more *offensive* than suggesting that Good, Ordinary, Decent Blokes with friends and family who love them might also be capable of exercising power over women to take what they feel they deserve.

One-fifth of all women over the age of fifteen sexually assaulted in their lifetime. Most of them by people they know.

Do the damn maths.

■

The only AFL figure to have come close to being made culpable for sexual assault is Stephen Milne, a former player for the St Kilda Football Club. In 2004, a young woman went to the police and alleged that Milne had raped her after a night out. The woman, who had been having sex with Milne's then-teammate Leigh Montagna, alleged that Milne snuck into the dark room. Pretending to be Montagna, Milne proceeded to initiate what she thought was round two. It was only midway through that she realised this wasn't the consensual sex she had signed up for with one man: this was assault perpetrated by a different man altogether. Fronting the police afterwards, Milne described her as 'just one of those footy sluts that runs around looking for footballers to fuck'. The charges were dismissed in what I would call 'dubious circumstances', and nothing more came of it.

Nothing more came of it, that is, until a decade later, when new rape charges relating to the incident were brought against Milne. This time, his teammates – the good and noble blokes of the St Kilda FC (which makes a pretence of supporting the White Ribbon Foundation and its supposed stance against gendered violence) – held a public fundraiser to help pay for Milne's legal costs. After all, boys have gotta stick together against the footy sluts, right? News of the fundraiser resulted in a modicum of backlash, but others came out in support of the team. 'What else are they supposed to do?' irate fans asked. 'What happened to innocent until proven guilty?!' 'Can't mates help each other out?!' As it turned out, proceeds from the drive might have ended up helping to pay the limp and pathetic $15,000 fine Milne was slapped with after he finally admitted fault and pled guilty to the lesser charge of indecent assault.

But despite the overwhelming public rush to urge respect for 'due process' when sexual assault allegations are made, admissions of fault aren't guaranteed to lead to any actual condemnation from either the legal system or the community at large. Despite Milne's guilty plea, Judge Michael Bourke's sentencing remarks not only made sure to mention that the act was 'out of character' (as if the way someone treats, say, their friends is automatically indistinguishable from the way they treat their rape victims) but also noted how much 'distress' the situation had caused Milne and his family over the last ten years. Being accused of an act for which some kind of responsibility is eventually claimed is apparently traumatising not for the victim of that act, but the perpetrator and his poor, beleaguered family. But, then, Bourke also referred to the assault as 'unplanned and spontaneous', saying 'there was no threatening or violent offending'.

Isn't it lucky that a male judge can make that call on behalf of a rape survivor for whom justice has taken ten years?

The reality of rape is that it's overwhelmingly more likely than not to be 'unplanned and spontaneous', and for a judge to decide that this makes it somehow 'not threatening or violent' is absurd. Threats transpire as more than just the use of physical force, and violence can be felt as more than just physical pain. Oh, but Judge Bourke did acknowledge that the victim had 'done nothing wrong' and 'did not deserve what happened to her' – language that is careless, obviously, but implies through its carelessness that there might be a circumstance in which she *did* do something wrong and thus 'deserved' it. This is the language that underpins rape culture, and it is shocking how many people are fluent in it.

This scene is frustratingly reminiscent of the trial of former Stanford University swimmer Brock Turner, a twenty-year-old man convicted in early 2016 of sexually assaulting an unconscious woman at an on-campus party one year earlier. Turner's assault of the woman, which occurred in public behind a dumpster and was so severe that doctors found abrasions, lacerations and dirt in her vagina, was interrupted by two graduate students passing by on their bicycles. Turner ran for it, but the men chased him and held him down until police arrived. His victim woke up hours later at the Valley Medical Center in San Jose. She would learn the specifics of the sexual violation later, after reading a news report about it on her phone.

As unprecedented as it seems to convict privileged young white boys of sexually assaulting drunk girls at parties, Turner's sentencing made international headlines for two major reasons. The first was because of the leniency of the sentence handed down by Judge Aaron Persky, himself a Stanford alum and former college sports star. Persky ignored requests from prosecutors for Turner to be given a minimum sentence of six years, saying, 'A prison sentence would have a severe impact on him . . . I think he will not be a danger to others.' Instead, he sentenced Turner to a measly six months in the county jail. With time served, Turner would be likely to serve less than three.

That a man like Turner found favour with America's legal system is hardly surprising – but it especially grated with what came next. That is, the publication of the twelve-page victim impact statement read to the court by his victim. In excoriating prose, 'Jane Doe' outlined exactly what Turner had taken from her that night.

'You don't know me,' she began, 'but you've been inside me, and that's why we're here today.'

Within days, her statement had been shared almost twelve million times. Rarely do we get to hear the voices of survivors, especially in such searing ways. The strength of her words seemed to cut through a culture more accustomed to treating survivors with suspicion rather than support, and cast Turner's pathetic sentence under an even harsher spotlight.

While it's encouraging to see a different response playing out in Turner's case, there are still signs of how much farther we have to go. Turner's family seem to be refusing to acknowledge the crimes of their son, with his father stating in a character reference that Turner didn't deserve to be punished for 'twenty minutes of action'. Like so many people, they blame a culture of binge drinking for 'causing' rape as opposed to, you know, rapists.

Meanwhile, I'm left to wonder how differently things might have played out had Turner chosen to perpetrate his crime in a secluded room instead of out in the open. If he had coerced a woman with a blood alcohol level three times the legal limit back to a bedroom (or worse, discovered her after she'd taken herself off to lie down) and violated her in private, would people be so quick to offer their support? Or would it be business as usual at Rape Culture HQ, with sceptics everywhere deciding that this was just another case of consensual sex gone awry – a decision fuelled by alcohol and lowered inhibitions and a slut who decided after the fact that she 'wasn't that type of girl'? If the graduate students who'd intervened had been women instead of men, would people be as inclined to believe them? Or would there be speculation about whether or not this was some kind of orchestrated plan, a collusion designed to ruin an innocent young man's life because Hell hath no fury like a woman scorned?

But the witnesses were men, and that gives them some kind of additional authority with which to judge. According to popular mythology, men have no reason to lie when they report rape. They can be the heroic bystanders intervening to rescue the damsel in distress, which proves immensely appealing for those men accustomed to seeing themselves centrally represented in almost every narrative the world offers them.

Perhaps that's why other stories of sexual violence and coercion play so poorly to broader audiences – without heroic male bystanders to intervene and save the day, men listening in after the fact automatically project themselves into the shoes of the only other men in the room: to wit, the rapists. Nestled in that uncomfortable dynamic, it becomes much more pressing to find ways to excuse or even nullify a behaviour that is far more common than men might like to admit.

Consider another football code and the liberties extended to those who triumph in it. In 2009, the ABC TV's *Four Corners* screened 'Code of Silence', a report into the sexual bonding activities present across some of Australia's sporting codes. Part of the report detailed a 2002 pack sex incident involving a young woman in New Zealand and members of the Cronulla Sharks, one of the teams in Australia's National Rugby League. The woman, referred to on *Four Corners* as 'Clare', was working as a barmaid at the time at a hotel where the players were staying. She allegedly consented to go back to a room with two of them. Over the next two hours, at least twelve players and staff entered that room despite having had no prior negotiation with the nineteen-year-old Clare. Six of them proceeded to 'have sex' with her, while the others watched and masturbated.

A statement from the *Four Corners* team later clarified, 'Most of the activity that took place during the incident is not disputed. Players and staff gave graphic accounts to police of the sexual activity. One player told police that at least one of them had climbed in through the bathroom window and crawled commando-style along the floor of the room.'

In fact, all that was disputed by the players was the issue of consent – they say she granted it. And large swathes of the public (none of whom were there) agreed. She had said yes, and this was accepted as a known fact. First of all, she'd gone back to the room with two of them, so we all know what she should have expected. And then there was the fact she hadn't fought back – this tiny nineteen-year-old woman suddenly faced with a procession of more than a dozen massive rugby players hadn't fought back against a pre-arranged deal she had no part in negotiating, and this was a sign she wanted it. Many argued that if Clare were telling the truth, she wouldn't have waited five days to report the incident to the police. They said that if there were a case to answer, the police would have laid charges, and the fact that they didn't apparently equates to incontrovertible evidence that nothing untoward happened.

Leaving aside the fact that charges of rape and sexual assault are particularly difficult to bring forward unless they bear the aforementioned hallmarks of Violent Stranger Rape, the fallout from the 'Code of Silence' broadcast illustrates another side of rape culture that's both infuriating and deeply concerning: namely, that there appear to be huge pockets of society who neither understand the complexities of consent nor the necessity for sex to be an unequivocally respectful exchange between two or more people. Equally worrying is how many people cling fiercely to the idea that initial consent means a green light for everything that comes after it. This sort of thinking not only holds that consenting to one person means consenting to any friends, teammates and colleagues who 'happen' to turn up during the event (undoubtedly for what Roy Masters, sports writer and former NRL coach, admits is seen as a 'vehicle for team bonding'), but that the presence of any form of initial consent at all is the equivalent of a contract written in blood that surrenders a woman's right to say no, to be respected, even to be considered *present* in the act as anything other than a conduit for male satisfaction and the facilitation of masculinity as performance.

The actions outlined in 'Code of Silence' were angrily defended by numerous fans as being little more than 'group sex', while producers and critics of the behaviour were (frighteningly) declared 'prudes'. But the following statement from Clare, evidently ignored by the aforementioned self-fancying libertines, really spoke to the heart of why this sort of coercive pack incident is closer to assault than the consensual group sex people explained it away as. Of the men who congregated either to fuck her or to enjoy watching each other fuck her, she said: 'They never spoke to me, they spoke just to themselves, amongst themselves, laughing and thinking it was really funny. When you have sex with someone, it's nice and you talk and you touch and this was awful. This was nothing like that.'

If group sex of any kind was occurring in a New Zealand hotel room that day, it was between men who had been conditioned to view women like Clare as little more than dehumanised fuckholes for them to humiliate, degrade and ultimately bond over. That there can be a defence of this kind of behaviour at all is utterly appalling. That it occurs in a society whose citizens vehemently denounce references to rape culture as part of some kind of nefarious feminist plot to demonise men is infuriating.

The rape apologists who thrive in a rape culture like to argue that there is no black and white when it comes to sexual assault, only shades of grey. And because of this, we're expected to direct the majority of our care to ensuring men aren't falsely accused or even punished for making 'one little mistake'. (As an aside, consider how quickly dominant social narratives rush to excuse men from making 'little mistakes' like raping women, while insisting that women be forced to carry easily remedied pregnancies to term because we have to accept the consequences of our actions.)

But shades of grey about consent can be very easily resolved by establishing whether or not your sexual partner is present in the situation, enjoying themselves and being afforded a dignity that recognises and respects their humanity. Coercive sex might not be exactly the same as perceptibly violent assault (and it's certainly harder to punish, despite what people fear), but it still relies on one partner asserting control over the other and denying them the sense of respect and value that should be fundamental to any consensual sexual encounter (regardless of whether or not it involves strangers, whips, alcohol or football teams). Degrading someone against their consent is really easy to do if you've already dehumanised them in your head. Informed consent therefore needs to move above and beyond simply securing a 'yes' to a place where we constantly ask ourselves, 'Am I treating my partner with dignity? Are they enjoying this? Are they present and equal? Are we experiencing this together?' Contrary to popular opinion, this won't wrap bedrooms in never-ending reams of bureaucratic red tape.

Up to now, responsibility for preventing sexual assault has always fallen to women and girls. We are instructed on how to modify our behaviour to avoid attacks and danger, lectured about the clothes we wear, the social activities we participate in, the men we choose to speak with or flirt with or even be mildly cordial to, whether or not we drink alcohol and to what level, the streets we walk down, the houses we go into and even the sexual situations we opt to wade into. When a woman is sexually assaulted, a forensic examination of her actions commences almost immediately while the person who assaulted her is sidelined almost to the point of being considered a stationary object observing her demise rather than an active perpetrator causing it. He becomes little more than a fence post or low wall she was silly enough to walk into because she wasn't paying proper attention to her surroundings. Even when some kind of cognitive awareness is ascribed to him, it's never positioned in a way he has control over. *She* made it happen, with her short skirt and drunken flirting and long hair and suggestive breasts and the fact that she was breathing and alive. What else was he supposed to do? And what else did she expect?

Of course, the truly audacious thing about this repetitive, condescending instruction is that girls and women already know how fucking unsafe the world is for us. We begin the long and painful process of knowing it sometime before we pass through the veil of childhood and into adolescence, before we've even begun to know ourselves. We learn it in the way we're told to close our legs when we sit down, in how we're suddenly not allowed to wear certain kinds of clothes, the ways we're told that boys who pick on us 'probably just have a crush' so we shouldn't fight back. We get an uncomfortable, creeping sense of it in the looks strange men start giving us on the street and the conversations we hear about how so-and-so 'dresses like a slut' and 'should take more care'. We feel it – literally – in the ways our bodies end up being touched and handled and groped, and this is made worse when our complaints are met with suspicion or laughter or urges to 'just ignore it'.

And this is just the beginning. Eventually, we absorb this message of danger so completely that we start to accumulate a bag of tools to protect ourselves. We learn to carry our keys between our fingers when we walk to our cars or front doors at night-time. To listen to music with one ear and footsteps with the other. To cross the street to avoid walking past a man or a group of men, even if it's just to prevent what soon becomes the inevitable expectation that they'll say something about our bodies and what they want to do with them. We become stoic and stony-faced when these words are thrown at us, pretending we didn't hear these men commanding us to show them our tits, suck their dicks, sit on their faces, lose some weight, stop being such a stuck-up fucking-cunt-bitch-didn't-want-you-anyway-you-fat-whore, to go fuck ourselves, the laughter the laughter the laughter. Stare straight ahead, keep walking, cross the street, arrange your keys between your fingers. Notice as another small part of yourself is ground down.

We know how unsafe the world is for us. We are like cliffs staring down at a raging sea, battered by winds and salt and spray and unable to wrench ourselves away from the supposed inevitability of it all. But though we may recede under the relentless thrashing, still we stand tall. The world and all its angry currents cannot break us, no matter how hard it tries.

Still, this erosion of the spirit is a bitter pill to swallow. Because despite knowing the dangers that face us, we're not allowed to talk about them. Patriarchy and the men favoured by it are empowered to tell women what we 'must' do in order to stop Bad Things from happening to us. When we take that narrative back for ourselves, we're further victimised as troublemakers, man-haters and fantasists. We're demonising men with stereotypes. We're overreacting to perfectly normal and reasonable situations. We're making it up to get attention. We're destroying men's lives with our false accusations and destructive attitudes. And worse, our storytelling makes them *feel bad*.

The irony is almost too great. How many times have you shared an experience of harassment or abuse only to be told you're being too sensitive? That the man or men involved were probably just trying to be nice to you? How many times have you been chided for talking about sexism because 'not all men' are like that? How many times have you had men straight up tell you you're making something up, that your fanciful story needs to be filed in the Things That Never Happened box, that it just doesn't even sound right because they've never seen anything like that happen or done it themselves and they would never be friends with men who behaved that way anyway?

And, in light of all that, how many times have you decided to stay silent about your experiences because the thought of being disbelieved or ridiculed or told off is simply too heartbreaking on top of all the other pain you have to shoulder because you were born into a world that is unsafe for you, but only in the ways that men are trusted to define it?

Yeah. Me too.

But enough is enough. I won't be silenced about this shit anymore. I'm sick and tired of men telling me that I don't properly understand the world I live in – the same world that tells me I have to be careful and make sensible choices, but that rears its head in outrage whenever I make mention of the role that men play in making this world unsafe for me. Men cannot have it both ways. They can't instruct us on how to behave to avoid danger from Bad People and then get outraged when we decide that this might include them. They don't get to pick and choose the folks and situations we have a responsibility to avoid while demanding we flatter them with our unquestioning trust. If men don't like the idea of being treated with suspicion by women on the streets, they should be working *with* feminists to bring an end to the rape culture that assumes men can be provoked by something as harmless as a short skirt or a late-night kiss.

The bandaid solution of making rape prevention the responsibility of women doesn't address the core issue of how and why it keeps happening. Telling a woman to protect herself from rape doesn't stop men from raping, especially not when the woman is also trained to doubt her own intuition and play nice at all times. Isn't it amazing how fiercely the world will police women and our behaviour just to ensure men are allowed to grow as wild and free as they please?

This is social law in action, and it is so pervasive and so rampant that many people still struggle even to see it. It's how two boys in a football town like Steubenville, Ohio, who dragged an unconscious girl from party to party, sexually assaulting her and at one point even urinating on her while people watched, can go on to be defended by almost their entire community because their young victim was a 'slut' whose choice to get blackout drunk destroyed the promising lives of two young boys. Indeed, it's why you can have a major news network refer to the shattering of those 'promising lives' when reporting on their sentencing – as if the real victims here were those boys forced to answer to their actions, and the real criminal the girl demanding they do.

It's how teenage boys in Auckland can start a group called the 'Roast Busters' in which they proudly and publicly boast of getting girls as young as thirteen drunk so they can sexually assault them. It's how that same racket can go on for more than two years, despite the group being known to the police, because some of the boys involved were the sons of influential men.

It's how boys and men have no problem telling girls and women who piss them off that they deserve to be raped, that they should be raped, that they want to be raped, that they're only angry because they're too ugly to be raped.

It's how boys and men who say these things can then turn around and claim they were only joking, that women need to lighten up, that they're just words and they don't mean anything.

It's how, in the western world, the only time these particular white men seem to give a fuck about women is when violence against them is being perpetrated by men of colour. There is a deep and rich fucking irony in the fact that the same men who vilify Islam for 'forcing' women to wear hijab or demanding four male witnesses be present to prosecute a rape charge or consider women inherently less important or powerful will also turn around and tell women to stop dressing like sluts if they want to avoid being raped, demand that adequate 'proof' be provided if a woman 'accuses' an ordinary bloke of assault and ridicule women whenever they feel like it because hey, it's just a joke.

Look at the way the conservative trolls crawled out from under their bridges to picket and protest groping attacks in Cologne on New Year's Eve in 2016 (attacks that, while horrifying, also turned out to be hyper-inflated and in service of perpetuating xenophobia against refugees). Many of these men suddenly outraged by street harassment and groping had documented histories of vehemently denying the problem of sexual assault on US college campuses, not to mention terrifying obsessions with violently trolling women on social media. These are the same men who claim false rape reports are a significant enough problem that we need to protect our sons against them, the same men who claim domestic violence is exaggerated and that the real victims are the men whose children are stolen from them by lying mothers. And we're supposed to believe they give a shit about women's safety on the streets? No. What they really mean is: get your filthy foreign hands off our property. Nothing spurs a bigot into false feminism quicker than the chance to flex their racism against men whose behaviour, were it being perpetrated by white men, would be dismissed as either a bit of a lark, the fault of alcohol or provocative women, or a fabrication entirely. Because women lie. And when they aren't lying, they're overreacting.

The world is unsafe for us girls – but so is acknowledging that. And this is the final way that rape culture operates: by telling us to take definitive action and then providing us with zero options. We cannot win the game that they're forcing us to play.

Here's the truth about Adrian Bayley and Jill Meagher.

If he had decided it was simply too risky to pursue her down Hope Street that night, she might have ended up safely at home with the all-too-familiar sense of being shaken but not stirred. She would have questioned whether or not her fear was misplaced and unfair. She might even have felt a sense of guilt at being automatically suspicious of his intentions, so trained are women to give men the benefit of the doubt.

But do you want to know what would invariably have happened later?

If Jill had taken to social media to tell this story, or even shared it with a group of friends at the pub later – this story of the creepy man who'd stopped her on the street and insisted on talking to her, the man to whom she'd been polite because self-preservation and self-doubt make remarkably compatible bedfellows, the man whom she could have sworn doubled back to talk to her, although she couldn't be sure and maybe she was just being paranoid – she would have been met with at least one person who chastised her for being too quick to judge. Someone who wasn't there, but who decided anyway that her interpretation was wrong or irrational. That Adrian Bayley was just a lonely guy who was probably looking to pick up or talk to a pretty girl with a nice smile and can he really be blamed for that? Some guys can't help it if they're socially awkward, and they don't *deserve* to be unfairly maligned just because they summoned up the courage to speak to a pretty girl on the street.

And Jill, being a woman living in the world, would have absorbed that message, the millionth in a series of messages about how she couldn't be trusted to interpret her own experiences, and she would have started to doubt it herself. Did it really happen like she remembered? Was he really that bad? Was she being unfair or unkind? The next time, she wouldn't be so quick to judge. She'd deny her instincts, ignore the alarm bells ringing in her head and tell herself she was being silly. And she'd smile and act nice and try to protect the man in front of her from having to feel any of the discomfort that was currently coursing through her.

Of course, that's if it even happened at all. I mean, it kind of sounds like she's making it up or exaggerating. Something about it just doesn't make sense.

You know?

—14—

IT'S OKAY TO BE ANGRY

Before you reach the end of this book, I need to tell you one of the most important things I've learned in my thirty-five years on earth as a human-being woman person. In fact, if you take just one message away from this book then I hope it's this one, because it might just be the cornerstone of everything. This is one of the hardest lessons for us to learn, but I urge you to embrace it. May it fill your heart and soul, may it keep you warm at night and may it carve itself in letters large across the breadth of your whole mind.

Are you ready?

It is okay for you to be angry.

I know. Revolutionary, right? All these years, people have been calling you 'angry' as if it's a shameful thing, when what they really mean is 'your refusal to be contained frightens me'.

It is okay for you to be angry.

It's okay for you to be angry because you are a human being who lives in the world and you are goddamn allowed to be angry about some of the things that happen here. It's okay for you to be angry because you have blood, bones and a beating heart and these things are messy and powerful and full of life. It's okay for you to be angry because being angry is not illegal, no matter how much it might make other people uncomfortable. It's okay for you to be angry because you're a woman and the world has given you a lot of fucking shit to be angry about.

It is okay for you to be angry.

To a world that instructs women to be passive and conciliatory, anger is a terrifying thing. Anger is unpredictable. It's uncontrollable. People are afraid of women's anger because they are afraid of confronting its source – inequality, violence, degradation, dehumanisation, misogyny. If you don't want to accept that these things exist, you won't want to accept the validity of women's feelings of rage about them.

And so it becomes much easier for those invested in the status quo to do what they've always done when faced with the 'extremity' of women's emotions, and that's pathologise them. Women who express anger are recast as mythically terrifying creatures. Hysterical banshees. Harpies. Fishmongers' wives. Squawking, screeching, shrieking she-beasts making the world unpleasant for everyone around them. We are grotesque, monstrous mountains of rage, engorged and swollen with our own irrational delusions about the state of the world.

We are ugly, and this is perhaps the most criminal aspect of our existence – because we're told that it's this ugliness that makes us so angry in the first place and causes us to lash out. In this reading of women's anger, our exclusion from the system has not been caused by the system itself but by the insufficiency of our own physicality. If we were pretty on the outside, we would be pleasant on the inside. If we were thin, we wouldn't have so much room inside us to harbour so much hate and toxicity. If we took more pride in our appearance, instead of being lazy, grizzly, fat, disgusting, ugly, angry old bitches, then men would want us. And if men wanted us, all our dissatisfaction and rage over being passed over would disappear and we would recognise just how wonderful this prison we live in really is.

From the time we are born until the time we die, girls and women are taught to be the simpering, smiling backdrop to the greater purpose of men's achievements. Men rule the world, while women decorate it. We aren't granted the flexibility of being able to play characters who can be complicated, messy, irreverent, assertive, admired and angry. These roles are reserved for men. We are expected to be their support in every way. We are the women they fight over, the women they lust after, the women who encourage them and the woman who applaud them. We are the stage on which they stand, the curtains that signal for silence or applause, the scenery that forms the backdrop to their adventures, the swelling music that heralds their success.

Why are you so angry?

I'm angry that this is even a question, because implicit in it is the suggestion that women have nothing to be angry about. It's so easy to stand within a system that favours you so completely that your privilege can no longer even been seen, and yet still have the arrogance to argue that those burdened by it are behaving unreasonably. Instead of responding to the legitimate grievances of half the world's population – the half that is marginalised, abused, discriminated against and oppressed – the responsibility to engage is shrugged off and once again turned into an issue of oversensitivity.

Why am I angry?

I'm angry because one in five girls over the age of fifteen will experience sexual violence, and yet the rape culture we raise them in leads them to believe this sexual violence is somehow their fault.

I'm angry because these same girls will hesitate to tell anyone what happened to them because if they don't already believe they caused it to happen, they're afraid that other people will.

I'm angry because girls and women are raped by groups of boys and men who colonise their precious bodies as a grotesque exercise in 'bonding', and yet are still later protected and defended by a community that wants to believe it's women who set out to 'ruin the lives of promising future leaders'.

I'm angry because entire sporting teams can decide that a woman who consents to sex with one of them is consenting to sex with the entire team, and that this entitlement is supported by a wider society that has no problem asking, 'What did she expect?'

I'm angry because a circumstance of pack sex in which men exert their physical and social power over a teenage girl can be defended by their supporters as 'consensual group sex', even when the girl ends up with a documented case of PTSD and ongoing suicidal thoughts.

I'm angry because the concept of consensual sex is so poorly understood by a world that favours male sexual dominance to the point where rape is excused all the time, and yet some people still react to the proposition of further education around consent with conspiracy theories about how the bedroom is being overrun by red tape and bureaucracy.

I'm angry because women and children are trafficked into sex slavery all over the world and are raped every day to make money for men who think of them as nothing but holes. I'm angry because other women opt into sex work and are shamed for it, subjected to greater levels of abuse but treated as though the nature of their profession means they deserve less respect and protection.

I'm angry because women are groped on the streets or in bars and told that they have to accept these interactions as compliments.

I'm angry because women are raped every day in their homes, by their partners, family members or friends, and yet people still think that avoiding rape is as simple as just saying no.

I'm angry because when feminists talk about rape, men tell us that we're just upset that no one wants to rape us. I'm angry because women who commit the egregious crime of being fat while raped are even more likely to be disbelieved, because 'why would anyone rape a fat chick?'. I'm angry because women of colour, trans women and women with disabilities suffer significantly higher rates of male-perpetrated sexual violence than almost anyone else, yet are given significantly lower levels of support across the board.

I'm angry because there are men who exploit the suffering of women of colour in other nations not because they care about the liberation of these women but so they can justify the white colonialist feelings of supremacy they have towards the men of colour who also live there. I'm angry because I've experienced these same men telling me they would laugh if I was gang-raped by 'a pack of Muslims'. I'm angry because it seems the real reason these men are upset is because they believe there are other men out there who are given permission to treat women the way they want to but can never admit to.

I'm angry because I have lost count of the number of women who have contacted me to tell me about the men who have raped them and got away with it. I'm angry because so many of these women are my friends.

I'm angry because rape and sexual violence is only one facet of how women are abused in this world. I'm angry because girls around the world are denied the right to education, to medical care, sometimes even to a fucking childhood. I'm angry at how so many of us are taught from so young to see our bodies as shameful and disgusting – nothing more than a dumping ground for men to unload their semen and insecurities into in equal measure. I'm angry at the fact we're expected to see ourselves as ridiculous. To laugh at the sneering jokes made about us and our inferior state and to pipe up in defence of the men who tell them whenever a flabby-mouthed harpy complains. I'm angry at how little we're valued as leaders and innovators. I'm angry that for thousands of years, men have taken credit for the work and discoveries of women to the point where we've been all but erased from history. Were we even there? As wives and mistresses, certainly. But all that other stuff we did? No one given the power to document matters of note saw us as important enough to bother with.

I'm angry that the sexist men who disregard women's immense contributions to the world insist that our gender has been responsible for creating nothing, building nothing, inventing nothing and designing nothing – because to them, the complicated, difficult task of growing an entire human being from scratch and then giving birth to it isn't considered that big a deal.

I'm angry that girls all over the world learn to hate themselves. Because we are taught that we are worth hating.

The examples I've given here are just a drop in the ocean of pain that some women spend a lifetime swimming through, just trying to find their way to safe land. These are real assaults and oppressions. This is a real culture of crime and degradation. If history did bother to document the lives of women, it would be written with the ink of tears that have flowed since the beginning of time.

These things aren't real, feminism's opponents will say to you, at least not in the way you pretend they are. Yes, this stuff sometimes happens but you're exaggerating most of it. Men can be victims too. A lot of these 'rape' stories are really just women regretting it afterwards. What do you mean, that's 'victim blaming'? I don't blame victims, not the real ones. And stop talking about 'rape culture'. Rape culture doesn't even exist; how can culture teach people to rape? Women just need to take more care, because there are bad people out there. No, of course you don't have to take care and be safe around me, that's absurd. I mean, how dare you? You're basically accusing me of being a rapist and that is so offensive. Don't you know that 99 percent of men are good, decent men who would never hurt anyone? Having said that, women still shouldn't wear short skirts and drink too much because you never know who might take advantage of you. Stop asking if that means around me as well – of course it doesn't mean around me! You can drink around *me*; I'm not going to hurt you. But don't get too drunk, because it's not nice when women get too drunk. Also, it affects their ability to respond to danger. That's why it's best if they stay sober, because you never know who's out there. NO, NOT ME! I already said that. No, he can't have raped her if she went back to his house. Because why else did she go back to his house? She should have known what to expect. I'm not saying what he did was right, but she shouldn't have been so drunk. Both people should take responsibility. Of course I can control myself around women, what kind of a question is that? Stop acting like women need to be on their guard around all men, as if we're all rapists! This is just about your vendetta. Your problem is that you hate men, and you're actually blinded by that. Yes, you're blinded by misandry. You're actually making the world more unsafe for women, because you refuse to let us issue practical advice about how they can protect themselves. Telling women to watch their behaviour isn't excusing rape – it's stopping it, if anything. God, why are you so fucking angry all the time? *What happened to you that made you so fucking bitter and angry?*

But anger is absolutely the appropriate response for women to have to a society that not only freezes us out of its core operations unit but seizes every opportunity to hurt and demean us. It is right that we be angry about our treatment as women in the world, because it means we still have control of our faculties and haven't been sucked into the Stepford hell that patriarchal order has always tried to box us into. We should be angry. Because if we aren't, we aren't paying enough attention.

But the problem here is twofold, because compounding this anger is the epic condescension and mansplaining that women have to endure from irate men who love nothing more than to waffle on and on about how sexism doesn't exist, misogyny is a myth and statistics about discrimination are all made up. It's bad enough that we have to live with the reality of this shit, but is there anything more infuriating than being told that you lack the proper objectivity to be able to rationalise your experience of the world so you need a man to do it for you?

Put up your hand if you've ever sat and listened, gobsmacked, as a man told you that something you found threatening or sexist – let's say, being yelled at from a car window – wasn't actually threatening or sexist at all but was in fact a light-hearted expression of appreciation or even a compliment, and to behave as if it was anything more than that isn't just a gross overreaction but actually an insult to the women who experience *real* oppression around the world. Right. Now, with that hand still raised, stand up and walk to the nearest window, open it and let out the bloodcurdling scream I know you felt building up inside of you as you read that sentence. Congratulations, that was the sound of the glass ceiling being shattered by thousands of angry women screaming at the same time.

It's okay to be angry.

We need to get over the stigma of what it means to be an angry woman. We've been taught to fear the label and all that it represents, which is supposedly a kind of hyper-emotional femaleness that lacks perspective and rationality. But our anger is not irrational. It's very concentrated and sensible, and it is a response to the pain of thousands of years of oppression and male supremacy. That doesn't mean that we are blazingly angry all the time. I mean, even I give myself a break now and then to watch *The Bachelor* or *Survivor*. My anger is not always explosive. But it is always with me.

It means I'm paying attention.

When I was young, my father used to tell me that I would catch more flies with honey than I would with vinegar, because sweetness was the shortcut to getting things done. Yet I never heard him offer the same advice to my brother. For that matter, I have never heard of any man being advised to be sweet and compliant in order to get his own way. Charming, yes. Convincing, of course. Powerful, assertive, confident, absolutely. But never to be sweet and passive, to flatter the person who has power over you by appealing to their sense of superiority.

It isn't for our own good that women are told to stop being so angry. This is the pretence, of course, but the objective isn't to protect us from the frightening capacity of our own rage. How could it be? More to the point, why would we in particular need to have our personalities babysat like this? We aren't delicate little flowers who need to be shielded from experiencing or expressing extreme emotions.

The truth is, women's anger is pathologised as dangerous because it represents a threat to the stability of the gender inequality that relies on its absence. Imagine the magnificent things women could achieve if we allowed ourselves to truly give in to our anger – if we turned our backs on 'sweetness' and harnessed instead the palpable rage that is our birthright.

And where has all that sweetness got us? As a collective, not especially far. I've no doubt it's helped individual women along the way, but even they must have had moments of frustration over how often they've had to fold themselves into a neatly pretty corsage just to get anything done. The truth is, our anger has been wrested from us using the same threats of isolation and rejection that have proved so effective against women trained to view our worth through the eyes of men. It isn't nice for women to be angry, so we try not to be. It isn't pretty for us to use our anger, so we don't. It doesn't recommend us to men to have anger within us, so we hide it away and pretend it belongs to those other kinds of women – the sexless, ugly, brutish ones whose hostility stems from being unappealing . . . or is it the other way around?

It is okay for you to be angry. You have a lot to be angry about.

And it's okay if being angry about these things makes some men feel bad or indignant or 'picked on'. It's not your job to shield them from the things women have to deal with every day. This isn't the same as forcing them to take personal responsibility for everything that happens, although a lot of guys will argue that this is exactly what you're doing. They do this in order to justify blocking their ears against what you're saying. A lot of them don't want to know about it, because they want to believe it has nothing to do with them. But they don't live outside the system. They can continue to do nothing within that system, but as I hope I've vehemently communicated in this book, doing nothing to change the structures of power that benefit you is just as bad as being part of the mechanism that keeps those structures in place.

Some of these people will tell you that this is all well and good, but your anger isn't helping your cause. They'll try to convince you that this anger is just pushing people away – people who would otherwise be interested in helping to create change, but who are put off because you make it so hard for them. Again, it isn't your responsibility to cushion the blow here. Most of the people you'll be having these conversations with are adults, so why are they expecting to be treated like children? Being angry isn't the same as being hostile or erratic. You can be patient while you walk people through this information, but you don't have to hold their hands and make sure their feelings are protected. All that does is give them permission to keep ignoring the gravity of the situation. If excessive care on your part encourages their belief that things aren't really that bad, they'll have all the excuse they need to refrain from doing anything about it.

Besides, why should women take it upon themselves to look after everyone else's feelings when no one ever looks after ours? Instead, we hear endless variations of 'you're overreacting' or 'stop being so sensitive' or 'toughen up' or (and I love this line, by which I mean it needs to be loaded into my magic desert sun cannon and blasted into space) 'your experience of that event is incorrect, let me explain to you what actually happened even though I wasn't there'.

The idea that women are protected from the world by men better equipped than we are to withstand its reality is such a myth. No one is wrapped more tightly in cotton wool than those men who express hostility towards feminism and women's rights. No one demands greater care when dealing with their feelings than the men who scream Not All Men! No one sets up parody accounts and trolling websites faster than the men whose entire argument is built on the back of the complaint that women are 'too sensitive'. And if we're going to talk about anger, hostility and extreme emotional overreactions, no one displays any of those things in greater quantities than the men who hate women, and feminists especially, so much that they dedicate hours every day to harassing us, abusing us and monitoring every single thing we say to use as 'evidence' of some greater conspiracy against men's freedom.

This aggression is palpable and obsessive. The intention of the people who wield it is to silence and scare us. I'm angry about that. In fact, I'm not just angry about it – I'm furious. It's as if a laser beam created from the testosterone, butt cheese and Mountain Dew sweat of Aggrieved Men is beamed all around the world to rally the troops whenever a woman opens her mouth. Amber alert! Amber alert! A woman is speaking about feminism! Quick, let's find her home address and post it online so we can TEACH HER A LESSON.

These men are consumed by an anger so intense that it's actually frightening. And that makes me furious too. The human race is thousands and thousands of years old, and yet there are some people so terrified of losing the marginal grip on power masculinity has given them that they devote their time and energy to telling women that if we don't shut up, someone will find us, rape us, kill us and then gloat about the victory to teach other women a lesson.

The good thing is that you don't have to listen. No matter how much they try to force you to (and they will, whether your interaction happens online or off) You. Do. Not. Have. To. Listen. Because in addition to it being okay for you to be angry, it's also okay for you to shut down conversations with people you don't want to talk to. You are not required to stand there and nod politely as a man lectures you on why gender inequality is a myth. It doesn't make your experience of life any less real or true if you walk away from sanctimonious dickheads. They don't want to have a discussion with you. Their only objective is to get you to admit you're wrong. I know exactly how frustrating and disempowering this is, because I am a woman and most women have spent their lives being taught to doubt their feelings and instincts. I am angry about the number of women who write to me to recount tedious conversations with arrogant men who won't let them get a word in edgeways, but who ultimately succeed in making these women second-guess themselves because 'You're overreacting' may as well be the first sentence we hear after 'It's a girl'.

I used to feel obligated to participate in these discussions. But I grew so frustrated at being spoken over, lectured and mansplained to that eventually I decided to stop doing it. Except in the rare situations where a dialogue has been initiated by someone who genuinely wants to learn more (even if they don't ultimately end up agreeing with everything said, which is their right), these conversations are mostly completely pointless. Nothing is achieved beyond yet more of your precious time being wasted on people who aren't there in good faith and don't have any interest in listening to what you have to say.

I might still have to deal with incessant demands that I 'defend my position', but I have the choice to ignore them. I used to think that doing so meant I was letting the side down or missing a valuable opportunity to educate, but then I realised you can lead a man to thought but you cannot make him think. This was a huge moment for me. Not only did it free up a lot of time, it also liberated me from a lot of the emotional trauma that came from being constantly ambushed by MRAs and other dingleberries. I can't tell you how satisfying it is to watch them grow more and more infuriated at being ignored. Truly, it gives me a lot of pleasure, and in this world we take what we can get.

So walk away. Walk away before the conversation even starts. Shut it down if they keep trying to goad you into it. Don't answer them and don't rise to the bait when they tell you that your refusal to engage is just further evidence that you have no argument (your status as a woman being the first and most damning proof of this). Face it, they already think you're full of shit anyway, and they're just chomping at the bit to tell you how there's no such thing as sexism, feminism is over, most 'sensible' women know that it's ridiculous, you just want superiority, you're just angry because you're ugly, if you gave it up you could get a boyfriend and (my personal favourite) 'real' feminists would be turning in their graves over what the movement's become. Yeah, because the suffragettes (all of whom encountered exactly the same kind of paternalistic lectures from whiny man-babies) were traditionally super into standing there and listening politely while men spoke at them. Try again, dickheads.

Like I said, it's okay to walk away. It's okay to ignore men, especially when they are furiously trying to put you back into the tiny little box they need to carry you around in so that they can feel comfortable and in control. It's okay to block men on Facebook and Twitter, to delete their emails without reading them, to tell them to Fuck Off on Tinder and basically to do whatever else you think is necessary to keep their toxic bullshit from seeping into your life. You are allowed to do all these things. It doesn't make you weak. It doesn't make you an enemy of free speech like some will argue (as if closing the door on a travelling evangelist who keeps yelling about how much of a fat cunt you are is an egregious form of censorship that shows how much you hate democracy). In fact, block with abandon. Walk away gleefully. Don't let people with shitty intentions suck your energy from you. Why should they have free access to it, especially when you get absolutely nothing from them in return?

It is okay for you to do all these things. It's okay for you to acknowledge your rage and give voice to it. It's okay for you to deny men your time and energy. It's okay not to care if they think you're fat and ugly. You are not responsible for other people's insecurities or the way they try to use them against you. It's okay for you to disagree with men. It's okay for you to tell men to fuck off. God, is it fucking okay for you to tell them to fuck off. Sometimes those two words are the only thing you need. I like to use them when someone's taken the time to send me an incomprehensible, illegible treatise on the dangers of feminism or how women have infiltrated the government and are now putting steps in place to prepare for the matriarchy (like, I wish that was actually happening). It's okay for you to make fun of them when they try to pick on you, to tease them when they act as if their approval has any bearing on your life whatsoever.

It's okay for you to reject men's attentions, to say no without explanation. You don't have to fabricate a boyfriend to make it easier for them to accept your lack of interest, as tempting as it might be. Men shouldn't need to view you as the property of another man in order to respect your wishes. You don't owe them anything. Of course, this can be dangerous. There are countless recorded cases of men killing women because they wouldn't go out with them (check out the website When Women Refuse). Elliot Rodger wrote an entire manifesto about that and then went on a killing spree in Isla Vista, California. It's terrifying. I get that. But you still don't owe it to them to ease the pain of rejection.

It's okay for you to have conversations about the pain and abuse that's inflicted on women without also having to acknowledge that these things happen to men too. Yes, men can be victimised. Yes, men can be raped. Yes, men can be targeted by family violence. Those are terrible things, and help should be given to the victims and survivors of such atrocities. But none of that negates the reality that women are victimised in different and more sustained ways, and the constant interruption to and attempts to derail that dialogue is just another form of violence. Why is it always seen as the responsibility of women to take on the burden of men's emotional labour, even (and especially) when it means putting our own problems to the side? History is one long laundry list of men's problems being put front and centre. In fact, women are the ones who have always led the charge to defend men from violence. It was largely women – mothers, wives, sisters and socialists – who marched against war and the policies of conscription that sent young men off to die and kill for colonialist governments. It's largely women who do the work of healing their broken communities. Women have always taken care of everyone else and will likely continue to do so. But the moment we start organising ourselves to address the serious, systemic issues that see us hospitalised and/or put in the ground, we're suddenly vilified for 'ignoring the bigger picture' while greedily siphoning off all the available funds into our own cause. Such a claim is ridiculous. Do you know how many women's health organisations and refuges have been defunded in the last decade? Compare that with the nationwide response whenever a young lad is randomly attacked on a city street and left to die. That situation is so intolerable to us as a nation that we even came up with a new phrase to replace the former description of being 'king hit'. Now these men suffer a 'coward's punch', because there can be nothing more cowardly than punching a man in the back of the head when he's just trying to enjoy a night out.

I have no objection to the rebranding of that behaviour. It's despicable. My heart breaks for the families who've lost sons and brothers to that kind of violence. I think it's commendable that our government has responded to it in such a proactive way. But domestic violence is still called domestic violence. Men who kill their wives or families and then themselves are still valorised in newspapers, praised for being 'good blokes' and 'family men'. Their old coaches and community sporting teams are still sought for comment on what wonderful team players they were. Everyone talks about what a terribly tragedy it was all round.

Women and children are put in the ground, and the feminists who campaign against these atrocities are abused for making it all about us.

Embrace your anger. Don't be pretty little flowers decorating the hallways of life. Women have spent too long burying our anger deep beneath those roots in the hope that we could stop it from affecting our blooms, but all it's resulted in is failure to thrive.

If you are a woman living in this world and you're not angry, you're not paying enough attention. Not to your own life, not to the lives of other women and not to the lives of the women who'll come after you.

Be angry. Be rageful. Be loud. Be unrepentant. Be assertive. Be aggressive. Be the kind of she-beast that trains her fire-filled eyes on the male gaze and burns it down. Be everything that women are always told not to be, and commit to giving zero fucks about who may or may not have a problem with that.

It is okay to be angry. *It is fucking okay.*

—15—

#METOO

When I was ten years old a man at least six times that number pulled me against him and pressed his hot, wet lips against mine. It was New Year's Eve, a rare night on which us kids were allowed to join the revelry of the grown-ups downstairs, and the clock had just tipped us into 1992. Around me adults swirled, jovial and drunk, as I had seen them become so many times before while peering down at our living room from between the shadowed rungs of our upstairs bannister. Between exclamations of 'Happy New Year!' and 'Can you believe it's 1992?' some of them were locked in their own embraces. No one had seen the man kiss me, or if they did they didn't think enough about it to feel uncomfortable. In the background, 'Auld Lang Syne' began to play. Everyone around me started to sing, so I did too.

I was wearing a knee-length floral dress that night, with puffy sleeves and a full skirt. Our mother had given my sister and me matching dresses especially for the party. I adored mine. I was a particularly frothy child, and I had coveted big, ostentatious dresses ever since I had seen Jennifer Connelly's Sarah float into the snow globe ballroom in *Labyrinth*. The movie was on high rotation in our house, my sister and I transfixed as much by the dangerous current of sexuality running between the adolescent Sarah and the much older Goblin King (played to spandex perfection by David Bowie) as by his ultimate defeat at her hands.

'Through dangers untold and hardships unnumbered,' I would recite sombrely in front of the mirror in my bedroom, 'I have fought my way here to the castle, beyond the Goblin City, to take back the child that you have stolen.'

It was one of many games I played alone in my room that year, closing the door to the outside world as I felt my way along the tremulous passage from childhood to adolescence. The magic that allows a child to commit fully to a land of make-believe had faded by then, but I wrung what I could out of the dust that remained. I put oranges in my top to mimic the silhouette of the breasts some of my friends had already started to develop, and strutted around my room pretending to be Tess McGill from *Working Girl*. The innocently crafted scenarios that had previously involved Barbie hanging out in her Dream House or going shopping for hours on end were now hurriedly rushed through in order to get to the new closing act: Barbie and Ken (or Barbie and one of her friends, or sometimes Barbie, Ken and one of her friends) mashing their bodies together in what I imagined frenetic, passionate sex-making was supposed to look like.

It was the season of John Hughes' movies and *Beverly Hills 90210*, and my sister and I watched these and more on the video tapes we begged our parents to bring home from the store. Clearly unacquainted at this point with the feminism that would later become the focus of my work, I lived on a steady diet of teen romance, ugly duckling storylines and third act kisses at the high school dance. Even at ten, I yearned to one day be transformed from a weird, awkward nerd into a beautiful prom queen, like the heavy-lidded, sugar sandwich-eating goth Allison, whose bathroom makeover leads to the school wrestling champion kissing her sweetly in the school parking lot at the end of *The Breakfast Club*. At the same time, I had an inkling that I might want to lock myself in a cleaning closet with Judd Nelson and his smart mouth and fingerless gloves and find out what he could do with them.

At ten years old, I had a sense of sex and how important it might one day become. I had watched it flicker at the edges of movie screens. Somewhere deep inside I had felt the sleeping beast begin to work its way towards wakefulness. I wanted someone to take me in their arms and kiss me, to fall so hard into the moment that I became oblivious to the people moving around me. I wanted to come up for air feeling like I had learned a new language, one that only I and the person I had created it with could speak. I wanted to be wanted. I wanted to want in return.

But I didn't want it be with the ageing, grey-skinned friend of my parents who lived a few doors down from us. I was a young girl in the first decade of her life; I didn't imagine my first kiss would come from someone who was in the last decade of his. That his fat, slippery lips would open over mine and deposit a slick glaze before quickly closing and pulling back, unseen by the circling crowd. Should auld acquaintance be forgot, and never brought to mind.

When we were growing up, my parents had always urged us to tell them if an adult did something that made us uncomfortable in any way. But there's a difference between understanding something theoretically and figuring out how to put it into practice when the hypotheticals become realities. I remember even at ten weighing up the circumstances. I had been open-mouth kissed (I think) by a man old enough to be my grandfather. I hadn't liked it and I didn't want to be around him in case it happened again.

But this man was also a friend of my parents. He and his wife were at our house a lot and nothing like this had happened before. I knew he'd been drinking, and didn't that make people do funny things? How could I be sure that this was the sort of thing my parents meant when they talked about 'feeling uncomfortable'?

It seemed easier not to rock the boat. Besides, I didn't feel damaged in any way. I may have felt uneasy about what had happened, but the feeling existed somewhere outside myself – like an object I could pull out of a drawer and examine, then return to its proper place once curiosity gave way to boredom. As I grew older and heard reports of more terrible encounters with men from friends who sectioned their memories off in darker, more hidden places, I began to feel embarrassed when I thought of my reaction. *It was just a kiss*, I told myself. *It's not like he raped you.*

In recent months, I've returned to that drawer time and again to pull out the memory that lies within. Turning it over in my hands, I've looked long and hard at the things I didn't consider interesting before. The sight of his wife standing nearby, laughing as he pulled me in close. The moment my jubilation at being allowed to stay up past midnight and play at being a grown-up gave way to confusion over what that apparently seemed to mean. But perhaps most instructive of all is the fact that this memory of mine is so commonplace among girls that I can barely comprehend why I held on to it at all. More to the point, it's a G-rated version of inappropriate conduct that sits within an entire genre of M+-rated abuse. Holding on to it, even as an example of something that just plainly acknowledges how treacherous the terrain of girlhood is, seems a little over the top.

Downplaying the gravity of the things men choose to do to us is a lesson most of us learn in one way or another. After all, it wasn't like this thing that happened to us was a big deal or anything. Not when you compare it to some other things we've heard. It was just a kiss, just a grope, just a few filthy words, just a hand up the skirt, just the brush of an erection against a thigh, just the offer to come sit on a lap, just a hug that was a little too tight and went on for a little too long. Don't cause a scene.

It wasn't that big a deal, whatever it was that happened to you. You were just meant to forget about it and move on. So how come none of us did?

■

I touched on the rise of the #MeToo movement in 'Birth of a feminist', but given its historic importance would like to expand upon it more fully here. 'If all the women who have been sexually harassed or assaulted wrote "Me too" as a status, we might give people a sense of the magnitude of the problem.' In October 2017, the actress Alyssa Milano retweeted this statement with the caption: 'If you've been sexually assaulted or harassed, write "me too" as a reply to this tweet.' When I searched #MeToo on Twitter, I found the hashtag's latest tweet had been posted only twenty-six seconds earlier. Three more appeared in the time it took me to write that sentence. A Google search for #MeToo returns almost 30 million entries, with the topic having evolved enough to include among its top three news stories the headline, 'Is #MeToo backlash hurting women's opportunities in finance?'

'The problem' was a reference to the circumstances that precipitated Milano's tweet. I say circumstances, but it was more like an explosion that ripped through America's entertainment industry, the shock waves toppling some of its most protected men. Shortly before Milano posted her tweet calling for solidarity among the survivors of sexual assault and harassment, Harvey Weinstein – who until the end of 2017 had been arguably the most powerful man in Hollywood for at least three decades – was exposed as a serial sexual predator and abuser. In an exhaustively researched article, *New York Times* journalists Jodi Kantor and Megan Twohey revealed the movie mogul had 'undisclosed allegations . . . stretching over nearly three decades, documented through interviews with current and former employees and film industry workers, as well as legal records, emails and internal documents from the businesses he has run, Miramax and the Weinstein Company'.

Weinstein and his lawyers were reported to have reached financial settlements with at least eight of the more than eighty women who have alleged sexual assault against him over the last thirty years. The producer amassed a number of alleged assaults whose patterns resembled each other so closely he may as well have been following a script himself. But where similar circumstances involving high-powered, predatory men typically involve unknown women whose stories have proved easy for the public to dismiss, Weinstein's accusers include some of Hollywood's most bankable stars, including Angelina Jolie, Gwyneth Paltrow, Lupita Nyong'o, Salma Hayek, Rose McGowan and Ashley Judd. A man has to be pretty assured of his untouchability to think he can get away with assaulting women who might actually be listened to, but I guess thirty years of invincibility can be pretty convincing. He must have been so confident none of them would ever speak out.

But then they did. And the impact of their accusations led not just to #MeToo but also to #TimesUp, a legal defence fund created in the wake of Weinstein with the aim of providing subsidised legal support to people who have been subjected to sexual harassment, assault and/or abuse in the workplace. *TIME* magazine dedicated its 2017 Person of the Year issue to the 'Silence Breakers', paying tribute not just to those women who spoke out against Weinstein but also those who had broken the silence surrounding any issue to do with sexual harassment. At the 2018 Golden Globes, attendees dressed all in black to show their support for the movement. A-list actresses walked the red carpet with community activists, and both groups used the time normally devoted to chatter about who's wearing who to discuss issues of sexual violence and harassment.

Present was Tarana Burke, a community leader and woman of colour from New York who has spent the last twelve years working with the young, mostly black and brown women in her community who are survivors of sexual violence. It was Burke who first coined the use of 'me too', and she has continued to front for her community despite the international recognition her name and the movement she founded now receives. In response to a backlash over what some see as the co-opting by a white woman of a movement begun by a woman of colour, Burke described Milano as an 'ally and friend', and says the actress 'acknowledges me as a founder and has often deferred to my vision and leadership'. However, she has also warned people not to focus on #MeToo as a recent phenomenon, because this framing erases not just the work of women of colour but also the suffering experienced by the girls of colour who are too often sublimated into a dialogue that places white women front and centre. It's one of the many conflicts of #MeToo and it speaks to the ongoing issue of whiteness, supremacy and social justice movements, a problem starkly displayed by the fact that, instead of being featured on the cover of *TIME*'s Person of the Year issue, Burke was relegated to the inside pages.

There are other frustrations too. There's no denying that in the months since women worldwide began posting their own #MeToo stories, a much-needed dialogue has begun about sexual assault, rape culture and the abuse of power. Given the startling, infuriating and often heartbreaking stories that have been shared since (not to mention the predatory and institutionally protected workplace and industry practices that have been exposed), it's hard not to see that silence as being forever broken. Yet it feels in some ways like we have been here before. In 2014 Elliot Rodger massacred six people in downtown Santa Barbara before turning his gun on himself. In addition to a YouTube channel full of disturbing videos, Rodger left behind a novel-length manifesto detailing his hatred for the women who had refused to 'give' him love and sex throughout his life. He described his premeditated murder spree as 'The Retribution', a plan that, had he been able to carry it out as he wished, would have seen him break into a nearby college sorority house and execute all the women inside.

Following Rodger's rampage, a slew of opinion pieces appeared drawing the connections between toxic masculinity, entitlement and misogyny. In response to the argument that 'not all men' are responsible – an argument that's made passionately every time women suffer gendered violence (made with more passion than the male voices speaking out against the violence itself, it has to be said) – a hashtag appeared. 'Not all men' may be guilty of sexual harassment or assault, but #YesAllWomen have certainly been subjected to it at some point.

For a while at least, #YesAllWomen was successful at prompting the same important and serious conversations about the reality of sexual and gendered violence that we're having again now. Women spoke out not just to share their stories but also to critique the paternalistic response those stories so often evoke in people. The calls just to ignore it, as if that works. To report it to the police, not to Twitter, as if the judicial system and its agents have historically always been on the side of women when it comes to the invasion of our bodies. And, dangerously, the admonishment to stop criminalising male behaviour – he probably just wants to take you out on a date but doesn't know how to ask. A website was launched to detail just how out of step this last message is with the reality of the world women live in. Called *When Women Refuse*, it continues today and details via personal and news-reported stories the terrible, sometimes homicidal, punishments men are capable of meting out to the women who reject their advances. (Indeed, only a month before Rodger staged 'The Retribution', a student named Christopher Plaskon fatally stabbed sixteen-year-old Maren Sanchez at the pair's high school after Maren turned down his invitation to junior prom.)

The #YesAllWomen movement was without question empowering, but like #MeToo it also involved women having to bleed metaphorically before a world of men in order to have our trauma understood. There is strength in standing up and giving voice to your experiences, but the recipients of that information often confuse the line between being invited to listen and being invited to judge. We don't share these stories as a way of asking permission to feel angry; we share them to claim our anger. In many ways, #MeToo the hashtag didn't seem like an extension of that conversation – it felt like deja vu. Just as with #YesAllWomen, men fell over themselves to express their astonishment, shock, outrage; they just 'had no idea' how bad things were. Self-proclaimed allies shared long-winded statuses on social media that affirmed their support for the women in their lives, and in response they were showered with praise, while those same women were met with abuse. (Never forget that, in Australia, all it takes for a man to be considered a feminist superhero is for him secretly to wear the same suit to work for a year.)

We have been here before. The men gaping open-mouthed at this new round of testimonies just let themselves forget about it, that's all. Still, stripped of the frustration posed by the two movements' similarities, the weight of #MeToo distributed itself differently to #YesAllWomen if only because it came at a unique point in political history. We were primed for an examination of the powerful men and the abuses they inflict, because less than a year earlier Donald Trump had been elected to the office of President of the United States. During his campaign, Trump behaved like an overgrown child with self-control issues. His campaign was punctuated by frequent moments of ostentatious braggadocio and rank misogyny; during the presidential debates, he stalked his opponent Hillary Clinton around the stage, blatantly attempting to intimidate her in a manner most women recognised. Unhappy with the refusal of Megyn Kelly to pitch him soft balls during the Republican primary debates, he described the veteran journalist as having 'blood coming out of her eyes, blood coming out of her wherever'. (Geddit? She's angry 'cos she's on her period! Bitches be crazy.)

Trump's view of women appeared fairly clear in the lead-up to the election, but a month out from voting day something even more extraordinary happened. Audio from a 2005 tape was released in which Trump could be heard telling the entertainment reporter Billy Bush that he couldn't resist beautiful women. 'I just start kissing them,' he said. 'It's like a magnet. Just kiss. I don't even wait. And when you're a star, they let you do it. You can do anything . . . Grab 'em by the pussy. You can do anything.'

You can do anything to women when you're famous, says the man vying for the most powerful office in the world. Those of us who were clearly overoptimistic felt sure this would finally bury Trump's chance at the White House. But it turns out that there are a whole lot of people who have no problem with a man sexually assaulting women as long as they respect both his race and his money. Surprise!

As children, we learn that bullies never win in the end, that the underdog with the heart of gold and the upstanding morals always rises to the top. So when Trump won, some people felt an almost childlike sense of betrayal, because it shattered all of those formative lessons absorbed about goodness and basic decency being the keys to success. It wasn't just that a man so rancid, racist and clearly misogynistic as Trump could become president – it was also that so many people cheered as he ascended to that position, cackling with glee at the realisation that they no longer had to hide their own similar proclivities. If the President of the United States can grab women by the pussy, why can't we all?

But what Trump's election also did was further galvanise the feminism that had been steadily reinvigorating itself over the last decade. By the time of Weinstein's fall a year later, women had already organised globally to march in protest not just against the pussy-grabbing commander-in-chief but also against the litany of inequalities that are represented by the white, straight, cis, paternalistic men like him who see it as their right to tell women how to behave and remind us of our duty to defer to their authority. In the shadow of Trump's oafish, crude success, the destruction of a similarly powerful man was just enough to turn those sparks into a roaring blaze.

It has always seemed as if power made a man indestructible. (And it's worth noting that at least sixteen women have come forward alleging sexual assault at the hands of Trump. While his approval rating is low – 42 percent at the time of writing – it has been on the rise recently.) But as a sort of mirror image of Trump, Weinstein showed that it was possible to hold a man accountable for his actions. It might take time, but there was hope.

Thus, while #MeToo might be the club that most women would rather not have been forced to join, Weinstein ensured there was no better time for those women to announce their membership. Then, the backlash.

■

In examining the backlash against #MeToo, it's helpful to look at a woman who has, for better or worse, emerged as a kind of blazing figurehead in the downfall of Weinstein. In 1997, Rose McGowan was celebrating the release of her film *Going All the Way* at the Sundance Film Festival when she met Weinstein for the first time. She was twenty-three years old and no doubt excited when the heavyweight producer invited her to meet him at a restaurant following the screening. Having Weinstein as a champion could launch a working actor's career. What ambitious young performer wouldn't have been thrilled to be noticed by him? But in a last-minute move that would later emerge as a favourite from the Weinstein playbook, the meeting was relocated from the restaurant to his hotel suite where, following thirty minutes of discussion about McGowan's career, Weinstein allegedly held the young woman down on the edge of a jacuzzi and raped her.

Referring to the alleged rape in her memoir *Brave*, McGowan writes, 'I felt so dirty. I had been so violated and I was sad to the core of my being. I kept thinking about how he'd been sitting behind me in the theatre the night before it happened. Which made it not my responsibility exactly, but as if I had had a hand in tempting him. Which made it even sicker and made me feel dirtier.'

McGowan's status as a silence breaker is an interesting one, and in many ways it represents a depressing reality for sexual assault survivors and how difficulty it can be for them to be taken seriously by the public. For as many supporters as she has (on Twitter, McGowan has amassed what she calls the Rose Army, not only speaking out against sexual assault but also calling out the people she sees as being complicit in silencing victims), she can also be volatile and unpredictable. She has reason to be. In November 2017, shortly after the Weinstein story broke, the *New Yorker*'s Ronan Farrow published a piece claiming Weinstein had hired private security agencies – including ex-Mossad agents – to gather information on the women and journalists seeking to expose his abuse. McGowan was one of the targets. She explained her 'growing sense of paranoia' to Farrow, telling him, 'It was like the movie *Gaslight*. Everyone lied to me all the time. For the past year, I've lived inside a mirrored fun house.'

An already traumatised and disbelieved woman is not made more believable by her claims of being tailed by spies, no matter how many receipts she has to prove it. Presenting women as 'crazy' and 'unreliable' has always proved effective for the people invested in maintaining power structures such as the ones Weinstein exploited, and this is no less true for the #MeToo movement than it was in the late nineteenth century, when abused and traumatised women were committed to mental asylums by fathers and husbands eager to be rid of them. To be believed about abuse (or if not believed, at least humoured), a woman has to be well behaved.

But McGowan behaves for nobody, even when it's to her detriment. She's been accused of focusing her anger on the wrong people after publicly flaying both Meryl Streep and Alyssa Milano (her former *Charmed* co-star). In February 2018, she was filmed launching a tirade against a trans woman during an appearance to promote *Brave* at a Manhattan bookshop. The audience member had asked McGowan to explain some comments she had made on a podcast hosted by the drag queen RuPaul, in which McGowan had said 'trans women are not like regular women'. McGowan was apoplectic in response, and the woman was removed by security. Later, McGowan accused the woman of being a spy sent by Weinstein.

She has been accused of hypocrisy for working on a movie in 2011 with director Victor Salva, who served time in the late 1980s for sexually assaulting a twelve-year-old boy who had worked on one of his films. In an interview with *The Advocate* recorded just prior to the start of production, McGowan said of Salva, 'Yeah, I still don't really understand the whole story or history there, and I'd rather not, because it's not really my business. But he's an incredibly sweet and gentle man, lovely to his crew, and a very hard worker.' It's a cringe-worthy comment to read, especially in light of McGowan's recent condemnation of Justin Timberlake for daring to wear a Time's Up pin despite having worked on Woody Allen's latest film.

Herein lies another tricky aspect of the #MeToo movement: all the people who have been empowered to break their silence on abuse, from the most famous of actresses to the most invisible of domestic labourers, are also messy, imperfect humans. The supporters of rape culture (which is to say, the people who help maintain its power by pretending rape is something that women not only provoke but also later lie about in exchange for fame and/or money) demand nothing short of purity from its victims. If you claimed to be assaulted by Harvey Weinstein (or Brett Ratner, or Matt Lauer, or Garrison Keillor, or Charlie Rose, or Don Burke, or Craig McLachlan, or Louis C.K., or any one of the dozens of men named as alleged predators since October 2017 – and that's just the ones working in entertainment) but opted to stay silent and keep working with him, then you apparently have no credibility should you subsequently point your finger at the man who hurt you.

The people most likely to be victimised by a power imbalance are also commonly expected to be the ones to stand up against it. In the wake of #MeToo, some people have wasted no time in pointing the finger not at the structural systems of inequality that allow for such abuses of power to occur but at the women who somehow 'failed' either to avoid it entirely or respond according to an approved script. Public sentiment has been full of classic victim-blaming tropes. Why didn't she say something at the time? Why didn't she stop him? Why was she dressed like that? Why had she been drinking? More reprehensible even than these spiteful offerings are the ones that suggest women victimised in the workplace were somehow complicit in their assaults by virtue of their own ambition. Even as I wrote this essay, *Monty Python* director Terry Gilliam joined the not-so-illustrious ranks of those who claim to be worried that #MeToo has gone #TooFar.

'Harvey opened the door for a few people, a night with Harvey – that's the price you pay,' Gilliam said in an interview with Agence France-Presse. 'I think some people did very well out of meeting with Harvey and others didn't. The ones who did knew what they were doing. These are adults; we are talking about adults with a lot of ambitions.'

Tell me, why is it that it seems women are the only ones required to let their boss or potential boss fuck them in order to fulfil their career ambitions?

But Gilliam isn't alone; #MeToo had barely been breathed into the ether before opponents lined up to discredit it, condemning it as a 'witch hunt' and the even more ludicrous 'war on flirting'. A group of French women comprising academics, performers and writers (including actress Catherine Deneuve) published an open letter decrying what they saw as a kind of 'American puritanism' over relations between men and women.

Even now, when months have passed and literally hundreds of thousands of words have been written and spoken worldwide about #MeToo, when numerous (although by no means all) prominent men named as perpetrators of sexual harassment (and sometimes violence) have acknowledged their behaviour and accepted some of the consequences that come with that, we still have to contend with the tedious and disingenuous fear that a global wake-up call on sexual abuse will somehow lead to men being too afraid to talk to women and women being so drunk on their newfound power that they'll think nothing of using it to 'destroy' the life of an innocent man.

In January, *The Australian*'s Angela Shanahan called it 'Hollywood virtue signalling' and a 'campaign of intimidation and vengeful finger-pointing' that reached 'bizarre heights of hysteria'. (Speaking of all those things, remember how *The Australian* dedicated 90,000 words of copy to hounding Yassmin Abdel-Magied after she made the simple observation that war is bad?) In February, the Oscar-winning director Michael Haneke condemned what he saw as a movement of 'man-hating'. In March, New Zealand's *The Press* published a cartoon by Al Nisbet featuring four witches riding brooms; the first announces, 'I'm goin' on a witch-hunt after men!' and the three witches behind her reply in unison, 'Me too!'

You don't have to listen too closely to pick up the dog whistles here – that women are liars, women are vengeful and women should not be trusted with the power to dictate to the society around them. In March, the South Korean actor Jo Min-ki hanged himself after admitting to molesting eight students at Cheongju University. His suicide led to a wave of abuse levelled at the student silence breakers, not to mention the repeated accusations that #MeToo was 'going too far'.

Let's be very clear about this: #MeToo is not and never has been a witch hunt. To suggest as much is to spit on the memory of the many thousands of women who were burned at the stake, executed by patriarchal orders because they challenged authority and protocol and, in some cases – ironically – embodied a sexual expression that these men considered demonic.

In her manifesto *Women and Power*, British historian Mary Beard explores how women's voices have been silenced throughout cultural history, going right back to Homer's *Odyssey*, written around 3000 years ago. In *The Odyssey*, Odysseus's wife Penelope awaits the return of her husband for decades, fending off a parade of suitors in the interim. When Penelope instructs a bard to play more upbeat music, her son Telemachus directs her to 'go back up into your quarters, and take up your own work, the loom and the distaff . . . speech will be the business of men, all men, and me most of all; for mine is the power in this household'. Beard explores how the attempts of women to take up political expression in the era of the Greeks and the Romans were often rewarded with ridicule, their femininity stripped away and replaced with what considered grotesque androgyny or freakishness.

The only exceptions made were when women spoke out to defend their menfolk or to protect their sectioned interests (a truth that continues today – think of the enthusiastic support given to anti-feminist women by anti-feminist men who normally demand that women 'shut the fuck up', or the rousing endorsement of these men for the autonomy of women who affirm their desire to stay at home with children). Conversely, speaking out against sexual assault resulted in terrible punishments for the women in classical mythology and canonical literature. In Ovid's *Metamorphoses*, a young princess named Philomela is raped. To prevent her denouncing him publicly, her rapist cuts out her tongue. Philomela ultimately makes herself heard by weaving a tapestry that depicts the rape committed against her, a plot twist that's no doubt responsible for the tedious trope of millennia of male writers exploring conflict in their female characters by first raping them and then deciding how they respond. (No such luck for Shakespeare's Lavinia, though. No doubt aware of Philomela's revenge, in *Titus Andronicus* Lavinia's rapist cuts off her hands in addition to ripping out her tongue.)

Thousands of years after Ovid traumatised Philomela, Australian writer Charlotte Wood published her allegorical novel *The Natural Way of Things*. Wood's frightening vision begins with the imprisonment of a seemingly random group of women on an abandoned station somewhere in the Australian outback. Under the watchful eye of two male wardens (who respectively represent misogyny wielded for pleasure and misogyny ignored for opportunism), they're forced to perform manual labour day after day under the harsh sun. There is no apparent purpose to the activity; they're building nothing, and their enquiries about what they're waiting for are met with only a vague reference to the arrival of 'Hardings'. Early on, we figure out that the women have something in common: they have all, in their own way, been responsible for the exposure of inappropriate or criminal sexual behaviour in a powerful man (or men) on the outside. As one of the main protagonists, Verla, is first becoming aware of her surroundings, she says to the menacing guard Boncer, 'I need to know where I am.' 'Oh, sweetie,' Boncer replies. 'You need to learn what you are.' Later, Verla recalls Boncer's words:

> In the days to come she will learn what she is, what they all are. That they are the minister's-little-travel-tramp and that-Skype-slut and the yuck-ugly-dog from the cruise ship; they are pig-on-a-spit and big-red-box, moll-number-twelve and bogan-gold-digger-gangbang-slut. They are what happens when you don't keep your fucking fat slag's mouth shut.

In Wood's (only half-) dystopian setting, these women represent a terrifying insight into modern society, built as it has been on classical ideals of public speech and authority and to whom these supposedly belong – indeed, who is even capable of properly wielding them.

For what are women? We are the silent, the claimed, the taken and the conquered. We are the spoils of war over whom victorious men have dominion. We are the cunts, the sluts, the fat pigs, the bitches, the whores, the slags and the crazies who lie about rape, who change our minds after the fact and cry rape, who are too ugly even to be raped in the first place. We are not protagonists. We exist on the sidelines, as supporting characters in the sweeping saga of human history. We are not the writers, and we are never allowed to tell our stories.

We were never, *are* never, meant to speak out against the system that created us.

■

Let me tell you an everyday story about one of the many things that can happen when girls are taught to hate themselves.

When I was thirteen, a man took me up to his apartment while his wife was out, gave me Pernod to drink and tried to manipulate me into touching him. I worked for this man in the ice-cream shop he ran below the apartment, and I had agreed to go upstairs with him after weeks of what can only have been careful grooming on his part. This period coincided with a severe eating disorder in which I'd strived to rid myself of the body I felt made me disgusting. His attention flattered me, and I felt grateful that he thought I was attractive.

Even getting the job had been a boon. It was common knowledge that only the best girls worked at Roger's shop – he had confirmed this himself, telling me how jealous his friends were that he got to work with so many 'pretty young things'. This was shortly before he tiptoed his fingers up the back of my leg one day while I slapped his hand away in peals of laughter, my insides burning with the warm glow of approval. It was definitely before he took me to the pub and plied me with snakebites (an odious mixture of lager, cider and grenadine that was favoured by the teenagers allowed to drink at seaside pubs in early 1990s Norfolk), my tongue slowly turning bright red as Roger talked to me about his 'frigid' wife. She had just had their second baby and was, according to Roger, no longer interested in sleeping with him. He told me about the sex workers he visited instead, and I listened sympathetically. It felt good to be treated like an adult, to be trusted with such adult secrets, to be looked at with such adult eyes.

It was late afternoon when Roger invited me upstairs to try the Pernod. The summer season was drawing to a close and long, grey shadows were beginning to wrap themselves around his living room. Up until now, Roger had been very careful to make me believe I was his equal and I had responded enthusiastically. But alone in his house, the power imbalance that had always existed between us revealed itself.

In many ways, I was easy prey: a young girl with poor self-esteem and the fervent belief that my worth and value was tied up in how attractive I appeared to other people. I had done everything I could to make my body desirably small, and now it was sitting alone and vulnerable in a house drinking hard liquor with an adult man who was telling me I was 'all talk' and betting me I wouldn't be brave enough to cross the floor to 'give him a hug'. I felt ashamed, because I knew he was right. I *wasn't* brave enough to go through with what had been implicitly building between us. I was a foolish little girl playing at being an adult and I felt like I had let us both down.

It was years before I realised that this wasn't my fault, and stopped describing Roger as this cool, older guy who was the best boss I'd ever had. The more I think about that period of time, the angrier I become. My absence of self-worth (perhaps coupled with the fact my family was due to return to Australia, making me a problem that would also be easily removed) made me susceptible to Roger's crude charms, but I was also more terrified of intimacy than determined to prove my fearlessness. He wasn't going to force me, but that doesn't make what happened okay.

I was lucky that day – and let's be clear that when the benchmark for luck is not being raped, you're dealing with extremely questionable parameters – but I shouldn't have been in that situation at all. My situation is not the only example of the dark tread that crisscrosses between adolescence and adulthood, but it's not that uncommon either. How many girls are preyed on by older men because those men correctly identify how desperate they are to feel like they matter?

There's a lot of resistance to feminism from people frightened of what a world with gender equality looks like, but one of the powerful things it does is to reframe girlhood as something that exists even when there is no one else around to look at it. Society offers protection against sexualisation to girls up to a certain age, but it whips it away without warning once that girl enters adolescence. Then, her body becomes public property and any attempts she makes to fight this are ridiculed or even responded to with violence. It isn't just abusers who behave like this. It's present in the way men holler out of cars at girls who learn to plow forward, steely-eyed and burning with shame. It's in the way we learn to laugh at jokes that mock our very humanity, because Cool Girls don't get worked up over that stuff. It's in the way angry women are told they just need a good dick, that fat women are an 'it', that old women are sour and bitter. It's an attitude deeply held across all of society, and if you are a man reading this and you don't believe me, then just turn to the nearest woman and ask her if she knows what this feels like.

I have encountered too many people throughout my life who insist that no one loves women more than they do, even as they mock women for daring to view themselves as human. These are the people who contribute to girls' feelings of worthlessness and dehumanisation. It is these people who make girls feel that they are worth hating. And it is these people whom girls will think of years later when they remember sitting in a living room at thirteen years old, clutching a drink they are too young to have, as a man who is decades older than them tells them to be brave.

■

In *Down Girl: The Logic of Misogyny*, the philosopher Kate Manne observes that misogyny is the system that enforces patriarchal social order, while sexism is the justification. Even prior to the explosion of #MeToo, it wasn't uncommon for feminists to hear that sexual violence could never be eradicated because the 'human nature' that accounted for it couldn't be kept in check by an artificial system of moral governance. If misogyny exists at all, the argument went, it is a system created and maintained by biological impulse. To fight against it is to fight against human nature, and such a battle can never be won.

This is the justification for people – and by this I mean mainly the class of men – throwing up their hands and declaring that nothing can be done. To pursue a movement like #MeToo in the face of such obvious and unavoidable defeat must therefore only be about pursuing a vendetta against men and ushering in the long-feared rule of the vengeful matriarchy.

Interestingly, and yet in keeping with the social conditioning that dictates who gets to write the stories, the fight against men's violence is never seen as futile when it is incorporated into the narrative of men. I have often observed the different ways in which people respond to women indulging violent revenge fantasies against the men who have wronged them and how men are treated when they engage in those same thought exercises. The women will invariably be berated for 'resorting to violence' – for which there is, as we know, 'never any excuse'. And men are allowed – encouraged even – to pursue retaliation against men who they feel have harmed 'their' women. When the father of a woman sexually abused by Larry Nassar launched himself at the disgraced former doctor of USA Gymnastics in a courtroom prior to his sentencing, people cheered.

It's a long-standing joke for fathers to wait on porches with shotguns when their daughters begin to date the young men whose minds these same fathers claim to know all too well. It's seen as culturally acceptable for men to defend their property – which, in this case, is considered to be the women around them – from the intrusion or violation of men. Men who behave in this way pose no threat to the power structure itself; they merely reassert the hierarchy that is part of it.

But there's no formal code of conduct in play when women defend ourselves against men. Our ability to fight back against this particular kind of oppression and to do it on our terms, as our own leaders, doesn't just threaten the hierarchy within a power structure, it poses a risk to the power structure itself. For patriarchy to be maintained, the actions and voices of women cannot be allowed to have the same power as those of men. This helps to explain why #MeToo is considered so threatening by so many people. If women realise the power we have as individuals and as a collective, we might be able to topple the whole damn house of cards. What began as the fall of one man has evolved in rapid time to a global call-out on the behaviours of men as they are conditioned by patriarchy. That's a terrifying prospect for those people who are invested in keeping that system invisible and very much alive.

What does this mean for those women with the least amount of privilege? Is #MeToo and the feminist fury that comes with it just another phenomenon that will create change for mostly white, mostly wealthy and mostly already privileged women while forgetting all the others? It's a fair question and it's a real possibility. You cannot dismantle patriarchy without also dismantling class oppression, white supremacy and capitalism. Weinstein might be no longer welcome in Hollywood, but exploitative, abusive men exist all over the world and they more often than not have power over women who rely on them for a wage.

But feminists have always been charged with providing all-or-nothing solutions to the problems we agitate against. It isn't enough that millions of women around the world are making visible a structural system that has worked against them for thousands of years; what are they doing to *fix it*?

As far as #MeToo is concerned, I'm more interested at this point in knowing what it is men choose to do to create lasting change. I keep hearing about these 'male allies' (to whom I'm also supposed to be nice to in order to keep them on side), yet I see very little evidence of this allegiance beyond a few supportive statements and maybe the odd well-worded tweet.

#MeToo has blasted its way through our global society, and it's left a bloody mess in its wake. It isn't the job of women to clean up that mess, to figure out once again how our various traumas can be tidied away and put out of sight, the house in which we all live clean once more. Women do not need men to protect us; we need men to stop protecting each other.

And yet despite the truth of this, we are still doing something. We're organising. The launch of the Time's Up fund was a meaningful commitment to providing economic and legal support to women who so frequently have neither. Journalists such as Tracey Spicer and Kate McClymont are ensuring that Australia's #MeToo stories are given a national platform. Along with Spicer, prominent Australian feminists have also recently launched NOW, an organisation similar to Time's Up that will connect women here with a range of services to help them take action on sexual harassment and abuse. Contrary to the suggestion this is just a movement for white and/or western women, women in Nigeria, Egypt, Mexico and South Korea have all used international news platforms recently to speak out about #MeToo, changing their own communities in the process.

In Hollywood, a group of women led by Maria Contreras-Sweet recently negotiated to purchase the Weinstein Company with the plan to include a $90 million victims compensation fund. The deal fell through when an additional $50 million of company debt was revealed, but the women are committed to making the production company happen. Having women in charge of creative projects does have an impact. A recent study conducted by the Geena Davis Institute on Gender and Media found that one in nine women globally (and one in four in Brazil) affirmed that 'positive female role models had given them the courage to leave an abusive relationship'.

If we are allowed to write the stories, we can have more control over the way they end.

As a ten-year-old girl, I was given my first taste of what #MeToo means. I had spent my days sitting in my room, using my dolls and toys and imagination to build worlds around me, worlds I imagined I might one day inhabit. In crafting these fantasies, I didn't think to myself, 'I wonder what my first sexual assault will look like? I hope it's not that bad.' When it came, I buttoned my lips and remained silent because I knew even then that women were not rewarded for pointing fingers.

What you are seeing right now is women reclaiming control over the stories told about our lives. It is not just about the women who are saying #MeToo in the twenty-first century. It's about all of us, stretching right back through history. We are the hands that Lavinia did not have. Together, we are weaving Philomela's tapestry and telling that story, and we will be heard.

(A version of this chapter appeared in the June 2018 edition of Meanjin.*)*

EPILOGUE

This book is a love letter to the girls. It's a letter to the bitches and the broads, the sluts and the whores. It's to the troublemakers and the rebels, the women who are told they're too loud, too proud, too big, too small.

Or not enough of nothing at all.

This is a letter to our mothers and our daughters, whose womanhood has been told it ought to reduce itself, to mute itself, to not wave but drown in a current that refuses to let us cast sail and find shores that will let us be free. It's a letter to all our friends and all our sisters, whose anger is recast as histrionics and caterwauling, a widespread madness that must be quelled for our own good and our own happiness.

This is a letter to the women we don't know but whose lives we do, because we live them too.

This is a letter to history, and to all of it that has been lost. History, you have been like a present passed around in a party game, layers and layers of you torn away and discarded because only a tiny part of you was ever considered to be of value. This is a letter to the women who were swept away in those layers, their stories crumpled up and thrown in the bin, rendered irrelevant to the bigger prize because of the assumption they were merely packaging. This is a letter to the people forced to relive that over and over, recycled into platforms for other people to scale and conquer, to plant a flag and declare ownership over while praising themselves for getting there on their own two feet.

This is a letter to all the girls born into this world only to be told that they don't belong.

Dear girls, I wish that I had written the rules.

If I had written the rules, the full expanse of human history wouldn't stretch out behind us as a list of White Men's Great Achievements. The trumpets wouldn't sound for the men who marched on to greater things, but for the legions of faceless, forgotten warriors who were assigned the thankless task of scrubbing out the bloodstains all those men left behind.

If I had written the rules, the progress of civilisation wouldn't be measured by the success of man's colonialism but by women's resistance to it. History books would be filled with the names of the women who fought back, those brave soldiers who rejected Man's arrogant quest to assume the status of God and remake the world in his own image.

If I had written the rules, there would be no God, no eternal father, no holy trinity designed to wrestle spiritual power away from the women who mock those aspirational conquerors with an ability to bear life from within.

If I had written the rules, women wouldn't be the first casualties of any conflict. We wouldn't be violated and abused as a means of sending a message, remembered only as a footnote in later renditions of Great Military Campaigners of Old and their Spoils of War. Our bodies wouldn't form a battleground for men to destroy because they think that stealing our power will make them stronger.

If I had written the rules, women would never have been traded as property, forced into marriages with men chosen by other men for the purpose of bearing new men to take over from the old and then thrown away if we failed to fulfil the obligations of a contract we had no part in writing. We would have been given leave to choose our own destinies, to forge our own paths and to believe from the first moment of our existence that our lives and our bodies belonged to us and us alone.

If I had written the rules, we wouldn't hear now about how women are so empowered. That we are so liberated, that we've been freed from the supposedly mythical 'patriarchy' and that anything beyond this is a dangerous tilt at supremacy. We wouldn't be told this while having to endure the indignity of also being told that merit dictates who wins and that if we aren't winning it's probably because we're not trying hard enough.

If I had written the rules, we wouldn't hear how the real problem is that women don't respect themselves enough, that we're asking for trouble, that our right to be treated as autonomous human beings with dignity and ownership of our bodies rises and falls with the length of our hemlines and we have no one to blame but ourselves. We wouldn't be told when we complain about this violence that we are 'making it up', that we're demonising men, that feminism has gone too far, that a compliment is just that, and can't a man even talk to a woman on the street anymore without being vilified, I mean, COME ON, how on earth will the human race possibly survive if men can't even talk to women on the street anymore? We wouldn't be told all that and then in the same breath be told that we lack common sense, that we all have to protect ourselves, that there are Bad People out there and if you leave your wallet sitting on the window sill of an unlocked car then you can't be surprised when someone steals it, it's just human nature, when when when WHEN will women learn?

If I had written the rules, the word 'shrill' would be banned from human vocabulary.

Instead, we would listen to everyone who is silenced, the chicks, the crips, the queers, the freaks, the people not born with white skin in white houses with white picket fences patrolled as fiercely as the borders that keep out people who didn't 'earn' their way into a life of arbitrary privilege.

If I had written the rules, the world would come to life with the volume of voices that we never get to hear, and the music of them all would ring in our ears for days.

I didn't write the rules. Instead, I wrote this book. I wrote it because I believe in the strength of girls and women. I know how deep those rivers of courage run – how deeply, in fact, they must run if any of us are to go on living in a world that demands we accept our own weakness and inferiority. Girls and women wake up and face the world with the kind of steely determination that can only be forged from years of bracing against whatever shit we expect to have thrown at us on any given day. Before we can even properly understand what it means to be a girl, we learn that such a thing is a source of shame and embarrassment. Girls are weak. Girls are boring. Girls are too sensitive. Girls are pathetic. To do something like a girl is to fail in some way. 'Girl' is an accusation that's used against boys to humiliate them. And the absolute proliferation of this in sitcoms, movies, books and pop culture has resulted in 50 percent of the world internalising the idea that not only are we somehow less than our male counterparts, we also occupy a state that's shameful and gross.

You dress like a girl.

You run like a girl.

You throw like a girl.

You fight like a girl.

What are we to take away from this, except the understanding that the very state of being a girl is a humiliation?

Girls have two choices available to them if they want to survive under this system. The first is to rebel against it, to exist as the aberration other people say they are and thus be hated openly, enthusiastically and greedily. This is a hard road, which explains why so few us of choose it. The second option is to capitulate to the powers that be. To accept our humiliating existence and agree that we are, indeed, a laughable waste of time. Many girls feel safer walking this path, because the hate foisted on them feels more manageable. What does it matter that they learn also to hate themselves? Isn't this what they deserve, after all?

Along the way, we learn that the quickest way to deflect attention from ourselves is to direct it to the other girls, the ones who commit the grave crimes of being either too girly or not girly enough. Whose ironed bows and penchant for pink draw as much withering disdain as the shapeless clothes and unpainted faces of those girls who 'don't take care of themselves'. We might sit there and laugh as boys throw around the words 'slut' and 'whore', wanting to believe that the offer of fierce support will be enough to protect us from their animosity. We learn to do it to each other, to use the language of hatred and misogyny against our fellow girls as a way of policing each other and elevating ourselves to the top of the pile.

We strive for happiness, but learn to equate its meaning with simply being 'the least hated'.

I think back on my teenage years now with a mixture of sadness and wonder. My face is frozen in artificial smiles across albums full of photographs, but inside is a swirling storm of anxiety, self-doubt and loneliness. I wanted desperately to be liberated from the discomfort I felt in my own skin, but I also didn't believe I deserved anything more than that. What had I done to qualify for a life defined by love and respect? I thought of myself as ugly, unwieldy, fat, monstrous, too loud, too brash, too freckled, too grotesque, too too too too *too*. I was a girl and that made me a joke. But I was also a failure at all the things that girls were supposed to be, and that made me worse.

I was a nothing-girl. And in a way, it didn't matter how much I perceived the world might hate me. It was nowhere near the depths to which I had learned to hate myself.

All those years spent feeling inadequate and ashamed, absorbing the messages that had dripped into me from birth and that told me I was right to feel this way, that the only way I could negotiate some kind of value for myself was by playing the game. To let myself become a conduit for other people to nurture their self worth and power, and to be grateful for the opportunity to do so. To blush with pride every time a man singled me out on the street, regardless of what he might be saying. To thrill at even being *noticed*, because if a girl isn't being looked at does she really even exist at all? Like Hans Christian Andersen's tragic mermaid, I looked beyond a glass ceiling to a world I yearned to become a part of. I signed my voice away and learned to swallow the pain of walking on a thousand knives. And so I went on for years, silenced against complaint and sliced into more manageable pieces.

Those days are long gone. My voice is strong and imposing, and my legs are powerful enough to hold up its weight. I wake up every day feeling assured of my right to not only participate in the world as an equal part of it, but to loudly reject the narrative that keeps trying to tell me to pipe down, fold in, shrivel up, simper, apologise and slink my way through life so as not to offend or upset anyone with the complicated, beautiful mess that is me. I have fought the odds to get here, empowered by the knowledge that every single woman who has come before me has fought her own battle in order to survive. We fight like girls. This is how we prevail. And this is why we're still standing.

This book is a love letter to the girls. I see you, even if history doesn't. I hear you, even when the present won't.

I wrote this book for you.

The future, we can write together.

ACKNOWLEDGMENTS

This book has been the culmination of so many things, not least of which has been the good faith and support shown to me by so many people over the years. Anything I say will be woefully inadequate in comparison to what they've given me, but I'll make an imperfect attempt anyway. Firstly, to the incomparable Jane Palfreyman at Allen & Unwin. I could not be prouder to be making this book with you and your team. Your encouragement has been a gift only eclipsed by the strength of your critical eye. Thank you for feeling like you needed to fight hard to have me, but I can assure you that the privilege has been entirely mine.

To Ali Lavau and Christa Munns, who took something that at times felt to me like a decaying lump of cow dung and shaped it into an elegant structure even the most self-critical author would be thrilled to put their name to. You killed my darlings for me and I am in your debt for the rest of eternity.

To Tami Rex, Karen Williams, Caitlin Withey, Louise Cornege and Catherine Donaldson: your combined talent and expertise is going to sell this book for me. I thank you sincerely for that, because I love money.

Thank you to Jacinta di Mase, who is quite literally the best agent anyone could ask for. Thank you for your guidance and support, and for navigating me through waters far beyond my ability to sail in alone. I look forward to your captaincy for years to come, if you'll continue to have me as a deckhand. Thank you also to Clare Wright, rebel historian and certified brainbox, who encouraged me to contact Jacinta and unlocked the next level in this whole process.

To Sarah Oakes, Candice Chung and Natalie Hambly, my editors at Daily Life. Thank you for being *unrelenting* in your willingness to back me over the years. I've said this to each of you, but I'll commit it to paper here: you will always have my loyalty. Daily Life has been so instrumental in reinvigorating feminist dialogue and activism in Australia and I am so proud and grateful to have been given a chance to be a part of that. The deepest of thanks also to Nat Reilly, who provided such fantastic editorial and emotional support during the first few years of Daily Life's existence. You rock my world.

Thank you to my girl gangs. Good golly, I am one of the luckiest girls alive to be surrounded by so many sensational women. To my Adelaidies: Melissa Vine, Anais Chevalier, Anna Svedberg, Penny Chalke and Emily Ohannessian. You were my gateway drug into feminism. May we still be drinking cheap wine and making cheaper jokes well into the nursing home years. To the members of the OSC, Celeste, Cecilia, Ruby, Jane et al.: thank you for being the sounding board for large-scale ranting and reassurance. I learn from you every day. To the What'sApp crew, Fyfey, Pop, Maim, Tui and

Swishy – you guys make me laugh and laugh. The world needs more close-up videos of lip flapping in slow motion, that's for sure.

To Rachel Thorne, you are the most beautiful woman alive and I want to marry you and kiss you all over your face. To Heather Stewart, who helps my heart to breathe easier. I cannot imagine a world in which you don't exist. To Michelle Dicinoski, who is one of the most frighteningly intelligent people I've ever met. I treasure you dearly. Thank you for being one of this book's first readers. You are beloved aunt to both of my babies, and I couldn't ask for better.

Thank you also to my dear friend Anna Branford, whose passionate reading of the first draft gave me the confidence to think I had something worth saying. Anna, may we share many more walks and craft days as the years go by!

Amy Gray, you are the light of my life. Thank you for the late-night chats, the endless coffee, the writing solidarity and companionship. I cannot wait to read my name in your acknowledgements list one day. Please note that I will never stop posting 'London Still' on your Facebook wall.

Thank you to the numerous people who so generously gave me keys to their empty houses so I could steal myself away and write furiously. To Marieke Hardy, Jenny Valentish, Justin Healey, Marion Campbell and Warren Walker, you are perfect humans. Thank you also to the team at Varuna, whose provision of a two-week residency allowed me the time and space to write major portions of this book. It is a great fortune indeed to be able to write in places like Daylesford, Castlemaine, Golden Beach and the Blue Mountains, and I thank you all from the bottom of my bottomless cups of tea.

To a special little girl, Anja Reine, who taught me that I have 'blood, bones and a beating heart'. You are wise beyond your years.

Thank you to the inspiring and fierce Caitlin Stasey, who taught me that it's not always about the people you're having the conversation with but the people who are listening. Thank you also to the equally brilliant Anne Thériault, who very generously allowed me to appropriate the title of her fantastic feminist website, The Belle Jar. Canada is lucky to have you, Anne. To Chilla Bulbeck and Kellie Grace – you were both my finest teachers, and I'm so grateful to have had you guiding me during those formative years.

My deepest love goes out to my family. To my father, Steven, who raised me to speak my mind even when he didn't always like what I had to say. Iron sharpens iron, and I love you so much for making me who I am today. To my brother, Toby, who let me sleep in his room on the nights I was afraid of the dark.

To my sister, Charlotte, who deserves a paragraph all of her own. How can I ever repay the gods for making you mine? You are a much stronger fighter than you realise. Thank you for loving me the way that you do. I am so proud to call you friend.

To my mother, Luciana, who fought harder than anyone should have to. You read books to us as children and then placed them under our pillows so the stories would filter into our dreams. Thank you for giving me a love of literature. I wish you were here to see this, but I know you're looking down from Orion. I hope I've done you proud.

Finally, thank you to my love and my champion: Jesse. You are the anchor that allows me to be the kite. You, me and the babbis – we are water from the same source.